D1104295

WITHDRAWN

CALVIN T. RYAN LIBRARY
U. OF NEBRASKA AT KEARNEY

TERRORISM
and
ORGANIZED HATE CRIME

INTELLIGENCE GATHERING, ANALYSIS, and INVESTIGATIONS

CALVIN T. RYAN LIBRARY
U. OF NEBRASKA AT KEARNEY

TERRORISM
and
ORGANIZED HATE CRIME

INTELLIGENCE GATHERING, ANALYSIS, and INVESTIGATIONS

Michael R. Ronczkowski, MPA

CRC PRESS

Boca Raton   London   New York   Washington, D.C.

Library of Congress Cataloging-in-Publication Data

Ronczkowski, Michael.
    Terrorism and organized hate crime : intelligence gathering, analysis, and investigations /
Michael Ronczkowski.
        p.   cm.
    Includes bibliographical references and index.
    ISBN 0-8493-2012-7 (alk. paper)
    1. Hate crime investigation--United States. 2. Hate crime investigation. 3.
    Terrorism--United States--Prevention. 4. Terrorism--Prevention. 5. Terrorism. I. Title.

HV8079.H38R66 2003
363.3'2—dc21   2003051577
                                                                                                        CIP

This book contains information obtained from authentic and highly regarded sources. Reprinted material is quoted with permission, and sources are indicated. A wide variety of references are listed. Reasonable efforts have been made to publish reliable data and information, but the author and the publisher cannot assume responsibility for the validity of all materials or for the consequences of their use.

Neither this book nor any part may be reproduced or transmitted in any form or by any means, electronic or mechanical, including photocopying, microfilming, and recording, or by any information storage or retrieval system, without prior permission in writing from the publisher.

The consent of CRC Press LLC does not extend to copying for general distribution, for promotion, for creating new works, or for resale. Specific permission must be obtained in writing from CRC Press LLC for such copying.

Direct all inquiries to CRC Press LLC, 2000 N.W. Corporate Blvd., Boca Raton, Florida 33431.

Trademark Notice: Product or corporate names may be trademarks or registered trademarks, and are used only for identification and explanation, without intent to infringe.

Visit the CRC Press Web site at www.crcpress.com

© 2004 by CRC Press LLC

No claim to original U.S. Government works
International Standard Book Number 0-8493-2012-7
Library of Congress Card Number 2003051577
Printed in the United States of America 1 2 3 4 5 6 7 8 9 0
Printed on acid-free paper

Dedication

For my wife Mary Ann (the reviewer) and children Steven and Jennifer, thanks for helping and understanding the importance of, and need for, this project. Also for my parents Bob and Gloria, who helped make this possible from the beginning.

Foreword

As I write this foreword, the entire world is focused on the Middle East and the continuing threat of more terrorist attacks against Americans, both here and abroad. And while the military continues its deployment of troops and equipment to address the possibility of war, law enforcement personnel in this country scurry to hire and train analytical specialists — individuals essential to our ability to address matters of homeland security.

The present-day practice with regard to the hiring and use of analytical specialists in law enforcement agencies is in stark contrast to the common practices in 1965 when I began my law enforcement career with the Miami-Dade Police Department (MDPD) in Miami, Florida. Throughout my 27 years in South Florida, I witnessed firsthand how detectives were forced to rely on personal contacts and individual practices to gather and analyze information. I still remember how, as a young General Investigations Unit lieutenant, I would sit at my desk every morning plotting burglary trends from the previous day's crime reports. I would gather the information, try to put it into some type of usable format, push pins into a district map in the uniform roll call room, and then provide the data to the uniform lieutenants for dissemination to their officers. It was the best that we could do at the district level in the mid-1970s.

What few analysts the department hired were devoted to organized crime analysis, and plotting the relationships among the various organized crime figures plying their trade in the Miami area. It was, in fact, the combination of the successes enjoyed in the organized crime investigations arena and the attendant frustration the rest of us were experiencing in analyzing crime data that finally caused the agency to recognize the need to have personnel specialized in gathering and analyzing information assigned throughout the department. I was the deputy director when I left MDPD in 1992. By then, the use of analysts in the agency was much more widespread. Not only was the intelligence unit beginning to realize the value of having professionally trained analysts, so were many of the criminal investigative units both at headquarters and throughout the district.

As police chief in Tampa, Florida, I continued to recognize the need to have an effective medium in which to gather, analyze, and share information among agencies. The Tampa Police Department (TPD) had an effective analytical function. They did a great job of gathering and analyzing information and disseminating it to internal units. Unfortunately, and through no fault of the personnel, they did not do a good job of sharing information as it related to youth gangs. In spite of the plainly visible graffiti and gang tags on walls throughout the city, the city administration remained adamant in its position that there was no youth gang issue in Tampa. Through detailed briefings with the political structure, I was able to convince those in the administration of the importance of acknowledging the problem so that we could deal openly with other local authorities, law enforcement agencies, social service agencies, and the judiciary. The chief judge for the Circuit convened a summit on youth gangs, and we were well on our way to confronting this serious issue.

Not only do local agencies have to share among themselves, they must also share with state and federal agencies. Local law enforcement frequently possesses information that may be germane to state and federal investigations, but the conduit to share it is lacking. In fact, many agencies still rely on personal contacts and friendships among detectives as means for sharing information. As director of the U.S. Marshal's Service (USMS) from 1993 to 1999, I observed just how many federal agencies are dependent upon information from local, county, and state agencies to address matters of national security and interests. Terrorism and threats to homeland security have been major concerns in Washington, D.C. for many years.

As director at USMS, I witnessed firsthand the impact that terrorists, foreign or domestic, can have on our society and way of life. The 1993 World Trade Center bombing, the Oklahoma City bombing, and the 1998 embassy bombings in Kenya and Tanzania strained the resources of dedicated federal investigators. And, while I was not the director during the tragic and violent 1992 incident at Ruby Ridge involving alleged members of the Patriot movement, I was involved in the subsequent review of the actions of the deputy marshals. I certainly came to recognize the continuing need to monitor and comprehend organized hate groups such as the Patriot movement in the United States. There has been a constant need for national intelligence and analysis after these tragic events, but also a new emphasis on information that can identify possible future attacks. However, much of the training and materials available to law enforcement have focused on preparing and responding.

There has been a training and analytical void in law enforcement on the full context of the terrorism and organized hate crime issues faced by officers and analysts. That was, until now.

This book is extremely topical and current. Mike Ronczkowski has spent 20 years in law enforcement — the last 8 years managing and teaching intelligence analysts. He serves as an adjunct professor at a local university, teaching a course on how to recognize and deal with terrorism. As he worked on his lesson plans, he came to recognize the need for a book like this. This book is relevant for law enforcement personnel around the world and, at the same time, appropriate for students seeking to learn more about one of criminal justice's hottest topics.

Material in this book undoubtedly provides personnel with an understanding and approach for gathering intelligence and conducting analysis on terrorism-related matters. The reader will also find that many of the concepts are applicable to other law enforcement investigations.

From a management perspective, I believe that hiring and training analysts is essential. I have seen many agencies promote clerical staff members into analytical roles and just assume that they would learn on the job. This is a fallacy. As this book points out, law enforcement managers and policy makers need accurate and quality intelligence. This will enable them to make informed decisions if they are to properly address issues. How can this be achieved without training and an understanding of the topic being analyzed?

I firmly believe that the author's approach, as detailed in this book, will greatly aid in addressing the analytical needs faced by agencies, filling in the gaps and voids that exist today.

In my current role as Commission Secretary for the Commission on Accreditation for Law Enforcement Agencies (CALEA), I have witnessed growth of an emphasis on agencies hiring, training, and even certifying analytical personnel to address such topics as homeland security, terrorism, and organized hate crime. The problem has been the lack of materials applicable to law enforcement — that is, until the author wrote this book. I congratulate him for addressing the needs of so many law enforcement agencies and for sharing his knowledge and experience with the rest of the law enforcement community. It has been an honor to review and write the foreword for this book, and I strongly recommend use of it by law enforcement practitioners, managers, and students.

Eduardo Gonzalez

Director, U.S. Marshal's Service (1993–1999)
Chief of Police, Tampa, Florida (1992–1993)
Deputy Director, Miami-Dade Police Department, Miami, Florida
(1965–1992)

Preface

Since September 11, 2001 the U.S. Federal Bureau of Investigation (FBI), as well as law enforcement agencies nationwide, have been thrust into the forefront of the "war" on terrorism. One may ask why law enforcement is fighting a "war" instead of "crime." For centuries, wars have been fought by the military. However, since the wave of "new terrorism" reaches beyond conventional boundaries by nonconventional methods, there is a need to attack from all fronts with all available resources. It has become apparent that a successful campaign against terrorism will require cooperation and coordination from military, law enforcement, and private civilian agencies. The subsequent passage of the USA PATRIOT Act in October, 2001 gave the role of traditional law enforcement a new direction. This enhanced the parameters in which agencies can communicate and gather good intelligence information. Since October, 2001 the FBI staff alone sought to hire nearly 900 agents and 400 crime and intelligence analysts, also known as investigative research specialists, in the wake of perceived deficiencies in the gathering, analysis, investigation, and dissemination of intelligence data. This initiative may thwart future attempts to attack the United States and its interests. Only time will tell.

In an October 18, 2002 *Miami Herald* article, these deficiencies were made apparent. During testimony taken before a joint congressional hearing on October 17, 2002, FBI Director Robert Mueller stated that the FBI does well at collecting information, "…but will be the first to concede that we have not done a good job at analyzing it."[*] This statement should not be viewed as an issue for only the FBI. Much of the information that the FBI gathers comes from the thousands of law enforcement agencies from throughout the United States and other countries. Based on this, it can be argued that if the FBI has not done a good job of analyzing the information, then law enforcement has not done a good job of analyzing the same information. However, this is not the case: the public had not experienced any revelations that their domestic security was compromised or breached. The public only encountered criminals, organized hate groups, organized crime, gangs, and the occasional "whacko," all of which could be addressed

---

[*] Frank Davies, CIA director warns of potential attacks, *Miami Herald*, October 18, 2002, final edition.

by local law enforcement. Therefore, there was no precedence to look for or monitor "terrorists" or "terrorist-related" activity, and therefore no one to analyze this type of activity.

Terrorism, although not a new concept, is a relatively new variable for law enforcement agencies to consider on a regular basis. The need to effectively analyze terrorist-related and organized hate group information in a timely manner is critical. However, to analyze a topic, particularly terrorism and organized hate crimes, an analyst must have an understanding of the subject matter. This is perhaps the reason, as Director Mueller stated, that the FBI has not done a good job of analyzing this type of information.

This book is written to bridge that gap, to provide law enforcement agencies here — nearly 18,000 in the United States alone — as well as those in other countries, with an approach to analyzing homeland security needs and to aid the law enforcement community in understanding the vital role it plays in the war on terrorism. References to domestic terrorism cannot be construed as being specific to any one country. In this modern era of technology, communication, and transportation, placing boundaries on investigating and analyzing a topic such as terrorism is counterproductive. Based on history, terrorism is not going away any time soon. Therefore law enforcement must develop methods and practices that address developing multifaceted links to local, regional, national, and international terrorism and hate crimes. Although many of the approaches detailed here focus on laws and practices in the United States, homegrown organized hate groups as well as domestic and international terrorism can strike in any country at any time.

Acknowledgments

This book would not have been possible without assistance from a multitude of people and entities. In no particular order, I would like to extend my gratitude to everyone who aided, directly and indirectly, this project over the past year: Sergeant Sean Holtz for his expertise in the area of cybercrimes and cyberterrorism matters as well as his technical wizardry; Intergovernmental Bureau Detective Ray Smith for his graphical and digital photography and cover designs; Criminal Intelligence Detectives Richard Edwards and Rich Hayward for their expertise and assistance on organized hate groups; Dan Helms, Crime Analyst, National Law Enforcement and Corrections Technology Center, Rocky Mountain Region and the Crime Mapping and Analysis Program (CMAP) for use of the GIS images; and Bair Software, Research and Consulting for the training project images. Thanks also to Julie Gonzalez for making the phone call and facilitating the foreword; Professor Jamie Price, David Kalinich, Ph.D., and Florida Atlantic University for giving me the opportunity to instruct in the Department of Criminology and Criminal Justice — in particular, the "Terrorism" course; the Miami-Dade Police Department in Florida; and the staff at the National Law Enforcement and Corrections Technology Center–Southeast in Charleston, South Carolina for providing working environments that allowed me to gain experience and hone my skills and abilities. A special thanks to the staff, particularly Mark Potok and Russell Estes, of the Southern Poverty Law Center for their assistance, immediate responses, and work on the Center's Intelligence Report.

I would also like to acknowledge the hard work of all the men and women in law enforcement, both sworn and nonsworn, and everyone in the armed forces who make sacrifices every day in honor of their country.

The Author

Michael Ronczkowski, M.P.A. began his law enforcement career in 1983 with the Miami-Dade Police Department in Miami, Florida, where he has risen through the ranks and continues to serve in an upper managerial capacity as a captain. He is an adjunct professor teaching courses on terrorism and the criminal justice system at Florida Atlantic University in the Criminal Justice Department. Recognized internationally for his analytical skills, techniques and practices, and crime-mapping expertise, Ronczkowski has presented analytical material at numerous conferences and workshops for various international associations and the National Institute of Justice. He managed a county-wide analytical intelligence unit for over 8 years and has written analytical policy, procedures, and training protocols and has developed analytical databases and information resources. He also served as a certified Florida law enforcement instructor, field training officer, and supervisor. Ronczkowski has supervised various criminal investigative units, including serving several years with the FBI and U.S. Marshal's fugitive task forces. He is an authorized Environmental Systems Research Institute (ArcView) instructor, and teaches crime and incident mapping and analysis for the National Law Enforcement and Corrections Technology Center (since January 2000). Ronczkowski is the coauthor of "The Robbery Clearinghouse: Successful Real-Time Intelligence Analysis" (*Police Chief Magazine*, September 1999) and *Tactical/Investigative Analysis of Targeted Crimes* (Advanced Crime Mapping Topics, NIJ — Crime Mapping and Analysis Program, April 2002). He earned a bachelor of arts degree in criminal justice and a masters of public administration degree from Florida Atlantic University.

Introduction

"Terrorism" is perhaps the one word that creates more controversy and thought-provoking research than any other word, no matter where it is discussed. Debated, defined, and studied for decades by scholars and academics, terrorism remains at the forefront of many discussions, government debates, and media outlets. Now those in the field of law enforcement are debating, defining, and studying what terrorism is and what it means to the first responders of the world.

World events have shaped public perceptions for years, and these events have aided in the establishment of a framework that law enforcement managers use in guiding their agencies. With the advent of modern technology, law enforcement has sought to enhance its security, ability to work faster, process and analyze data, and develop avenues for sharing and consolidating information; working "smarter" and more efficiently.

Events surrounding recent terrorist activities now force law enforcement agencies to expedite and expand technological initiatives in order to aid in operational, tactical, investigative, intelligence, and deployment strategies. Facilitating methodologies with which to process these new demands within the law enforcement arena has led agencies across the country to hire specially trained criminal and intelligence analysts.

Since 1979 law enforcement agencies have sought to improve delivery of their services by standardizing practices and procedures through the development of the Commission on Accreditation for Law Enforcement Agencies (CALEA). The importance of crime analysis is noted in CALEA's documentation on accreditation. Based on this, many agencies have established crime analyst positions. The importance of these positions has not gone unnoticed. In 1996 Crime Analyst was listed as a "Hot Track" position in law enforcement, and the International Association of Crime Analysts was cited as saying "the demand for these technical whizzes has risen 10-fold in 15 years."[*]

For individuals in the field of analysis, this was not a surprise. The International Association of Chiefs of Police (IACP) also recognized the importance of designing and implementing a standardized policy governing

---

[*] Katherine T. Beddingfield et al., 20 Hot job tracks when baby boomers retire, *U.S. News & World Report*, October 28, 1996, p. 96.

crime analysis, and has developed a blueprint for agencies to follow. In this document, which became effective on October 1, 1993, the IACP outlined a Model Policy for law enforcement agencies to use as a guide in its development of analytical protocols. IACP's Model Policy notes that crime analyst techniques began to emerge as early as 1972 in Dallas, Kansas City, and Sacramento. For nearly 20 years analysts have honed their skills, usually on the job and with little managerial direction. Many analysts anecdotally stated that their agencies were uncertain of how to utilize the talents of those in this largely non-sworn position. They also failed to see the importance of having a dedicated unit responsible for identifying patterns, series, and trends, usually without going on the street and generating statistics, such as arrests. However, this changed with the IACP's Model Policy. The crime analysis process was organized into five categories: data collection, data collation, analysis, report dissemination, and feedback/evaluation.* This policy provided direction and helped define the role of the analyst within the agency.

Now that the concept of crime analysis has been with law enforcement for at least 30 years, and has been widely embraced in the past 10 years, why does it seem that agencies are still reactive rather than proactive? Perhaps it is because although the law enforcement community has implemented methods to standardize and categorize the analytical process, lack of understanding, education, and training of personnel throughout the ranks has impeded the process. How can one provide analysis for a topic for which one lacks knowledge, understanding, or formal training?

Traditional law enforcement methods have tended to be reactive rather than proactive, with an emphasis on identification and arrest of an offender in a specific jurisdiction. Analytical practices have enhanced this process; however, through experience, training, and technological advances, analytical personnel can aid the law enforcement community in looking at crime from a proactive posture across jurisdictional boundaries. Now that law enforcement agencies accept and rely upon analysts for the gathering, analyzing, and disseminating of "crime" information, a more exotic term has been added to the mix: "terrorism."

What is terrorism? How do we handle it? What information should we gather? How do we analyze it? For what are we looking? Why are crime analysts analyzing terrorism? These are just a few of the questions that an analyst outside of a federal- or military-based agency might have. Analytical-based training for law enforcement analysts investigating crimes, although growing, has been limited over the past 30 years. Therefore, the importance of understanding "terrorism analysis" is exponential. The criminal relationships associated with crime, the knowledge and understanding of the topic, and the subject to be analyzed are of immediate importance if law enforcement agencies are to play a vital role in the war against terrorism. Waiting

---

* IACP National Law Enforcement Policy Center, *Crime Analysis*, International Association of Chiefs of Police, Washington, D.C., May 1996.

30 days, or 30 years, runs the risk of missed information and perhaps many injuries or deaths. Provided in this book is a framework for answering and addressing these questions. Law enforcement now must target these much-debated issues and focus on understanding and defining its new and enhanced role in the war on terrorism.

Table of Contents

chapter one

A need for understanding and analysis

Prior to September 11, 2001 the terms "terrorist," "terrorism," and "terrorist activity" were reserved for "other" countries and third-world locations struggling for an identity. This was especially true in the United States and the rest of the Western world. However, this perception could not have been further from the truth. Although only a country for over 225 years, the U.S., just like many other countries, was born through the "revolutionary acts" of ordinary people. While viewed as revolutionary acts by citizens, according to modern definitions of terrorism those acts could be seen as terrorist activity today.

The U.S., as well as other countries, has seen the need to gather and monitor terrorist-related activity and intelligence for many years. In the U.S., the Central Intelligence Agency (CIA) was tasked with this mission for locations and groups outside the country. However, the need for internal monitoring was not seen as critical until September 11, 2001. With the demise of the Soviet Union and the end of the Cold War, the U.S. was viewed as the only remaining superpower — or in the eyes of some extremists, Satan. Being a superpower as well as a melting pot of cultures, surrounded by two oceans and neighbored by two cordial and passive countries, it is easy to become complacent and develop an "it can't happen here (or to me)" attitude. Now that this myth has been shattered forever, law enforcement is redefining its mission and purpose not only locally but also with respect to this international crisis.

What took so long for us to wake up? The U.S. was aware of terrorist activity and international reaches. It even convened a committee to investigate research on terrorism. The research was undertaken by a nonprofit institution, RAND, which formally initiated terrorism research in 1972 in response to two significant terrorist events that horrified the world — the Japanese Red Army's attack at Lod Airport in Tel Aviv, Israel, and Black September's attack at the Munich Olympic Games in Germany. This research was in response to then President Richard M. Nixon's creation of a Cabinet Committee to Combat Terrorism.[1]

Approximately 30 years later, we are still struggling with defining, dealing with, and addressing terrorism and the roles of officials and agencies in combating terrorism. Why is this? Is it because of politics and legal concerns? It is certainly not due to a lack of academic and scholarly research and writings. Countless publications have been written in the past 30 years covering virtually every aspect of the terrorism topic. However, outside of the field of terrorism research or military arenas there is a lack of awareness, especially by law enforcement personnel, as to how to best deal with and analyze terrorism and terrorist-related activity. Therefore, how are we to expect law enforcement personnel to identify something about which they do not have a conceptual understanding? Law enforcement academies have always focused on training and developing an individual so he understands every aspect of what he can do and what is expected of him in criminal-based situations locally, according to state guidelines. So how can law enforcement personnel be expected to effectively address the international reaches of terrorism without proper training and awareness of what they are attempting to identify and analyze? Much of the current law enforcement training focuses on the first responder handling hazardous materials and weapons of mass destruction instead of obtaining information and gathering intelligence. Providing training and a clear understanding of what needs to be gathered and analyzed are essential to effective management.

The mission

For many years, many law enforcement agencies have employed civilian and sworn status personnel as crime and intelligence analysts. The role of these highly specialized individuals has gone largely unnoticed in the realm of law enforcement until now. Accredited law enforcement agencies currently follow the guidelines set forth in the *CALEA Standards Manual*, Chapter 15, "Crime Analysis," as well as the IACP (International Association of Chiefs of Police) Model Policy, as blueprints for its respective personnel assigned to performing crime and intelligence analysis. Chapter 15 of the *CALEA Standards Manual* alludes to the mission of an analyst as being that of a "support" position, stating that "The information obtained by analyzing the data is used to support management and operations."[2] Additionally, it is noted that the information obtained from analysis is to be used in strategic planning for topics such as crime prevention. However, is crime prevention the same as terrorism prevention? Much crime prevention is completed within the jurisdictional parameters of the respective agency. If this is the case, and local agencies are focused on a limited geographical area, the chances are that terrorism prevention is not a part of the mission.

The barometer often used as a measure of effectiveness and analyzed by an array of personnel is the FBI's Uniform Crime Report (UCR). Through the use of the UCR, law enforcement managers are capable of performing statistical management to gauge the effectiveness of their mission to reduce crime, to instill a sense of security in their citizens and the community they serve, and to follow a set of standardized procedures.

However, there is a flaw. There are just over 18,000 law enforcement agencies in the U.S. According to the U.S. Department of Justice, the FBI has attempted to collect basic crime and arrest data since 1930 from these agencies, but only over 17,000 of them have complied.[3] Although standardized, the voluntary nature of compliance and the various ways that states compile and submit information to the UCR leaves a gap in the basic collection of raw numbers. Given this gap in the collection of basic raw crime figures, the 18,000-plus independent law enforcement agencies are less able to define methods and practices designed to facilitate analysis of terrorism-related issues in a manner suitable to fit the immediate needs of concerned parties.

The missions and roles of analytical personnel and their duties need to be clearly defined in every agency's standard operating procedures for all employees to follow. Regardless of whether or not an agency employs analytical personnel, the need for information and analysis of data associated with terrorist-related activities or terrorists is vital to the interest of national security. Furthermore, it is imperative that this information be forwarded to concerned parties in an expeditious manner.

Actionable intelligence is essential for preventing acts of terrorism. Thorough analysis and expedient dissemination of information about domestic and international terrorists and their activities will improve the government's ability to disrupt and prevent terrorist acts and will provide useful warning to the private sector. Currently, the U.S. government does not have an institution (such as the CIA, which performs analysis regarding terrorist threats abroad) primarily dedicated to systematically analyzing all information and intelligence on potential terrorist threats within the U.S. This will undoubtedly change with the establishment of the Department of Homeland Security and the restructure of numerous government agencies. According to the documents establishing the Department of Homeland Security, working together with enhanced capabilities in other agencies such as the FBI would make America safer by compiling intelligence from a variety of sources.

Consolidation of resources is essential to any collective attack. In this mission, however, there are several underlying factors impeding the process that must be considered. The factors that stand in the way of effective homeland security and terrorism analysis are as follows:

- The Constitution
    - Freedom of speech, press, and religion, and protection against unreasonable search and seizure
    - The First Amendment
    - The Fourth Amendment

- Traditional law enforcement approach to investigating crimes
- Reactive vs. proactive style of policing
- Lack of or insufficient number of crime and intelligence analysts
- Law enforcement that traditionally analyzes after the fact
- Proactive behavior or attitude when analyzing which is usually met with skepticism
- Local law enforcement that is often consumed with local, civil, and community issues, e.g., racial profiling
- Proactive attitude requiring a change in philosophy, which law enforcement has not been traditionally quick to change or to accept

Currently, law enforcement analyzes and responds to the here and now. With homeland security, organized hate crime and terrorism analysts will need to be proactive and ready for the long term (at least 18 months) and look for nontraditional suspects.

Intelligence analysis units

For several decades, intelligence analysis units existed in law enforcement. In *Applications in Criminal Analysis*, Marilyn B. Peterson provides historical background on intelligence, and she reports that it found its way into law enforcement in the 1920s and 1930s.[4] This was in response to the need to collect information on anarchists and mobsters operating during that time. Intelligence units operated sporadically in the U.S. until the advent of computers and adoption of analysis by many state and local agencies in the early 1980s. In the 1990s, perhaps the greatest growth and organization of intelligence units was seen. This was the decade in which the birth of many professional associations dedicated to intelligence and analysis, many of which still operate today, was seen. There were also several books written on the topic, and training programs began to emerge. Then came the new millennium. Just prior to the end of the century, everyone was consumed with the Y2K bug and computer meltdowns. Law enforcement was busy preparing for chaos and anarchy. Intelligence units, for those agencies who had them, were working around the clock in hopes of averting a catastrophic event. Today, these units are preparing for terrorism and threats to homeland security. However, "today" has been taking place for at least 10 years. Peterson dedicated a section of her book to terrorism, noting that it had blossomed in the previous 25 years as a threat, and she pointed out that groups such as the Skinheads and the Ku Klux Klan were then being considered domestic terrorist groups.[4]

While many agencies have intelligence units in place, many still do not. Or, if they have them, they fail to use their skills and abilities to the fullest. Another consideration is logistical. An informal cursory poll of analysts throughout North America over the preceding 3 years revealed that many analytical units are removed from the general investigative work area. They are usually relegated to a back room, or they work off-site in federal or state government intelligence centers. In order to be effective, analysts must be accessible.

Whether seeking to develop an analysis unit or to optimize an existing one, police administrators should strive to place these units in open areas that are readily accessible to their personnel. This is true whether the unit is composed of one person or several squads. Another practice to avoid is the use of cubicle jungles. Besides location and accessibility, the second most important factor for successful units is communication — which is greatly diminished by the use of any wall, including 6-ft cubicle walls. Interaction is essential to any intelligence unit.

With the logistics worked out, police administrators and managers — through the use of intelligence units — will be assisted in working smarter and in directing enforcement efforts of their organizations toward the right issues for the right reasons. Law enforcement is in the throes of an information age that is forcing the design or purchase of complex records management systems. Much of what law enforcement does is process information, but this does little to combat crime or to assist with terrorism matters without an effective intelligence analysis unit. To be effective, these units also require high-end computers, laser printers, plotters, and other peripheral devices, and complex software packages. All of these items are costly, and some managers fail to see the benefits of using scarce budgetary funds for a unit that does not produce traditional results — arrests. However, these items interpret the vast volumes of information collected annually. This interpretation pays dividends that indirectly drive a successful agency by providing direction that will lead to arrests and increased clearances. Properly outfitted units can also aid many facets of law enforcement, particularly special enforcement programs, including those dealing with terrorism, homeland security, and organized hate groups. This is done through Analysis Driven Enforcement (ADE). ADE relies on technology and the use of advanced crime analysis techniques, such as crime mapping, to identify critical need areas of policing. Managers then utilize this information to make informed decisions that will assist in dedicating resources to the endeavor at hand.

Intelligence analysis units will never lead an agency in statistical categories such as arrests, seizures, or citations. Intelligence units come with a cost and require a dedicated staff. Regardless of an agency's size, these units play an invaluable role with contributions that will be realized indirectly. This role will become evident as managers embrace ADE and analysts train to look for criminal occurrences that may be linked to terrorist and organized hate crime activities.

Defining analytical positions and roles

With the mission defined, it is now necessary to standardize and establish working definitions for personnel assigned to perform the duties essential to developing effective and timely intelligence. This assignment would seem to be a relatively easy task. However, law enforcement agencies have spent the past two decades struggling with it. Job descriptions and requirements across the U.S. vary as much as the color and style of uniforms and badges.

Just as with uniforms, many agencies have written job descriptions and requirements to meet the needs of their particular agency. These have not impeded the level of service realized by any one jurisdiction, but if we as a country are to effectively tackle the issues surrounding homeland security and terrorism, it is essential that analytical requirements, practices, and procedures be standardized so that everyone is "speaking the same language." The importance of analysts has been realized locally by many agencies, and now this sentiment is echoed in the halls of the nation's capital. Analysts help protect the interests of the country through the development of useful high-quality analysis. The question that has lingered for years is, what is the difference between crime and intelligence analysis?

For many years, analytical and law enforcement practitioners have accepted the working definitions detailed in *Crime Analysis: From First Report to Final Arrest* by Gottlieb, Arenberg, and Singh, as best practices for their personnel. Written in 1994, these definitions were insightful. However, some of the details mentioned in the book may have been overlooked at the time. One such detail that was probably overlooked, or even questioned, was the mention of terrorism in the working definition of intelligence analysis. This occurred some 7 years before most people realized that this would be something for law enforcement to consider, or even what the term "terrorism" meant. The definitions cited in the book are outlined below:[5]

- *Crime analysis*: Allows the analyst to determine who is doing what to whom by its focus on crimes against persons and property (homicide, rape, robbery, burglary, theft, etc.)
- *Intelligence analysis*: Aids in the determination of who is doing what with whom by its focus on the relationships between persons and organizations involved in illegal, and usually conspiratorial, activities (narcotics, trafficking, prostitution rings, organized crime, gangs, terrorism, etc.)

These definitions were incorporated into various job descriptions and policy protocols along with the premise that the world of analysis only encompasses administrative, strategic, and tactical practices. For law enforcement, this was true until September 11, 2001. We can now add another method of analysis, homeland security, which is actually a hybrid of the above types of analysis.

Throughout the years, differences in analytical definitions could be attributed to the fundamentally different missions experienced by various agencies employing analysts. The military, federal, state, and local law enforcement agencies employ analysts, but the job functions vary by agency. No matter how different the daily functions concerning administrative, tactical, and strategic analysis are for the various agencies, they now have one thing in common to strive for, and that is homeland security analysis. Regardless of the definitions used, an effective analyst will be part researcher, part psychologist, part historian, part investigator, and part linguist. In simple terms, any analyst is, or should be, a mulitasker.

In a 1997 document, 15 axioms for intelligence analysts were published by a member of the CIA Directorate of Intelligence and should be considered valuable insight into what principles can be used in everyday analytical conduct. Outlined below are the principles that should be used as guidelines for all analysts in their daily duties, regardless of agency size:[6]

1. Believe in your own professional judgments.
2. Be aggressive, and do not fear being wrong.
3. It is better to be mistaken than to be wrong.
4. Avoid mirror imaging at all costs.
5. Intelligence is of no value if it is not disseminated.
6. Coordination is necessary, but do not settle for the least common denominator.
7. When everyone agrees on an issue, something is probably wrong.
8. The consumer does not care how much you know, just tell him what is important.
9. Form is never more important than substance.
10. Aggressively pursue the collection of information you need.
11. Do not take the editing process too seriously.
12. Know your community counterparts, and talk to them frequently.
13. Never let your career take precedence over your job.
14. Being an intelligence analyst is not a popularity contest.
15. Do not take your job or yourself too seriously.

Not all 15 axioms will be employed by everyone or be applicable in every agency all the time, but they should be used as guidance in defining roles and missions of analytical personnel. There is, however, one more axiom that might be added to the list: Possess a fundamental grasp of the topic. Many of the cited axioms will be expanded upon in detail in subsequent sections. Use of the axioms is directed to the analysts, but they are only one piece of the whole. Agency leaders and command staff personnel also play vital roles in defining analytical positions and how they are used. In *Psychology of Intelligence Analysis*, former CIA employee Jack Davis stated in the Introduction (p. 7) that "… to ensure sustained improvement in assessing complex issues, analysis must be treated as more than a substantive and organizational process."[7] Definitions mean little if the agency's leaders do not establish an organizational environment that utilizes an analyst in his intended role. It is incumbent upon these leaders to ensure that analysts are used to their fullest capabilities, are certified and trained properly, and are not relegated to mundane data entry duties.

What is homeland security and terrorism analysis?

Undertaking and employing analytical methods is a bold concept that can be construed as proactive and controversial. Both of these are contrary to traditional law enforcement practices of being reactive to crime and being wary of controversial situations. Now we are adding the exotic world of homeland security and terrorism that by necessity requires law enforcement personnel to be proactive. Waiting could have detrimental effects that would be felt beyond traditional jurisdictional boundaries of any one particular agency. It is usually after a tragic event that we observe many different people and agencies analyzing the occurrence and looking for what went wrong, what could have been done prior to the event, as well as what a law enforcement agency neglected to do. Performing analysis after a significant event, for law enforcement, is done to identify deficiencies and best practices and to improve future performance. However, with modern training, technology, and professional analysts, law enforcement has the ability to make an informed and educated statement to predict or anticipate future behavior.

One way of looking at analysis is that it is to law enforcement as market research is to business. Just like market research will investigate every aspect of a business from customer-based demographics to target market, analysts charged with homeland security and terrorism need to look at every available variable. Traditional analysis seeks to build probable cause in substantiating criminal charges, usually after developing some sort of investigative lead. With homeland security and terrorism analysis, law enforcement personnel cannot afford to wait for the lead to come in. They need to proactively seek not only terrorist activity but also potential terrorists, links, and targets.

Traditional law enforcement has been reluctant to share information due to jurisdictional reasons, confidentiality constraints, and case ownership. With a routine case, items such as case ownership are not seen as negatives and generally do not have detrimental effects on criminal cases. This is not the case with homeland security and terrorism. In homeland security and terrorism analysis and investigations, these limitations need to be overcome. Due to the nature of the assignment and the sensitivity of the materials to be analyzed, information must be handled carefully. Personnel need to understand that the intelligence they are dealing with is not limited to any one jurisdiction. Knowledge may be power, but in the world of homeland security failure to share this knowledge, understand what needs to be analyzed, and think globally could have a devastating impact.

Understanding what needs to be analyzed

Since the advent of computer technology, law enforcement agencies have sought to enhance their capabilities to increase efficiency and effectiveness by implementing technological initiatives within their jurisdictions. However, due to bureaucratic and budgetary restrictions, many agencies strive to purchase the best systems possible from the lowest bidders. This has the potential of leaving an agency with outdated systems that meet the needs of their agency but lack compatibility with other agencies seeking to share information. Also, due to implementation phases and working out the bugs, many analysts may find themselves being trained only in the basics and learning the rest on the job. It is one thing to know which buttons to push but another to understand the topic you seek to analyze. In order to completely understand the topic, one must have a basic understanding of history, theories, practices, and needs prior to analyzing.

Not all terrorists or their organizations emanate from overseas. In *Countering the New Terrorism*, Ian O. Lesser stated that "In the U.S., right-wing militia and survivalist movements are a prominent source of terrorist risk, and are increasingly networked with like-minded groups worldwide."[8] Law enforcement should therefore look in its own backyard before looking overseas for terrorists or terrorist-related activity. Terrorist groups, domestic and foreign, as well as organized hate groups constantly seek to enhance their membership and expand their reach of violence. What better way to reach the U.S. or any country than by locating, associating with, and collaborating with groups that have an antigovernment stand. This might be a shocking concept for some law enforcement agencies. After all, the media portrays a terrorist as someone coming from the Middle East who does not look or sound like the average American. Are we being publicly misled? Should we be looking in our own backyards or only overseas? The answer to these questions will probably vary from place to place, but one thing is certain. We are dealing with groups full of hatred that have a transnational reach or following. Therefore, law enforcement will not be able to deal with terrorism the same way it deals with crime. Also, an analyst is more apt to identify activity in an expeditious manner if armed with a fundamental understanding of terrorism and a skill for reviewing variables without prejudice or bias.

David C. Rapoport (1988) pointed out that he started preparing a terrorism report for the Canadian Broadcasting Company in 1969. Fifteen years later when he wrote and edited the book *Inside Terrorist Organizations*, he noted that the "academic enterprise" grew exponentially in such a short time.[9] More than 30 years later, with considerably more academic research and publications available on the topic, law enforcement is beginning to realize the magnitude of the field. Why reinvent the wheel? Many of the "who, what, where, when, why, and how" questions were answered for us. All we have to do is understand how to implement and use this vast knowledge and research to our advantage.

Keys to analyzing

Analysts employed by law enforcement agencies throughout the country utilize various approaches, methods, and techniques when analyzing crime.

These methods will probably not have a negative impact in the world of crime fighting. The fundamental approach is relatively simple. If we cannot prevent the crime, then we must do what we can to identify, apprehend, and prosecute the subject. With this approach, analysts review an array of reported-crime reports and information usually submitted by their personnel. Whether this is done manually or through the latest technology is irrelevant, because unless a serial criminal is involved, time is often on the side of law enforcement when building a case. Many crimes go unreported, and law enforcement does not seek this type of information. This is more of a "how can we analyze something we don't know" issue. The same cannot be said for homeland security and terrorism analysis.

There are six keys to analyzing information for intelligence that will remedy the need to get beyond street crimes. The first key is to seek reported and unreported information in an expeditious manner in order to thwart any potential activity that may penetrate homeland security or cause terrorist-related activity. We are still seeking to deter, prevent, and arrest, but the difference is that we are doing it without delay.

Martha Crenshaw said that "Intelligence failures may preclude warning of impending attack, or, paradoxically, an overload of warnings, especially if they are imprecise, may induce complacency or the 'cry wolf' syndrome."[10] Although these are valid concerns, it is up to the analytical and intelligence community to maintain a professional decorum, enhance training efforts, educate itself and its colleagues, streamline and standardize practices, and validate and document all information. The second key is to validate the authenticity and the accuracy of information received and never discount anything without checking it against all variables or leads.

Specific tactical terrorist warnings of impending attacks are rarely received. Based on Crenshaw's publication, "Governments often know that a terrorist attack is probable and what the likely targets are, but cannot predict the day or hour of the attack" (p. 15).[10] Pursuant to this, the third key is to know your data, resources, and capabilities. An analyst who has an in-depth or intimate knowledge of the data is more likely to take a little bit of information and transform it into a viable piece of intelligence that may aid in operational and deployment strategies in order to curb terrorist or hate crime activity. Also, he will be able to corroborate and challenge information as it is introduced, by analyzing it against a wide array of variables. Analysts who know what resources are available will be able to identify potential targets and their associations as well as recognize oddities.

The fourth key is to avoid becoming a one-dimensional analyst, and instead look at all global factors, including the organization at hand. Analysts who look at only one facet or variable will inevitably fail. With homeland security and terrorism analysis, analysts need to look beyond

the potential of identifying a terrorist or a terrorist's target. Terrorist organizations cannot survive without support and membership. Crenshaw
stated that "Organizational analysis explains not only why terrorism continues regardless of political results but why it starts" (p. 21).[10] We need
to identify what would make it hard to recruit and keep loyal members,
and we need to identify their weaknesses. Many law enforcement agencies
did this for years by tracking gang members and their affiliations. It can
be argued that many groups classified as terrorist or hate organizations
today may have been viewed as elaborate gangs or extremist movements
just 10 years ago.

The fifth key is not to jump to extremes. We cannot look only for those
things that may lead to weapons of mass destruction (WMD). In the 1970s,
the U.S. Army developed a spectrum of conflict. As demonstrated in
Figure 1.1, terrorism is right after riots and disorders and before guerilla
warfare on its Spectrum of Conflict. WMD are at the end of the spectrum,
so why is the public focusing on the end? Is it because WMD is more
sensational than terrorism? Whatever the views the public may have, law
enforcement needs to remain focused, and approach the situation systematically, with care and caution. The media cannot be allowed to dictate the law
enforcement analytical process when dealing with terrorism.

The sixth and final key is to immerse oneself into the process. No matter
what technology is used, the human factor is essential and cannot be
replaced. Analysts possess experience, preconceptions based on assumptions
and expectations, and know the makeup and limitations of a jurisdiction.

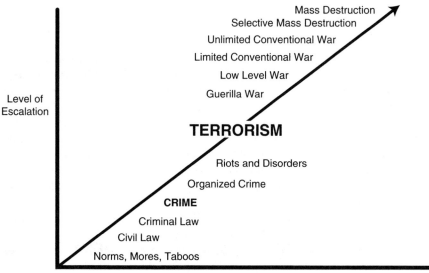

Figure 1.1 U.S. Army spectrum of conflict.

Deterrence, prevention, arrest, and target hardening

"In meeting a threat, government has two basic alternatives: *defense and deterrence*."[10] This statement was published in 1988 by Martha Crenshaw (p. 16) when speaking of terrorism, and remains relevant for the government and law enforcement today. However, for law enforcement it is often construed as *prevention* and deterrence. Crenshaw noted that "The exercise of prevention is based on estimates of enemy intention as of capabilities" (p. 16).[10] In this section a modern, all-inclusive approach to prevention being used by analysts when aiding their agencies dealing with the criminal element will be expanded upon. This approach can be applied to terrorism-related matters as well as organized hate groups. Based on a review of earlier scholarly and academic publications, analysts will be able to be multidimensional by looking for variables that will enhance deterrence, prevention, arrest, and target hardening for homeland security, organized hate crime, or terrorist-related matters. These four components were also discussed in detail in a publication sponsored by the National Law Enforcement and Corrections Technology Center's (NLECTC) Crime Mapping and Analysis Program. They were discussed in the context of tactical and investigative crime but are applicable to matters of homeland security and organized crime. The publication *Advanced Crime Mapping Topics* was the result of a symposium held in 2001 consisting of a panel of experts from around the country. These experts came from all areas of the criminal justice world, including analytical practitioners, police managers, cartographers, academics, and policy makers. Outlined below are the four concepts presented at the symposium.[10]

Deterrence

"Analytically, deterrence of anything from street crime to biological terrorism may rely on fear of consequences such as prison or execution imposed by governments or on fear of social condemnation."[11] In the realm of law enforcement, when dealing with street crime the above statement is accurate and is often a goal set by agencies seeking to address a particular trend. Whether through the use of social programs such as the drug abuse resistance education (DARE) program, or rehabilitation measures, law enforcement and governments continuously strive to find programs that will deter crime. The above statement regarding biological terrorism should not be discounted, even though this form of terrorism seldom occurs and will probably never be encountered by many of the thousands of law enforcement personnel. The best chance of deterrence when dealing with terrorism will come in sound analytical practices designed to place a stranglehold on terrorists' financial means and access targets, and limit their ability to recruit new members. Terrorists have little fear of social condemnation or execution. Their beliefs and their desires to be viewed as martyrs for their cause dramatically reduce the likelihood of any form of deterrence. If a person is willing to become a homicide bomber and die for his beliefs and his group, there is little that government can do in the form of sanctions to curb this activity. However, by proactively analyzing all terrorist-related information without undo delay, law enforcement personnel should be able to indirectly deter potential terrorists.

Prevention

Of the four areas of concern discussed in this section, prevention through proper and timely analysis of information is where law enforcement can have the greatest impact. Due to the structure and management of terrorist organizations, which will be discussed in depth later, the likelihood of law enforcement infiltrating a cell or column is highly improbable. This, coupled with the concept of a leaderless resistance or a lone wolf, would leave law enforcement personnel virtually handcuffed. However, through effective and accurate analysis, command staff and government personnel will be armed with intelligence that will greatly aid operational and deployment strategies designed to prevent a future attack.

There are three methods of prevention:[12]

1. Monitor groups suspected of planning terrorism in order to prevent their actions, or to arrest and incapacitate them.
2. Deny such groups what they need to access and to carry out acts of terrorism.
3. Monitor the acquisition of various supplies, information, or access that terrorists need, and then use that information to detect groups more likely to be contemplating acts of terrorism so that the group can be watched.

These three methods of prevention, although broad-based, can be readily adapted by virtually any law enforcement agency by expanding databases and documenting all potential information received. With these methods, the initial step in identifying potential leads for developing further intelligence and for enhancing investigative practices would be realized.

Just as law enforcement needs to successfully identify and prevent terrorist-related activity, a terrorist needs to successfully complete his mission. Prevention of terrorism requires depriving the terrorist of one or more of five specific conditions required to achieve his ends:[12]

1. Locate the target.
2. Get to the target.
3. Accomplish this with needed associates.
4. Have the necessary information, equipment, and facilities.
5. Expect enough safety to justify taking the risks.

Knowing that these conditions exist for a terrorist, it is important for analytical personnel to be aware of terrorists' needs when reviewing information for possible intelligence leads.

Arrest

In the world of law enforcement, locating and arresting a subject is the goal. In the realm of homeland security and terrorism, an arrest may come too late. We cannot afford to wait for an incident to be planned or to occur. Therefore every effort should be made to focus on prevention, deterrence, and target hardening.

Arrest with regard to organized hate group members can pose logistical and intelligence problems. Hate group members are often investigated and monitored in the same fashion as gang members. For law enforcement, opportunities for gleaning intelligence from the ranks of organized hate group membership are far greater than those for gleaning intelligence from a foreign-based terrorist organization. This is partly because hate groups publicly expose their beliefs and sometimes their actions. Once arrested, a larger issue of where and how to detain these individuals is created. Foreign-based groups are often incarcerated on a military installation or in a maximum-security federal penitentiary. Organized hate group members usually end up in county jails and state prisons. Hatred permeates so much from the ranks of these groups that several correctional facilities have implemented extensive databases and geographical mapping applications designed to capture hate group information while members are incarcerated.

Target hardening

The intent of target hardening is to reduce the possibility of attack by strengthening the perceived weakness of a given target. However, this is not a perfect science. As demonstrated through the course of history, terrorists do not shy away from secure or fortified targets, also known as hard targets. This is evident by the numerous attacks on military installations and equipment, such as the 1996 bombing of the Khobar Towers in Saudi Arabia or the attack on the U.S.S. Cole in October 2000, which killed 17 American sailors. Keeping this in mind, do not overlook or underevaluate any potential target. Another group of targets that requires consideration is what can be referred to as soft targets, such as hotels, restaurants, and public venues. These potential targets are often taken for granted and are seen as locations that have little notoriety to offer if attacked. However, in the world of terrorism nothing can be taken for granted.

By analyzing the array of information available to law enforcement, it is possible for government officials to identify likely targets of potential terrorists. Armed with this information and with the use of a wide range of intelligence tools, officials charged with preventing possible attacks can make better informed decisions and can assist identified targets in strengthening weaknesses that may cause them to be an attractive choice for a terrorist attack. When initiating a proactive target hardening posture, all aspects should be reviewed. Physical as well as psychological targets need to be evaluated and addressed. Items such as access control, security, identifications, and ingress and egress are all part of target hardening. Terrorists are not just looking to inflict bodily harm, they also count on the psychological impact a tragic event will have on the public. Whether it is direct or indirect intent, terrorists know that through their course of actions they may injure or kill a small number of individuals in any one particular incident. They know that their actions will be repeatedly played in the media, creating a psychological impression on the public. All one has to do to see this is look at the impact felt by the airline industry after September 11, 2001, when the number of passengers dramatically decreased. The reason for the decrease in passengers was fear, and this is something that cannot be addressed with target hardening.

Chapter concepts

1. The mission of analytical personnel is that of support, and the information obtained is used for strategic planning. Also, the topic to be analyzed, and what is meant by homeland security analysis, need to be understood.
2. Currently, the U.S. government has no institution primarily dedicated to systematic analysis of intelligence on potential terrorist threats within the country.
3. Intelligence has been used by law enforcement since the 1920s. There is also a need to define analytical roles within an agency and to know the difference in the working definitions of crime and intelligence analysts.
4. Fifteen axioms for intelligence analysts are described. They provide valuable insight into what principles can be used in everyday analytical conduct.
5. Six keys to analyzing information for intelligence remedy the need to get beyond street crimes.

References

1. Jenkins, B.M., *Countering the New Terrorism*, Lesser, I.O. et al., Eds., RAND, Santa Monica, CA: 1999, p. iii.
2. The Commission on Accreditation for Law Enforcement Agencies (CALEA), *Crime Analysis*, The Commission on Accreditation for Law Enforcement Agencies, Washington, D.C., January 1999, Chap. 15.
3. U.S. Department of Justice, Bureau of Justice Statistics, *Bridging Gaps in Police Crime Data*, Washington, D.C., September 1999, p. 1.

4. Peterson, M.B., *Applications in Criminal Analysis*, Greenwood Press, Westport, CT, 1994, pp. 3, 115–117.
5. Gottlieb, S., Arenberg, S., and Singh, R., *Crime Analysis: From First Report to Final Arrest*, Alpha Publishing, Montclair, CA, 1994, p. 11.
6. Watanabe, F., How to succeed in the DI: fifteen axioms for intelligence analysts, *Studies in Intelligence*, 1, 1, 1997.
7. Heuer, R.J., Jr., *Psychology of Intelligence Analysis*, Center for the Study of Intelligence, Central Intelligence Agency, 1999; http://www.cia.gov/csi/books/19104/art1.html (February 17, 2003).
8. Lesser, I.O. et al., *Countering the New Terrorism, Implications for Strategy*, RAND, Santa Monica, CA, 1999, p. 104.
9. Rapoport, D.C., *Inside Terrorist Organizations*, Rapoport, D.C., Ed., Columbia University Press, New York, 1988, p. 1.
10. Crenshaw, M., *Inside Terrorist Organizations*, *Theories of Terrorism: Instrumental and Organizational Approaches*, Rapoport, D.C., Ed., Columbia University Press, New York, 1988, pp. 14, 15, 16, 21.
11. Cooper, J., Nelson, E., and Ronczkowski, M., Tactical/investigative analysis of targeted crimes, in *Advanced Crime Mapping Topics*, National Law Enforcement and Corrections Technology Center, Denver, CO, April 2002, p. 28.
12. Heymann, P.B., *Terrorism and America: A Commonsense Strategy for a Democratic Society*, MIT Press, Cambridge, MA, 1998, pp. xi, xii, 84.

chapter two

Understanding and defining terrorism

In the late 1970s, Michael Stohl authored an introduction to the book *The Politics of Terrorism* entitled "Myths and Realities of Political Terrorism." He noted, referring to terrorism, that "The burgeoning journalistic and scholarly literature that has resulted from this increased awareness has unfortunately not been accompanied by a commensurate increase in the understanding of the phenomenon."[1] Here we are some 20-plus years later, and has anything changed? Does the law enforcement community understand any better? The short answer is "no." If academics and scholars continually struggle to understand terrorism and its repercussions, it is probable that law enforcement personnel are just beginning to understand and address the matter. This chapter is designed to aid the law enforcement community in understanding and defining terrorism, terrorist activity, and potential threat.

It has been explained that the terrorist and his adversary act in ways to change each other's behavior, and if a terrorist group fails it is because the government has virtually eliminated any possibility that its actions will be rewarded. If law enforcement personnel, particularly analytical and intelligence, have a sound foundation and understanding of terrorism, terrorist activity, and what a terrorist is, then government will be able to identify and change or eliminate the behavioral opportunities of those seeking to violate or encroach upon homeland security measures.

Terrorist organizational leaders may be reluctant to see their purpose accomplished and the organization's utility ended. Terrorists may look for incremental gains to sustain group morale but not to end members' dependence on the organization, which is similar to how many street gangs work. It is important that law enforcement personnel have a keen awareness of this because traditionally, with the arrest of a criminal, there will be closure to a crime series. Many crimes occur because there are opportunities for them to take place. However, with terrorism the activity or event is usually well planned, and once committed the organization will regroup and initiate a strategy for its next move. Just as the definition of terrorism changed over the decades, the causes of some groups have changed with time. This affords them the opportunity to garner support from different sectors and reinvent themselves in an effort to sustain life, enlist new members, and gain financial means. Defining terrorism is extremely difficult because it changes with time and historical context.

Defining terrorism

Defining terrorism has been greatly debated and written about for decades. Countless books have entire chapters dedicated to this topic. There are many working definitions of terrorism. In *Terrorism: An Introduction*, Jonathan R. White gives six "official" definitions of terrorism. Five of these are from various U.S. government agencies. Which is the most accurate? It depends on your position, mission, and the period in which you seek to define terrorism. Three of the more commonly cited definitions come from the FBI, the U.S. Department of State, and the U.S. Department of Defense, and they are outlined here:

> The FBI defines terrorism as "… the unlawful use of force and violence against persons or property to intimidate or coerce a Government, the civilian population, or any segment thereof, in furtherance of political or social objectives."[2]
> The U.S. Department of State defines terrorism as "… an activity, directed against persons involving violent acts or acts dangerous to human life which would be a criminal violation if committed within the jurisdiction of the U.S.; and is intended to intimidate or coerce a civilian population; to influence the policy of a government by intimidation or coercion; or to affect the conduct of a government by assassination or kidnapping…"[3]
> The Department of Defense defines terrorism as "… the calculated use of violence or threat of violence to inculcate fear; intended to coerce or to intimidate governments or societies in the pursuit of goals that are generally political, religious, or ideological."[3]

The similarities are evident, but which is correct, and why is it that one government cannot have just one definition? The answer is simple: their missions are fundamentally different. However, one should not get hung up on having an all-inclusive definition of terrorism, but rather focus on an understanding of what makes up terrorism. Phillip B. Heyman pointed out that there have "… been many attempts to define 'terrorism' as clearly as we define murder, robbery, or rape. The effort has been less than successful."[4] In this section, the analytical practitioner and law enforcement investigators will be given a foundation from which to work in their daily duties concerning terrorism and terrorist activity, as well as a historical perspective of the topic.

Snow give us the logical and simple explanation that "the root of the term terrorism itself is from the Latin word terrere, which means 'to frighten.'"[5] Looking at modern criminal statutes such as robbery, you will find terminology like "the taking of property by force or fear." Has law enforcement been dealing with terrorism for many decades without realizing it? Lesser et al. noted, "Terrorism is, among other things, a weapon used by the weak against the strong."[6] Again, using the robbery reference, many officers and detectives would argue that most robbers are intellectually and emotionally weak and use their social inabilities against those they see as financially strong in order to further their cause of financial gain.

Providing a definition of the root of terrorism can cause great debate and confusion. Deciding which definition should be adopted is another dilemma. Therefore, it is suggested that law enforcement agencies and analysts use a standardized and broad definition, if they must have one. The following definitions of terrorism, according to U.S. Code 22 USC Sec. 2656f(d), are straightforward and can be used by all parties when dealing with terrorism and terrorist activity:

> The term "terrorism" means premeditated, politically motivated violence perpetrated against noncombatant targets by subnational groups or clandestine agents, usually intended to influence an audience.
> The term "international terrorism" means terrorism involving citizens or the territory of more than one country.

Even though having a written definition of terrorism can be helpful, agencies should not dwell on the definition. Remember, this has been debated for decades, changed throughout the years, and is not going to be changed by any one law enforcement agency overnight. Besides, this is just one facet that needs defining. Terrorist activity and terrorists must also be defined.

Defining terrorist activity

Terrorist activity is designed to make a statement. This activity is a form of propaganda because the terrorist knows that the media will cover sensational and tragic events. Media coverage serves as a venue for expressing not only what physically can be done, but also what will likely psychologically affect those who view the activity. Terrorist activity takes many forms, including assassinations, bombings, arson, sabotage, hostage taking, property damage, and anarchy. According to White's citing of Gurr's empirical analyses, most terrorist activity lasts 18 months from the onset of violence.[7] Preparation to initiate the terrorist activity may go on for months, if not years, before the first incident. This is important for the law enforcement community to note, because law enforcement has traditionally been reactive to events. With terrorist-related activity, if you are not proactive, your community can be adversely affected. However, terrorist activity in the world of law enforcement has gone unnoticed, or has it? The fact is that many agencies have been gathering information on many activities classified under various other guises, such as labor movements, anarchy, social unrest, and anti-civil rights actions. The FBI does not measure criminal terrorism, but it has gathered information on numerous reported hate crime violations since the 1990s. Looking back, is it possible that some of these crimes could have been viewed as terrorist activity then, or even now? What is a working definition of terrorist activity? Let us look at how the U.S. Department of State defines terrorist activity from Section 212(a)(3)(B) of the Immigration and Nationality Act:[8]

> ...(ii) TERRORIST ACTIVITY DEFINED — As used in this Act, the term "terrorist activity" means any activity which is unlawful under the laws of the place where it is committed (or which, if committed in the United States, would be unlawful under the laws of the United States or any State) and which involves any of the following:
>
> (I)   The hijacking or sabotage of any conveyance (including an aircraft, vessel, or vehicle).
> (II) The seizing or detaining, and threatening to kill, injure, or continue to detain, another individual in order to compel a third person (including a governmental organization) to do or abstain from doing any act as an explicit or implicit condition for the release of the individual seized or detained. (III) A violent attack upon an internationally protected person (as defined in section 1116(b)(4) of title 18, United States code) or upon the liberty of such a person.
> (IV) An assassination.
> (V) The use on any:
>   (a) biological agent, chemical agent, or nuclear weapon or device, or
>   (b) explosive or firearm (other than for mere personal monetary gain), with intent to endanger, directly or indirectly, the safety of one or more individuals or to cause substantial damage to property.
> (VI) A threat, attempt, or conspiracy to do any of the foregoing.

Although some activity noted above would appear to be an obvious fit for terrorist activity, those on the front line — law enforcement and analytical personnel — should not overlook anything as a potential for terrorist activity. It does not take the actions of an entire group to justify terrorist activity. It only takes one. Just like a 1000-piece puzzle, at the beginning it appears confusing, but as the pieces are put together the picture becomes more obvious. Lose one piece and the picture will never be complete. Analysts will be dealing with those pieces right out of the box, so it is important to maintain them and arrange them without delay. One piece of the puzzle that must be identified is the form of terrorism or terrorist activity being investigated.

Forms of terrorism

Terrorism comes in many diabolical forms that are as diverse as the definitions of terrorism. Whether to lessen the blow or to identify why a terrorist activity took place, being aware of the forms of terrorism assists the mainstream populous in identifying and cataloging serious events. It is hoped that this knowledge will help deter and apprehend suspects.

Over the years, the term terrorism has been redefined and reinvented on many fronts. One word that will often be at the top of the list of definitions is "political." In Alex Schmid's review and analysis of 109 terrorism definitions, he reported that "political" was the second most common element used when defining terrorism, with a frequency rate of 65%. Only violence and fear had a higher frequency rate (83.5%).[9]

Political terrorism is not the only form of terrorism. Most definitions of terrorism have an underlying tone of politics associated with them. There is a need to expand upon political terrorism as a direct form of terrorism. Terrorism comes in many different forms, styles, types, and methods. However, for purposes of the law enforcement community, only six forms of terrorism will be discussed. These forms are the ones that most law enforcement officials are likely to encounter. Outlined below are working definitions of the six forms of terrorism enumerated in this section.

1. *Political terrorism* — An act or series of acts directed toward bringing about political or policy change through the use of force, intimidation, or threatened use of force.
2. *Ecological terrorism* — An act or series of acts designed to slow, impede, or halt the growth or harvesting of a nation's natural resources.
3. *Agricultural terrorism* — The use of chemicals or toxins (biological means) against some component of the agricultural industry in an attempt to disrupt distribution or consumption of goods by the general public.
4. *Narco terrorism* — Terrorist acts conducted in an attempt to divert attention from illegal drug and narcotic operations. This term is usually applied to groups that use the drug trade to fund terrorism.
5. *Biological terrorism* — The threat of use of biological or chemical agents designed to injure, maim, or cause death.
6. *Cyber terrorism* — The use of computer resources to intimidate and infiltrate public, private, and government computer-based infrastructures through the use of viruses or code breaking in an attempt to disrupt service, destroy, or compromise data.

Political terrorism

In Ted Robert Gurr's study of political terrorism, he noted several characteristics found in groups operating in the 1960s. Although this was roughly 40 years ago, many of the characteristics that he identified still ring true and are applicable to some modern-day groups.

Political terrorism has often been seen as a left-wing movement that virtually faded away in the U.S. after the 1970s. Individuals associated with these movements were considered political activists associated largely with underground movements. Although somewhat true for that era, political terrorism has existed for centuries. It is just now that we are coming to understand what makes up this form of terrorism and are identifying and developing methods of stymieing its activities.

Based on Gurr's characteristics of groups in the 1960s, activities associated with political terrorist or left-wing groups can be misclassified and labeled as other forms of terrorism. This is due to their methods of operation and their use of explosive and incendiary devices, the archetypical weapons of political terrorism.[10] In order to avoid this confusion, Gurr identified three objective elements associated with political terrorism and stated that all three elements must be present. The three objective definitional elements based on his definition of political terrorism are:[10]

- Destructive violence is used by stealth rather than in open combat.
- Some of the principal targets are political.
- Actions are carried out by groups operating clandestinely and sporadically.

Gurr went on to state that many of the targets of political terrorism are politicians, the military, and police, and that most terrorist campaigns were short-lived.[10]

Ecological terrorism

Incidents of ecological terrorism are sometimes reported publicly as random acts of destruction, and are seldom seen as having an underlying agenda or cause. Individuals operating in these groups are viewed as radical environmentalists (tree huggers and elves, as in the Earth Liberation Front [ELF]). These groups and individuals are not necessarily interested in garnering public support. They have little belief that any policy or legislative changes posed by the government will bring about sufficient social changes. They follow the premise that the ecosystems have an inherent worth that cannot be judged in relation to human needs, and that if action is not taken to effect changes there will be mass extinctions.

Two of the more prevalent target groups of ecological terrorists are the U.S. Forest Service and the logging industry. Many groups that carry out this form of terrorism dismiss the fact that they are violent and deny being terrorists. They consider actions such as setting large fires or inserting metal spikes into trees slated for harvesting as needed deterrents designed to keep logging companies from cutting down trees and destroying the environment. Their intentions are allegedly not designed to injure or kill individuals, but they cannot control the fires that are set or the lack of precautionary measures which could be employed to suppress the actions of outsiders.

Agricultural terrorism

Agricultural terrorism, or agroterrorism, is a relatively new form of terrorism that has many potential deadly scenarios. This form of terrorism has the potential to have a far greater impact on the multibillion dollar economic and international trade of a country due to contamination and disruption of the export of goods than the bombing of a single building. Opportunities to target designated sites are plentiful. There are approximately 1,912,000 farms and 87,000 food processing plants in the U.S. alone.[11] Most locations, e.g., farms, would be considered soft targets, and a terrorist act may go undetected for days or even weeks. Potential targets for agroterrorists include food handlers, processing facilities, grocery stores, restaurants, farms and ranches, livestock, crops, and food or agriculture transportation systems. This form of terrorism also includes the introduction of diseases to livestock.

Narco terrorism

Narco, or narcotic-related, terrorist activities are performed to further the aims of drug traffickers. These aims include financial gain, avoiding detection and apprehension, and establishing control over territories. This form of terrorism has been the focus of law enforcement and militaries from a wide array of countries for many years. Narco terrorist activities are often directed toward judges, prosecutors, politicians, and law enforcement officials in the form of assassinations, extortions, hijackings, bombings, and kidnappings.

Biological terrorism

Biological or chemical terrorism has received the majority of media attention in recent years largely due to its association with weapons of mass destruction. Just the thought of anthrax, smallpox, or some form of plague being spread can have crippling psychological implications. Biological agents gather a lot of media and Internet attention. Nearly 350,000 record results were returned in a recent Internet query with just one search engine. In reality, bioterrorism opportunities are perhaps the least likely scenarios to be encountered by law enforcement. However, due to the catastrophic potential of biological or chemical terrorism, law enforcement needs to become familiar with and prepared for the many different types of hazards that exist and the methods by which toxins can be ingested.

Cyber terrorism

Cyberterrorism, which will be detailed in a subsequent section, provides terrorists with the ability to operate in distant locations and to gain access to identities and financial records anywhere in the world. Terrorists operating in cyberspace are capable of accessing many secure data banks and stealing or altering information or destroying valuable data. Access to law enforcement, government, or military data files can aid a potential terrorist in avoiding detection. Cyber attacks may be geared toward disruption or denial of service, or financial gain. Financial gain is sometimes associated with identity theft or reallocation of funds from accounts, both of which are considered white-collar crimes and do not receive much attention from law enforcement agencies or the general public. Cyberterrorist acts, although void of mass casualties, have the potential to inflict mass hysteria and economic fallout that can be detrimental to global economy.

History and roots of modern terrorism

With a working definition of terrorism and terrorist activity in hand, it is important to know some of the historical content from which terrorism evolved. This will provide some insight into the growth of the term terrorism as well as how terrorism has become a modern-day obsession.

The Latin meaning of terrorism was explained above. However, the French are often credited with coining the term terrorism. The term terrorism grew out of the French Revolutionary period in the late 1700s known as the "Reign of Terror," and it has its roots in the Enlightenment Period of the 18th century. The Reign of Terror was the name for the bloody violence imposed upon the French citizens by their revolutionary leader, Maximilien Robespierre.

By the mid 1800s, the term changed to describe violent revolutionaries who revolted against governments. In the early 1900s in the U.S., the term was used to describe labor organizations and anarchists. The anarchists garnered perhaps the most attention from law enforcement. Labor organizations were fighting for the working class and sought to improve the work environment, employee rights, and financial equality. Although some labor organizations disrupted the flow of society, they generally did not create mass hysteria or death. Anarchists, on the other hand, did what they could to disrupt society by whatever means possible in order to achieve their end, regardless of who got in their way. Many of these anarchists eventually were rounded-up and deported.

After World War II, the term changed again to be associated with nationalistic groups revolting against European domination. During the turbulent 1940s and 1950s, known as the postcolonial era, Europeans felt the repercussions of terrorism by nationalists seeking to end colonial rule. The two hardest hit countries were France and England — both had colonial settlements on various continents. Two of the major problem areas of the time were in Algeria and Kenya. The French suffered greatly from terrorist attacks in Africa against colonialism in Algeria by the National Liberation Front (FLN). English colonies in Kenya were targeted by the Mau Mau. Also during the 1940s, the State of Israel was being formed in the Middle East. When the British replaced the Ottomans as the governing colonial force over the Palestinians and Jews in Palestine in what became known as the Balfour Declaration of 1917, they promised the Jews a home in Palestine. Over time, this grew into a conflict that saw the Jews trying to remove the British. They turned to urban terrorism and established the Irgun Zvai Leumi, commonly referred to as the Irgun, as an underground terrorist organization to conduct actions against the British. These terrorist actions continued until about 1948, when Israel was recognized as a nation. Becoming a nation did not end the problem in the Middle East for Israel. Various groups, particularly the Palestinian Liberation Organization (PLO), continue to struggle against non-Arabs in the region.

As the Middle East conflict continued, much of the world saw a rise from the left. From the mid-1960s to the early 1980s, the term terrorism was associated with activities of left-wing groups worldwide, many of which were opposed to conflicts such as the Vietnam War. Much of the activity experienced in the U.S. during this period was viewed as the work of left-wing groups, also referred to as "radicals," "revolutionaries," or "extremists," such as the Symbionese Liberation Army. As left-wing groups diminished, the rise of religious extremists came into being with the Iranian Revolution in 1979 and the transformation of Iran into an Islamic republic. Shortly after the transformation, the Ayatollah Khomeini declared a holy war against Westerners. Iran is also said to have had an important role in the establishment of two current terrorist organizations, Hizbollah and Islamic Jihad. Today, terrorism is associated with large groups, such as Hizbollah, capable of working independently from a state, with members considered to be violent religious fanatics or extremists.

Terrorism was also characterized by changes in the ways intellectuals approached social problems and class-based revolutions or revolts, such as the Russian Revolution. One thing is certain: the meaning and style of terrorism has changed with society over time. Regardless of who defines terrorism, this fact is agreed upon consistently. Other driving forces that changed the meaning of terrorism over time are the media, communication capabilities, advancement in sophisticated weapons, and various socioeconomic factors.

The evolution of domestic terrorism

Domestic terrorism is not a new phenomenon, and it did not suddenly appear on the shores of the U.S. on September 11, 2001. It has been around for over two centuries. The meaning of terrorism has changed with time. The differences in definitions of terrorism and in social viewpoints has led to many incidents of domestic terrorism being categorized as actions by extremists, anarchists, radicals, and revolutionaries, and even unions. Depending on the time and era, incidents we would now consider terrorism were seen as antigovernment or antisocial behaviors or were perceived as improving a way of life for a fledgling nation.

One of the first incidents of antifederal behavior in the U.S. occurred in 1791, when the federal government levied an excise tax on the production of whiskey. It has been said that this led to the Revolutionary War. However, the actions taken against the King of England were seen as revolutionary, not terroristic. Revolutionary, martyr, leader, and terrorist are all subjective labels.

Throughout the history of the U.S. there have been numerous incidents of antigovernment behavior that by today's standards would be considered terrorism. Prior to the Civil War in the early 1800s, an anarchist group known as the "Know Nothings" operated in the east. They were a secret society with an anti-immigrant agenda, committed to a white Protestant ruling class. No matter how many anarchist incidents they initiated, the membership would regularly claim that they were not involved, thus avoiding apprehension by law enforcement. Deborah Able reported that the "nativist" movement associated with the Know Nothings became the basis for a conservative political party known as the American Party.[12] This is the same party under whose auspices Millard Fillmore ran for President in 1856.

Violent ideological extremism also dominated many issues in the 1800s, up to and during the Civil War. Much of the war activity was geared toward southern states seeking to keep their rights. Most southerners were not fighting to preserve slavery, but rather to keep the power of local governments. Upon the conclusion of the Civil War, Revolutionary terrorism and Repressionist terrorism made appearances as labor movements and grew in the post-Civil War era. Primarily during the 1870s and 1880s, rural movements were complemented by labor violence, and anarchism from the left began to emerge. In the early 1900s, anarchists wrought havoc in the U.S. with one incident that led to the assassination of a President. The response at the time was to round up the anarchists and deport them, usually back to Europe. The assassination of President William McKinley in 1901 by anarchist Leon Czolgosz is just one example of the long history of political violence in the U.S., but until recently it was not interpreted as terrorism.

In the era immediately preceding World War II, nationalistic movements were viewed as terrorist groups as they revolted from European authority. Throughout the decades, particularly in the 1960s, the character of American terrorism began to change. It became known as a radical phenomenon, even though the antigovernment behavior went beyond mere picketing and demonstrations. Left-wing terrorism began to sunset after the Vietnam War, and modern right-wing extremism began to emerge and came to fruition around 1984 with the violent activity of the Hate Movement. Upon arrival of the new millennium, terrorism became associated with large groups possessing strong beliefs based on religion and violent fanaticism based on a particular cause such as the environment.

Although this section only begins to scratch the surface of terrorism in the U.S., domestic terrorism has been present for decades in many forms. Even though there were numerous changes over the years, the structure and makeup of domestic terrorist groups and classifications of domestic terrorists have remained relatively consistent for the past 25 years. Based on this consistency, the FBI ultimately developed a broad listing for the types of terrorist groups or terrorists found in the U.S. The three types of domestic terrorists according to the FBI are as follows:

- Left-wing
- Right-wing
- Special interest (e.g., abortion clinic bombings)

Table 2.1 demonstrates the characteristic and demographical differences between left-wing and right-wing members. Special interest terrorists are often seen as lone wolves or members of a leaderless resistance with views that are extreme and skewed and may be originally based on either the left or right wing. They randomly select their targets based on the presumption that they are associated with a segment of the population that opposes their point of view.

Domestic right-wing terrorist groups often adhere to the principles of racial supremacy and embrace antigovernment and antiregulatory beliefs. They generally engage in activity that is protected by constitutional guarantees of free speech and assembly. Many of these groups attempted to tame

Table 2.1 Profiling Terrorists

Characteristic	Right Wing	Left Wing
Social change perspective	Reactionary	Revolutionary
Social class membership	Lower/middle	Lower/middle/upper
Leadership	Male dominated	Egalitarian
Marital status	Married	Single/divorced/separated
Age	16–76	25–45
Educational level	High school	College
Religious belief	Fundamental	Agnostic/atheist
Criminal planning	Impulsive	Meticulous

Source: T. O'Connor, North Carolina Wesleyan College (http://faculty.ncwc.edu/to-connor/392/spy/terrorism.htm, Nov. 2002). With permission.

their rhetoric in order to appeal to a broader segment of the population. Left-wing groups, on the other hand, generally profess a revolutionary socialist doctrine and view themselves as protectors against capitalism. Special interest groups in the 1980s through the 1990s were often associated with abortion clinic attacks. Today, these groups are seen as anarchists and extremist socialist groups seeking to resolve specific issues rather than effect widespread political change. Groups and individuals often emerge from the extreme fringes of the animal rights, pro-life, and environmental movements. Although much of the terrorist activity seen in the U.S. could be categorized into the above categories, terrorist activity is too broad to be limited to just three types.

In 1987, the FBI expanded upon these three types of terrorism. In the *FBI Law Enforcement Bulletin*,[12b] John Harris named five categories of domestic terrorist groups, which are summarized below. These groups that were recognized by the FBI in 1987 are still applicable today:

- Left-wing (white leftists)
- Right-wing extremists
- Puerto Rican leftists
- Black militants
- Jewish extremists

When reviewing the list of current domestic terrorist groups, one can readily associate the group to a category. But just as with the FBI's types of domestic terrorists, it can be suggested that a sixth group category could be that of "special interest."

In the U.S., there are as many as 400 groups with anywhere from 10,000 to 100,000 members in right-wing groups that can be classified as domestic terrorist groups. In a speech before the Senate Select Committee on Intelligence on February 6, 2002, Dale L. Watson, executive assistant director of counterterrorism and counterintelligence for the FBI, reported that in the preceding decade right-wing extremism overtook left-wing terrorism as the most dangerous domestic terrorist threat to the U.S. He went on to note that two special interest extremist groups, the Animal Liberation Front (ALF) and the ELF committed approximately 600 criminal acts in the U.S. since 1996 resulting in damages in excess of $42 million.[13] Interestingly, in this statement to the Senate these two extremists groups were viewed as domestic terrorist threats, but their actions were described as criminal. This can be attributed to the lack of coordinated and direct information available on domestic groups.

According to MILNET, the open-source military information database, no U.S. Government agency maintains a formal list of domestic terrorist groups. However, there are two private nonprofit organizations that monitor groups in the U.S. under the designation of organized hate groups, the Anti-Defamation League (ADL) and the Southern Poverty Law Center (SPLC). The SPLC documented 676 active hate groups in the U.S. in its 2001

Intelligence Report.[14] In 2002 this number increased nearly 5% to 708 organized hate groups.[15] This is a dramatic rise from the 240 reported in 1996. The actual active membership numbers for hate groups are tough to ascertain because conservative estimates reflect 25,000 members, but there are possibly as many as 150,000 "armchair racists" who espouse the beliefs without necessarily taking any action.[16] The fact that there is no officially designated government agency that maintains a formal list is significant. Should some intelligence be developed regarding a domestic terrorist group, it may be hard to qualify and quantify the information within official government ranks.

In recent years, much has been written about international terrorist groups but little is available on known domestic terrorist groups. Domestic terrorist groups may be dismissed as a conglomeration of radicals, whiners, extremists, fanatics, and hate groups. No matter what the reference, they are dangerous. In a statement for the record before the U.S. Senate on May 10, 2001, then director of the FBI Louis J. Freeh remarked that domestic terrorist groups represent interests that span the full spectrum of political and economic viewpoints as well as social issues. He stated that FBI investigations into groups are based upon information regarding planned or actual criminal activity, not on information regarding beliefs.[22] This may be why little is officially documented concerning domestic terrorist and hate groups. Based on Freeh's remarks, it is probable that local and state law enforcement agencies are more cognizant of groups that would fall into the category of domestic terrorists, especially organized hate groups, because they may have operated in or near their jurisdictions.

A sampling of known domestic terrorist groups, many of which are also viewed as organized hate groups, is outlined below and explained in further detail in Appendix A.

Known domestic terrorist groups[17]

- American Coalition of Life Activists
- Animal Liberation Front
- Army of God
- Aryan Nation (aka Aryan Republican Army)
- Branch Davidians
- Christian Identity Movement
- Colorado First Light Infantry
- Colorado Militia
- Citizens of the Republic of Idaho
- Covenant (aka. Sword and Arm of the Lord)
- Earth Liberation Front (ELF)
- Freeman
- Ku Klux Klan
- Michigan Militia

- Militia of Montana
- Mountaineer Militia
- National Alliance
- North American Militia of Southwestern Michigan
- Patriot's Council
- Phineas Priesthood
- Posse Comitatus
- Reclaim the Seeds
- Republic of Texas
- Southern California Minuteman
- The Order (aka The New Order)
- Unnamed California and Texas Militias
- Viper Militia
- World Church of the Creator

The sheer number of potential groups or movements in the U.S. is alarming, and unconfirmed. An Internet search on general topics such as militias will garner over 200,000 results with use of just one search engine. There are militia groups scattered throughout America, and their numbers are growing. Bruce Hoffman, citing works from the mid-1990s, stated that there are "an estimated 800 other similarly oriented militias — with a total membership claimed to be over 5 million, though more realistically put at no more than 50,000."[18] According to the SPLC's 2001 Intelligence Report, there were 158 identified active "patriot" groups (see Appendix B, this book) with cells in many states, active in 2001, and of these 73 were classified as "militias."[19] These numbers decreased in 2002, with "patriot" groups dropping to 143 and "militias" to 54.[15]

Barbara Perry, in her book *In The Name of Hate: Understanding Hate Crimes*, cited the militia movement as being fueled by religious fanaticism and willing to kill, and referred to it as a "full-scale terrorist underground."[16] Despite not having a definitive number to work with, law enforcement personnel need to exercise caution when monitoring information on these groups. It does not take a group to commit an act of terrorism; one person can also do a lot of damage. You only have to look at a homicide bomber to be convinced of this. Just as important, not every group or its members has terrorist ties or expounds violence, but they are at best unstable and pose fertile ground for the growth of domestic terrorism.

Domestic terrorism

With the ambiguity in defining terrorism, how can we possibly define domestic terrorism? One of the few working definitions of domestic terrorism comes from the MILNET Web site, a research tool used by researchers, historians, and academics:

> Domestic Terrorism is the actions by persons seeking to persuade or dissuade the government or people of their home country using violent means that intend to frighten or coerce, ranging from threats to outright acts of violence such as kidnapping, beatings, or murder.[20]

This definition clearly fits many groups, from as early as the 1960s through today, and would surely fit everything from abortion clinic bombings to the Oklahoma City bombing.

However, much attention has been and continues to be focused on international terrorism and groups that are based overseas. Although the federal government has the means and authority to investigate and follow up on terrorist-related activity overseas, local law enforcement agencies do not, and they may fail to see the correlation between domestic or local events in the big picture of terrorism. The media focus on terrorist subjects from other countries as being the bad guys at the root of the entire epidemic known as terrorism. This may make a more attractive news angle to follow, and our citizens may find it easier to deal with than reading that one of their own could side with the enemy. After all, terrorists cannot look like mainstream law-abiding citizens, right? The truth is that domestic-related terrorism has taken place for many years and by those who would fit the mainstream citizen category. However, it is often classified as a routine crime somewhere in the criminal justice system.

It was not until the passage of the Uniting and Strengthening America by Providing Appropriate Tools Required to Intercept and Obstruct Terrorism (USA PATRIOT) Act in October, 2001 that many American citizens came to understand a working definition of domestic terrorism. Although the text is laden with many enhancements designed to increase the effectiveness of law enforcement in the war on terrorism, domestic terrorism is not directly addressed until about three-quarters of the way into the document. For the purposes of this book, the following definition of domestic terrorism from the USA PATRIOT Act is suggested for use by law enforcement:

(A) Involves acts dangerous to human life that are a violation of the criminal laws of the United States or of any State
(B) appear to be intended
   (i) to intimidate or coerce a civilian population
   (ii) to influence the policy of a government by intimidation or coercion; or
   (iii) to affect the conduct of a government by mass destruction, assassination, or kidnapping; and
(C) occur primarily within the territorial jurisdiction of the United States.[21]

This second definition is specific to the U.S. and its citizens, whereas the MILNET definition is more broadly based and can be adopted by almost any country.

A third definition to consider is that presented by Louis J. Freeh:[22]

> The unlawful use, or threatened use, of violence by a group or individual that is based and operating entirely within the United States or its territories without foreign direction and which is committed against persons or property with the intent of intimidating or coercing a government or its population in furtherance of political or social objectives.

Defining domestic terrorism and what constitutes domestic terrorism is increasingly becoming more complicated to achieve. Therefore, it is suggested that the definition overwhelmingly adopted in the USA PATRIOT Act be established as the standard used by law enforcement throughout the country.

The complex nature of terrorism and the transnational capabilities of virtually every person in the world are increasingly eroding traditional boundaries. Many so-called international terrorist organizations have sprouted roots in many countries, including the U.S., and have tried to fall into the mainstream to avoid detection, reap financial gains, or exploit laws designed for law-abiding citizens. Elaine Landau pointed out that there are not many differences between domestic terrorists and the highly publicized terrorist bands operating in other parts of the world.[23] This also muddies the waters when trying to define domestic terrorism, but caution should be used, and the best way to monitor such groups is through categorizing and monitoring with link analysis in order to develop associations.

As noted earlier, domestic terrorism in the U.S. by American citizens has been prevalent for several years but has often been classified somewhere else in the criminal justice system. Walter Laqueur advised that statistics concerning terrorism focus on international terrorism. He said that terrorism statistics over the years are dependent on who is collecting the figures and what criteria are being used, but noted that "This is not to argue that statistics on terrorism are altogether useless."[24] Terrorism statistics are no different than many law enforcement statistics, which are at times subjective and completely dependent upon the reporting or collection criteria. What is important about statistics is that they are cited and compared with like variables. Outlined below are some statistics and examples of domestic terrorism, according to the Council on Foreign Relations, that show how prevalent it has been in the U.S. before September 11, 2001:[25]

- Between 1980 and 2000, Americans accounted for about three-quarters of the 335 terrorist acts committed in the United States.

- Weapons of mass destruction were used. In 1984, followers of the Bagwan Shree Rajneessh cult sprayed salad bars in Oregon with salmonella, causing 751 people to become ill.
- In April 1995, the Oklahoma City bombing took place.
- In July 1996, the Atlanta Centennial Park bombing took place.
- In the summer of 1999, shooting sprees targeting minorities in Chicago and Los Angeles took place.

In December 2002, former FBI associate deputy director Buck Revell pointed out several factors that are changing and increasing the domestic terrorist threat. One point of particular interest is that "antigovernment reactionary extremists have proliferated and now pose a significant threat to the federal government and to law enforcement at all levels."[26] This point is well taken, but today's reactionary extremists were the turn-of-the-century's anarchists. People classified as anarchists were seen as opposing all forms of organized authority, including government, and they advocated the use of violence in order to improve a class of society, usually the working or lower class. Revell also noted that had it not been for modern-day non-government agencies such as the SPLC and the ADL, the federal government would have been totally clueless about right-wing extremists. It is these extremist or organized hate groups that can provide a conduit to international terrorist organizations seeking to expand their terror campaign into a country such as the U.S.

Americans do not have immunity to the lure of violent ideologies or hatred. At the beginning of the new millennium, there were several U.S. citizens allegedly associated with known terrorist organizations such as al-Qaeda. Two of the more prevalent were the individuals who came to be known as "the American Taliban" and "the Dirty Bomber." The connection for each of these individuals was said to be religion. The Dirty Bomber reportedly converted or was exposed to an extreme version of Islam while incarcerated in a Florida prison. This does not mean that every disenchanted prisoner will join an international terrorist group, but prisoners' hatred often runs deep and represents a valuable recruitment source of potential candidates to join organized hate groups and antigovernment movements.

Organized hate groups and crimes

As alluded to in the evolution of domestic terrorism, organized groups such as gangs and crime families have a long-standing presence in the U.S. The roots of modern hate have been around for centuries. From the early settlers of the U.S. to one of the first organized hate groups, the Ku Klux Klan, which has been around for over 135 years, hate has festered and been a contributing factor to many illegal actions. However, the presence of these groups has been seen as a crime threat, not a terrorist threat, but times have changed.

In a speech before the U.S. Senate, Louis J. Freeh reported that on a national level, formal right-wing hate groups such as World Church of the Creator and the Aryan Nations represent a continuing terrorist threat. These two groups have formal followings throughout the country and probably have even more informal followers. Small splinter factions, such as the South Florida Aryan Alliance, spawned from the larger groups described above. These groups have continuously become more vocal and blatantly display their cache of weapons in photographs or public domains. Concern over hate crimes and actions of hate groups such as these prompted the FBI to initiate data collection on hate or bias with the Hate Crimes Statistics Act of 1990 through the Uniform Crime Reporting system.

In 2001, the FBI reported that there were nearly 10,000 reported incidents of hate within the U.S. According to some private nonprofit associations that monitor hate crimes, this number may actually be as high as 50,000 per year. The discrepancy in numbers can largely be attributed to reporting practices and lack of training or awareness on the behalf of law enforcement. Measures are in place to remedy this discrepancy but only time will tell if the issue has been addressed. Many reported hate crime incidents are focused on gender, race, and ethnicity, and they are reported as being committed by an individual rather than a group. This is contrary to the way terrorism-related actions are reported. In these instances, you hear more about the group than the individual who committed the act.

During her tenure as attorney general of the U.S., Janet Reno identified a need and requested that the FBI work in concert with state and local law enforcement agencies to develop a model hate crime training curriculum. This was in response to her deep concern about the problem of hate crime in the U.S. and perhaps to address the alleged differences in data. The result was four new training curricula for patrol officers, detectives, policy-level officers, and a mixed audience of all three levels. Interestingly, analytical personnel were not included. Regardless of this criticism, many personnel were trained on a variety of topics, including group characteristics that should be shared with analysts tasked with analyzing hate groups. Outlined below are some known characteristics of organized hate groups:

- Group structure is loose on a local level and highly structured internationally.
- A substantial number of members are white males under the age of 30.
- Leaders tend to project a mainstream image.
- Many are technologically savvy and use such venues as cable television and computers to promote their rhetoric.
- Group members are often loosely affiliated and take inspiration and direction (e.g., Skinheads).
- Groups focus on issues of concern to Middle America as a way of cloaking and marketing hate.

- Members of these groups believe in an inevitable global war between races.

Another matter that needed to be addressed was a definition for hate crime. Much like defining terrorism, defining hate crime led to numerous working definitions. Some of the more prominent definitions come from the Hate Crimes Statistics Act of 1990, Bureau of Justice Administration in 1997, the ADL, and the National Education Association. For purposes of law enforcement, the FBI definition is widely used as a standard:[27]

> A criminal offense committed against a person, property or society which is motivated, in whole or in part, by the offender's bias against a race, religion, disability, sexual orientation, or ethnicity/national origin.

Louis Freeh, in his statement before the Senate, also noted that anarchists and extreme socialist groups have an international presence and pose a potential threat to the U.S. This is important to note, because foreign-based terrorist organizations that wish to attack on American soil must first gain access to the U.S. As demonstrated with some disenfranchised American citizens such as those who joined the Taliban and al-Qaeda in Afghanistan, foreign-based groups recruited Americans and thereby reached American soil. Monitoring hate groups and their members, publicly and in prison, is vital. These groups represent potential recruitment grounds for well-financed foreign-based terrorist organizations that have hatred toward the U.S. and who can build upon this cause in an effort to solicit members of domestic-based groups to perform acts of terrorism. The hatred of domestic-based groups did not evolve overnight. It has been around for decades and without a doubt poses a great risk to homeland security.

American organized hate groups are not only proprietary to the U.S. Several groups have established chapters overseas and recruited members in many European countries, including England, Germany, and Austria. This is similar to the actions of terrorist organizations that are extending their reach to the U.S. The roles these various groups play in the terrorism theater is expanding domestically and internationally.

Role of organized hate groups in domestic terrorism

Terrorism of any magnitude has an underlying tone of hate. All organized hate groups have beliefs or practices that attack or malign an entire class of people, and such is the case with terrorist groups like al-Qaeda, whose members overwhelmingly hate Americans.

Numbers concerning known militias and patriot groups are staggering. With potentially hundreds of home-grown organized groups active in the U.S., law enforcement agencies should strive to categorize groups along the following suggested domestic ideological parameters, in addition to the FBI's domestic types, rather than treat them as individual organizations:

- White supremacy
- Hate groups
- Neomilitia or Patriot movements
- Sovereign Citizen movements
- Militias
- Tax protestors
- Foreign or state sponsored groups

Use of the suggested parameters will aid analytical and investigative personnel in narrowing criteria when tracking and monitoring activity as well as members. There are other categories available, but for analytical purposes most groups will fit into the above list. Categorizing domestic groups along these lines will also aid in identifying splinter groups, membership transfers, or groups that may associate with one another based on a common belief or hatred. Law enforcement is accustomed to using labels for such groups as career criminals. The difference is that most career criminal labels have structured guidelines and are usually progressive, so there is no need to change the category. When categorizing organized hate groups, law enforcement needs to be aware that members may change groups or associate with multiple groups. Therefore as new information concerning changes becomes known, it is important that a mechanism exist to facilitate the change in order to keep intelligence accurate.

Figure 2.1 depicts a hate map. Symbols are used to identify groups following the SPLC categories. The information demonstrates how virtually every area of the U.S. has been touched by organized hate groups. Categories used by the SPLC differ slightly from those just outlined. The SPLC's categories are valid but broad-based, and they may be too limiting for future analytical consideration. However, they should not be discounted. The SPLC uses the following organized hate group categories and definitions:[28]

1. ***Ku Klux Klan*** — The Ku Klux Klan, with its mystique and its long history of violence, is the oldest and most infamous of American hate groups. Although blacks have typically been the Klan's primary target, it also has attacked Jews, immigrants, homosexuals, and recently Catholics. Since December 1865 when it was formed, the Klan has typically seen itself as a Christian organization. However, in modern times Klan groups are motivated by a variety of theological and political ideologies.
   Started during the Reconstruction at the end of the Civil War, the Klan quickly mobilized as a vigilante group to intimidate Southern blacks (and any whites who would help them) and to prevent blacks from enjoying basic civil rights. Outlandish titles (like Imperial Wizard and Exalted Cyclops), hooded costumes, violent night rides, and

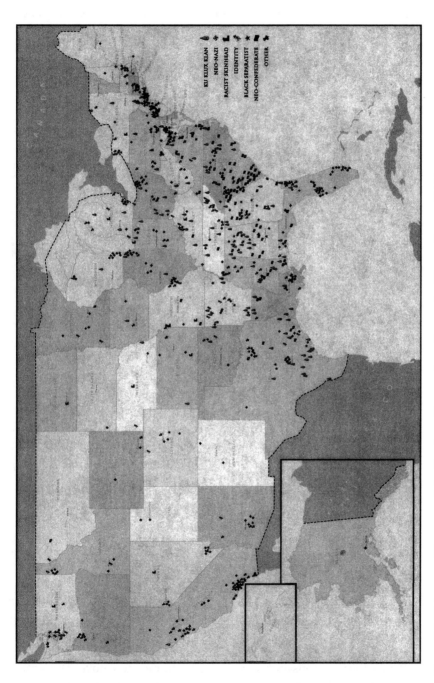

Figure 2.1 Hate map. (Courtesy of the Southern Poverty Law Center, *Intelligence Report*, 2003.)

the notion that the group comprised an invisible empire conferred a mystique that only added to the Klan's popularity. Lynching, tar-and-featherings, rape, and other violent attacks on those challenging white supremacy became hallmarks of the Klan.

After a short but violent period, the "first era" Klan disbanded after Jim Crow laws secured the domination of Southern whites. However, the Klan enjoyed a huge revival in the 1920s when it opposed (mainly Catholic and Jewish) immigration. By 1925, when its followers staged a huge Washington, D.C., march, the Klan had as many as 5 million members and considerable political power in some states. A series of sex scandals, internal battles over power, and newspaper exposés quickly reduced its influence.

The Klan arose a third time during the 1960s to oppose the civil rights movement and to preserve segregation in the face of unfavorable court rulings. The Klan's bombings, murders, and other attacks took a great many lives, including four young girls killed while preparing for services at the 16th Street Baptist Church in Birmingham, Alabama.

Since the 1970s, the Klan has been greatly weakened by internal conflicts, court cases, and a seemingly endless series of splits and government infiltration. While some factions preserved an openly racist and militant approach others tried to enter the mainstream, cloaking their racism as "civil rights for whites." Today, the SPLC estimates that there are a total of 5500 to 6000 Klan members split among scores of different and often warring organizations that use the Klan name. The total number of groups counted in 2002 was 133 compared to 109 in 2001, a 22% increase.

2. *Neo-Nazi* — Neo-Nazi groups share a hatred for Jews and a love for Adolf Hitler and Nazi Germany. While they also hate other minorities, homosexuals, and sometimes Christians. They perceive "the Jew" as their cardinal enemy and trace social problems to a Jewish conspiracy that supposedly controls governments, financial institutions, and the media. While some neo-Nazi groups emphasize simple hatred, others are more focused on the revolutionary creation of a fascist political state. Nazism, of course, has roots in Europe, and links between American and European neo-Nazis are strong and growing stronger. American neo-Nazi groups, protected by the First Amendment, often publish material and host Internet sites that are aimed at European audiences. These materials would be illegal under European antiracism laws. For this reason, many European groups have their Internet sites on American servers to avoid prosecution under the laws of their native countries. The most important neo-Nazi group in the U.S. is the National Alliance, founded by William Pierce, the infamous author of the futuristic race-war novel *The Turner Diaries*, a book believed by some to have served as the blueprint for

the 1995 Oklahoma City bombing. The total number of groups counted in 2002 was 220 compared to 209 in 2001.

3. **Racist Skinhead** — Racist Skinheads form a particularly violent element of the white supremacist movement and have often been referred to as the "shock troops" of the hoped-for revolution. The
classic Skinhead look is a shaved head, black Doc Martens boots,
jeans with suspenders, and an array of typically racist tattoos.

The Skinhead phenomenon began in the industrial cities of 1960s
Britain as a working-class movement strongly marked by contempt
for hippies and middle-class youth. Though drugs and violence
were always part of the Skinhead scene, Skinheads originally embraced Afro-Caribbean music and were of different races. British
fascists were able to precipitate a split in the movement between
racist and antiracist elements — a split that has endured to the
present day in Britain and in the U.S., where "Skins" arrived in the
early 1980s. Racist Skins are referred to by their enemies as "bone-
heads." Antiracist Skins are often referred to as SHARPS, a reference
to a now essentially defunct group known as Skinheads Against
Racial Prejudice.

Racist Skinheads in the U.S., like those in other countries, often
operate in small crews that move from city to city with some reg-
ularity. The largest and most dangerous Skinhead group today is
Hammerskin Nation, with thousands of members and extremely
violent track records in North America and Europe. The total number of groups counted in 2001 was 43, and in 2002 this number
reduced to 18.

4. **Christian Identity** — The Christian Identity religion asserts that
whites, not Jews, are the true Israelites favored by God in the Bible.
In most of its forms, Identity theology depicts Jews as biologically
descended from Satan, while non-whites are seen as soulless "mud
people" created with the other Biblical "beasts of the field." Christian
Identity has its roots in a 19th-century English fad called British
Israelism, which asserted that European whites were descended from
the ten "lost tribes" of Israel and were thus related to Jews, who were
descended from the other two Hebrew tribes mentioned in the Bible.
However British Israelism, which was initially friendly to Jews, was
adopted and transformed in the 20th century into a rabidly anti-Semitic creed by a number of racist preachers in the U.S.

For decades, identity has been one of the most important ideologies
for the white supremacist movement. In its hardest-line form, it asserts that Christ will not return to earth until the globe is swept clean
of Jews and other Satanic influences. In recent years deep doctrinal
disputes, the lack of a central church structure, and a shift among
white supremacists toward agnosticism and racist variations of
neo-Paganism weakened the Identity movement and reduced its

number of adherents. The total number of groups counted in 2001 was 31 and in 2002 was 27.

5. *Neo-Confederate* —Many groups celebrate traditional Southern culture and the Civil War's dramatic conflict between the Union and the Confederacy, but some groups go further and embrace racist attitudes toward blacks and, in some cases, white separatism. Such groups are listed in this category.

   The League of the South, founded in 1994 and counting some 9000 members by 2001, is at the center of the racist neo-Confederate movement. Calling once again for Southern secession, the League's leaders say minorities are destroying the Anglo-Celtic (white) culture of the South. They oppose most non-white immigration and all interracial marriages. Founder Michael Hill, a former college professor, called blacks "a deadly and compliant underclass" and embraced well-known white supremacists such as North Carolina attorney Kirk Lyons. The total number of groups counted in 2001 was 124 and in 2002 was 91.

6. *Black Separatist* — Black separatists typically oppose integration and racial intermarriage, and they want separate institutions — or even a separate nation — for blacks. Most forms of black separatism are strongly anti-white and anti-Semitic, and a number of religious versions assert that blacks, not Jews, are the Biblical "chosen people" of God.

   Although the SPLC recognizes that much black racism in America is at least in part a response to centuries of white racism, its members believe that racism must be exposed in all its forms. White groups espousing beliefs similar to Black Separatists would be considered clearly racist. The same criterion should be applied to all groups, regardless of their members' color. The total number of groups counted in 2001 was 51 and in 2002 the number reached 82, a 61% increase.

7. *Other* — Included in this category are hate groups with a hodgepodge of doctrines. Some, like the National Association for the Advancement of White People, are white supremacist groups masquerading as mainstream groups, with an interest in issues such as black crime, busing, and affirmative action. Others embrace racist forms of neo-Pagan religions such as Odinism, a pre-Christian theology that is largely focused on the virtues of the tribe or race.

   The Council of Conservative Citizens is a reincarnation of the White Citizens Councils that sprang up in the South in the 1950s and 1960s to oppose school desegregation. Like the League of the South, a neo-confederate group to which it has many links, the 15,000-member Council tried without success to mask its white supremacist ideology to further promote a right-wing political agenda. The total number of groups counted in 2001 was 109 and in 2002 this increased to 137.

Calculations and determinations that make up the SPLCs categories are based on group activities such as criminal acts, marches, rallies, speeches, meetings, and publications. Whether a group advocates or engages in violence or criminal activity is not applied. Therefore, use of the first seven domestic categories might be more applicable for matters of homeland security and terrorism analysis. However, for informational purposes and general relationship correlations, the SPLC categories would be of value pending further analysis.

As reflected in their maps, the SPLC also uses symbols to demonstrate the type of group being identified. Although these symbols are generic, few people have not seen these and know what they are intended to reflect. Although these symbols are used generically, they are hybrids of actual symbols used by the various organized hate groups located within the U.S. (Appendix C). Symbols have played an important role in groups for decades and are used as badges of honor, often worn on clothing and uniforms, reflected on flags and banners (such as depicted in Figure 2.2), or painted on buildings. Some members go as far as tattooing the symbols on their bodies. Many symbols have been modified even further and adopted by street-level gang members and inmates incarcerated in correctional institutions. Symbols, however, are not proprietary to U.S.-based organized hate groups. They have also been used by numerous international-based terrorist groups, such as the Irish Republican Army (IRA), and they can be found prominently displayed on buildings in areas controlled by the related organizations.

The use of symbols and knowledge of their meanings will be discussed in Appendix C. Identification of symbols in large international groups, organized hate groups, or even street gangs, may provide information into associations, relationships, or terrorist activity signatures. It is also important for law enforcement personnel to remain cognizant of international or foreign-based terrorist organizations, such as those listed in Appendix C, that may have fostered relationships or support of domestic groups or are active in the U.S. If a foreign-based terrorist organization is looking for a way to infiltrate the borders of a country, gaining access to an organized group of malcontents filled with extreme hatred opens new horizons for recruitment.

Now that we have an understanding of the types of terrorists and terrorist groups that exist, and where they exist, there is one last general

Figure 2.2 South Florida Aryan Alliance banner.

challenge for law enforcement. What is a terrorist? After all, there is no stereotypical terrorist appearance, race, religion, or ethnicity.

What is a terrorist?

One person's terrorist is another person's freedom fighter. In some cases, a terrorist may be seen as a leader, martyr, or visionary. However, in the world of law enforcement this argument is not necessarily a concern. "Criminal" is not usually thought of as an option for how a terrorist is seen. According to Brent Smith, terrorists remain criminals but are motivated by ideology, religion, or political cause. If one were to look at just eight pictures — Osama bin Laden, Timothy McVeigh, Yassar Arafat, Mohammad Atta, Che Guevara, Menachem Begin, Yahweh Ben Yahweh, and William Pierce — there would be much debate as to who the terrorists are. The perception would depend greatly on the year and the definition of terrorist that is used. Two of the individuals, Timothy McVeigh and Yahweh Ben Yahweh, were not initially viewed as terrorists at the time of their alleged atrocities. These individuals were seen as radicals, extremists, and criminals. All one has to do is check their criminal records, and you will not find them labeled as terrorists, the way we label sexual predators or career criminals. They were charged with crimes and sentenced accordingly. On the other hand, bin Ladin, Arafat, Atta, Guevara, and Begin do not have criminal records, at least not in the U.S.. Menachem Begin, the former prime minister of Israel, is described in the media, published documents, and the Internet as being active in Jewish guerilla activity, fighting for Jewish independence, and a member of the Irgun. The Irgun was considered one of the more relentless groups of the 1940s. The Irgun can be classified as a terrorist group, yet Begin is not referred to as a terrorist. As for Arafat, Atta, and Guevara, their descriptors run the gamut. Arafat and Guevara are described as guerilla fighters, freedom fighters, revolutionaries, martyrs, and terrorists. William Pierce, also known as Andrew MacDonald, writer of the *Turner Diaries* (1978), the book that Timothy McVeigh was allegedly in possession of at the time of his arrest, was perhaps one of America's most notorious neo-Nazis. He was the leader of the West Virginia-based National Alliance. To some he was known only as a professor holding a Ph.D. in physics, which he once taught at Oregon State University — not your stereotypical vision of a terrorist. This listing of eight individuals is just a sample of the controversy that can be stirred on the topic of what a terrorist is.

When it comes to identifying a terrorist, one area that was alluded to is organized hate group leaders or members. This is not an indictment that all individuals associated with these groups are terrorists, but many of those in leadership ranks expound extremism beliefs in America similar to those of terrorist leaders in the Middle East. There are also some similarities between many hate group leaders and terrorists. Their educations, personas, and exposures to military tactics are similar to many known terrorists. A recent review of 20 individuals seen as leaders and associated with extremism in America, according to the ADL, showed that several were highly educated and had authored several publications and books. In addition, some sought to become mainstream by running for political office. The party ticket of choice was often the Populist Party. However, some ran under the traditional Republican and Democratic Parties. Two ran for the presidency. One was elected, and served as a state representative in the Louisiana legislature. One ran and won a primary in California, and one won a large percent of the first ballot when running for the Arkansas office of lieutenant governor. Several served in the armed forces. There is no definitive way to identify a terrorist, hate group member, or potential recruit. They come from all walks of life, social classes, and educational levels. Regardless of their diverse backgrounds or locales, there are approaches that can be employed by analysts or investigators that will aid in identifying who might be a terrorist.

In order to initiate any form of analytical or intelligence-based undertaking, law enforcement personnel need to have a starting point for gathering and cataloging individuals and their activities. One starting point would be beliefs. In 1988, essentially three types of terrorist beliefs were identified that apply to virtually any individual who can be construed as being a terrorist or belonging to a terrorist group:

- Nationalistic
- Ideological
- Theological

The U.S. military recognizes and describes nationalistic and theological in their general terrorism training courses, both of which are applicable for use in law enforcement. "Nationalist terrorists seek to form a separate state for their own national group, often by drawing attention to a fight for 'national liberation' that they think the world has ignored."[3] Many members of nationalist groups are not viewed as terrorists but rather are seen by the populous as freedom fighters. An example of a nationalist group would be the Irish Republican Army whose members began their struggle not as a Catholic vs. Protestant religious conflict but rather as a fight for independence and establishment of an Irish state. As for ideological terrorists, their actions are simply based on their beliefs. The differences between nationalist and ideological are usually found in their goals. Many ideological terrorists expressed frustration toward social structures and capitalism, and they seek a new order. The third type of belief group is theological or religious terrorists who believe they speak and work for their chosen deity. They "seek to use violence to further what they see as divinely commanded purposes, often targeting broad categories of foes in an attempt to bring about sweeping changes."[3]

Once a belief or point of view is established, analytical personnel need to avoid grouping these individuals in general terms based on membership in a left- or right-wing movement. Terrorists are multifaceted. They often approach their mission much like a business. They have beliefs, and businesses have mission statements. They have economic needs and seek funding, and a business is always looking at the financial bottom line. They develop geographic bases of support, and businesses often look for location, location, location. Terrorists develop tactics to take advantage of others, and businesses develop tactics to outdo the competition and convince the consumer to buy their product. Terrorists selectively choose their targets, and businesses look for the target audience. Another consideration is that they may even change affiliations or beliefs. With this said, how can analytical personnel in the field of law enforcement differentiate between a terrorist and a criminal?

Terrorist vs. street criminal

Jonathan White offers a comparison of terrorist vs. typical street criminal.[7] Although it may not be all-inclusive or fit every situation, the information provided will greatly aid analytical personnel when categorizing individuals. This categorization is done much the same way as agencies decide what constitutes a gang member or career criminal. The difference is that we are now looking for the characteristics that might constitute a terrorist.

Differences between typical street criminals and terrorists[7]

- Terrorist
  - Fighting for political objective
  - Motivated by ideology or religion
  - Group-focused
  - Consumed with purpose
  - Trained and motivated for the mission
  - On the attack
- Typical street criminal
  - Crimes of opportunity
  - Uncommitted
  - Self-centered
  - No cause
  - Untrained
  - Escape-oriented

Members of the law enforcement community would probably readily agree about what constitutes a typical street criminal. It is the terrorist with whom those in the law enforcement community are unfamiliar and, except for a select few, have encountered. Using the above list, law enforcement personnel will be able to inquire about these variables when determining whether to document someone as a terrorist. This information will also enhance opportunities of developing interrelationship links. Determining whether or not a suspect fits the category of terrorist requires investigators and analysts to ask the fundamentals — who, what, where, when, why, and how — when encountering individuals. Chances of developing a profile that will fit most terrorists are highly unlikely. Asking the proper questions is essential when encountering individuals in order to identify differences, but these differences will not always be apparent. Such was the case with the September 11, 2001, terrorists.

September 11, 2001 — subjects, criminals, or terrorists?

The 19 subjects from the September 11, 2001, attack on America were undoubtedly terrorists as opposed to criminals. However, in order to demonstrate the effectiveness of the above terrorist vs. criminal comparison, all one has to do is look at the activity that led up to the tragic events, and look at a profile of the September 11, 2001, terrorists. These terrorists did not commit any violations of state or federal statutes (other than traffic and immigration violations) that would have classified them as criminals in a traditional law enforcement sense. Following is a profile of the terrorists:

- Ranged in age between their early 20s and mid 30s
- Primarily originated from Middle Eastern countries, traveled and resided in several different countries
- Were affiliated with an international group, al-Qaeda, known for its dislike of the American government
- Were motivated by religious beliefs and extreme ideology
- Usually had one spokesperson for the group
- Mainly used bank branches located in highly populated Muslim areas
- Usually came into banks as a group to open an account
- Wanted to deal with one person at the bank
- Nineteen hijackers opened over 20 domestic bank accounts at four different bank branches
- Opened bank accounts with a few thousand dollars within 30 days of arriving in the U.S., with three to four members present
- Did not have Social Security Cards, and used nonpermanent addresses
- Many lived within the same region, not all in one jurisdiction, and rented apartments
- Primarily had wire transfers done from United Arab Emirates (UAE), Saudi Arabia, and Germany, and used identification from these countries
- Made numerous balance inquiries
- Made overall transactions that were below federal banking guideline reporting requirements

- Purchased travelers checks overseas, brought them to the U.S., and deposited a portion of them in accounts
- Consumed with their mission and purpose, even willing to die for it
- Trained at several aviation schools as well as known terrorist camps

Based on the limited information above, there would be little if any reason for law enforcement to be concerned, especially if they were only looking for evidence of a crime. They were not what traditional law enforcement personnel were trained to detect and monitor, which are street criminals. There were no red flags. Analytical and investigative personnel need to be cautious when reviewing and discounting any information. What appears to be legitimate activity by law-abiding individuals may turn out to be something more if looked at over time or with a certain perspective.

It is apparent that financing placed an important role in the activities of the terrorists. Much of the money they obtained came via other operatives, also known as supporters and sleeper cells, operating in various European countries. These individuals obtained the money through legitimate businesses and employment, such as masonry work and automobile sales and repair. Other terrorists with al-Qaeda affiliations stated that they received training on criminal activities such as bank robberies and fraud schemes to fund their activities. They were also instructed in street crimes, such as residential and vehicle burglaries, as well as the use of stolen telephones and credit cards in order to facilitate their communication needs.

What appears to be noncriminal and run-of-the-mill may just be the piece of the puzzle needed to avert a catastrophic event. Remember, you are not just looking for street criminals anymore, and terrorists do not work alone. There is an infrastructure of support for every active terrorist. You must look at the big picture based on verified information, and you must avoid stereotypes. Terrorist groups are not just a ragtag bunch of individuals with fanatical or extreme beliefs. They are organized groups with structure and a management component.

Terrorism structure and management

Much like corporations, businesses, governments, and paramilitary or military organizations, terrorist groups have a structure and management component, as loose as it may appear to be.

In the 2003 government document "National Strategy for Combating Terrorism," a basic structure of terror was presented, which is demonstrated in Figure 2.3. "At the base, underlying conditions such as poverty, corruption, religious conflict, and ethnic strife create opportunities for terrorists to exploit."[29] Terrorists use these conditions to justify their actions and expand support. An organization's structure, membership, resources, and security determine its capabilities and reach. Open borders, and to some extent technology, allow for access to international resources and

Figure 2.3 National Strategy for Combating Terrorism structure.

new recruitment arenas. But no matter what, an organization must have a base of operation. Some organizations receive such bases of support, either physical or virtual, from states and countries all over the world. Groups such as al-Qaeda were able to establish and maintain bases and terrorist training camps in Afghanistan, and many others have done likewise in the Bekka Valley in Lebanon.

The leadership component becomes the catalyst for terrorist action. Regardless of size or structure, most organizations tend to utilize a chain-of-command style of management. Many terrorist groups, domestic and foreign based, and hate organizations also tend to follow a paramilitary or military organization when it comes to their training, structure, and tactics. The corporation or business world component is often displayed on the financial side of a terrorist organization. A tremendous financial need exists for an organization to keep a handful of operatives in the field, let alone to sustain the entire group. Therefore, many groups have turned to traditional criminal methods for gaining the capital they need to survive, committing crimes such as flimflams, credit card fraud, Internet scams, and robbery. However, these methods bring unwanted law enforcement attention to members of an organization. Therefore, many groups turned to business world ventures, such as nonprofit organizations. Law enforcement personnel and scholars would probably argue that these so-called business ventures are an exploitation of a capitalistic and free society. Many international groups that have a pure hatred for the U.S. and everything that it stands for have exploited the use of nonprofit religious and aid groups within the U.S. in order to increase their financial coffers.

Similar to Maslow's Hierarchy of Human Needs, terrorists have needs, too. Jonathan White demonstrated the use of James Fraser's (former U.S. Army counterterrorist specialist) and Ian Fulton's analyses and writings from 1984. This was done in the form of a pyramid, similar to the National Strategy for Combating Terrorism and to Maslow's Hierarchy, to explain the structural needs of terrorist organizations. Fraser pointed out that terrorist organizations are divided into four distinctly separate levels dependent upon each other: Command, Active Cadre, Active Supporters, and Passive Supporters.[7]

Figure 2.4 shows the four levels of an organization as developed by Fraser and Fulton. The Command level is at the top and is the smallest. Just like many businesses, it does not exercise direct day-to-day operational control of activities and individuals. Command-level members would be well-educated planners, financial monitors, and target selectors. The second level is the Active Cadre. This is the hard-core component of the organization that consists of the field soldiers and, as some communities have come to experience, suicide/homicide bombers. It is at this level that the mission gets carried out. Active Cadre members are aware of the existence of other members and the organization's beliefs but will have limited knowledge of missions beyond their roles. The third tier in the hierarchal structure is made up of the Active Supporters. These are the individuals charged with logistics, field support, and intelligence gathering for the Active Cadre. In order to keep one terrorist in the field, it takes several individuals to actively support the mission. The largest group is the Passive Supporters. They are used to muster up political or financial support. Many of these individuals do not even know they are supporting an active terrorist organization. Therefore, it is difficult to capture and identify verifiable intelligence on individuals who fall into this classification.

Organizational size varies. Terrorist organizations may have a handful of members or may have as many as 10,000 or more. Dealing with and managing such numbers of personnel is difficult enough in a legitimate business but in a covert terrorist organization of this size, opportunities for leaks exist. Leaders within these organizations realize the importance of being inconspicuous. Therefore, leaders keep communication, access to information, and mission details on a need-to-know basis, and often use small units, referred to as cells. The use of cells restricts the likelihood that law enforcement or spies can gain access to an organization. Cells are generally composed of four to six members, all with specialties to enhance the mission, and each member has limited knowledge of the overall mission. This ensures that if one is captured or intelligence is leaked, the entire mission is not jeopardized. It also makes infiltration of the group by law enforcement or a source of human intelligence nearly impossible. Similar to the military, where squads make up units and units make up divisions, a group of terrorist cells makes up columns. This form of command structure allows many

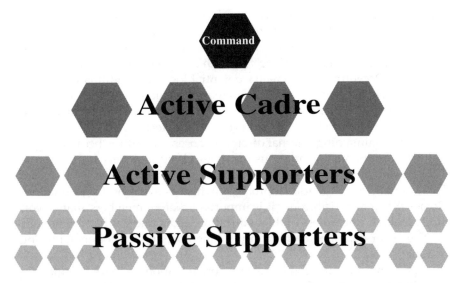

Figure 2.4 Command, active cadre, active supporters, and passive supporters.

individuals with various specialties to be under a single command. This is important for an analyst or investigator to know when developing leads and initiating a link analysis.

The makeup and structure of a terrorist organization make it ripe for dissent and problems. Management is difficult enough in the public sector, but couple it with a cloak of secrecy and you have a recipe for potential failure. Understanding the problems associated with terrorist management will give the law enforcement community the knowledge necessary to exploit the weaknesses of the enemy and to potentially turn these weakness into advantages.

Terrorist groups face several managerial problems. Outlined below are some of the more common problems of terrorist management:[7]

- Communicating within an infrastructure of secrecy
- Coordinating activities despite decentralization
- Maintaining internal discipline
- Avoiding fragmented ideologies
- Maintaining logistics
- Training
- Financing

Terrorist leaders face many special operational problems. Communicating within an infrastructure of secrecy is perhaps an organization's primary weakness. Even with technological advances such as satellite telephones and the Internet, terrorists find it difficult to communicate because they are decentralized. With every communication they run the risk of being intercepted and compromised. Although secrecy is a tactical advantage, terrorists still need some form of communication to survive.

A second problem for terrorists involves coordinating activities, without centralization. This is something to which many law enforcement agencies can relate. Decentralization creates potential logistical nightmares and mishaps. Large-scale terrorist operations require a coordinated effort in order to be successful. Decentralization combined with the first problem, communication, increase the likelihood of errors and detection.

Third, maintaining internal discipline poses difficulties, because organizational leaders must continuously strive to keep members focused on the mission as well as on the group's ideology in order to prevent defection. This overlaps with the fourth problem, which is avoiding fragmented ideologies. For a terrorist group, it is important that all members share a common ideology. Regardless of their education, economic status, or nationality, the one factor that often bonds a group's membership is a common ideology or belief system.

The fifth problem faced by terrorist organizations is that of maintaining logistics. It takes 35 to 50 support personnel to keep one terrorist active in the field.[30] Support personnel are essential for providing food, transportation, funding, communications, and housing. Housing is perhaps the greatest challenge, because in order to avoid detection it may be necessary for a terrorist to relocate numerous times before completing a mission.

Training, the sixth problem faced in terrorist management, is as vital to a terrorist as it is to a law enforcement official. It is one thing to adopt a belief system, but it is another matter to be effectively trained in how to handle situations. Many law enforcement officials who have faced deadly scenarios and survived are cited as giving credit to their training. They noted that their training caused their instincts to take over. The same holds true for just about anyone with an extensive training background, including a terrorist. However, the problem of training for a terrorist is compounded by logistics and secrecy. Establishing a training facility especially for conducting a deadly terrorist act is no easy task and can bring unwelcome attention to the group.

Financing is the seventh and final problem faced in terrorist management, and it applies to all managers, legitimate and terrorist-related. Financing lies at the heart of any operation. Terrorist attacks do not materialize overnight; they must be well planned and organized. They require considerable funding to sustain momentum. Financial means are needed for travel, lodging, food, supplies, training, and payoffs.

Using the above information, analysts and investigators must consider and evaluate these weaknesses. For every weakness in a terrorist organization, there is strength to be gained by law enforcement. It is up to the law enforcement community to become cognizant of terrorists' needs when gathering and analyzing information in order to effectively exploit a weakness and to seize the opportunity to thwart a tragic terrorist event.

Chapter concepts

1. For years, the definition of terrorism has been debated without concurrence on its meaning. This is because it has been defined within political and social contexts and has been influenced by history.
2. Terrorism has many different forms, including political, ecological, agricultural, narco, biological, and cyber.
3. Domestic terrorism is not a new phenomenon. It has evolved since 1791 and has gone through several different stages.
4. Different types of domestic terrorist groups are left-wing, right-wing, Puerto Rican leftists, black militants, Jewish extremists, and special interests.
5. Organized hate groups play a role in the context of domestic terrorism. These groups are categorized into white supremacy, hate groups, patriot movements, sovereign citizen movements, militias, tax protestors, and foreign sponsored.
6. There are three types of terrorist beliefs: nationalistic, ideological, and theological, and there are differences between a terrorist and a street criminal.

References

1. Stohl, M., *The Politics of Terrorism*, Stohl, M., Ed., Marcel Dekker, New York, 1979, p. 1.
2. Justice Department, Federal Bureau of Investigation, http://www.fbi.gov/publish/terror/terrusa.html (February 21, 2003).
3. General Military Training, Terrorism, N.p., n.d., p1-3-10, pl-3-14, and pl-3-16.
4. Heymann, P.B., *Terrorism and America: A Commonsense Strategy for a Democratic Society*, MIT Press, Cambridge, MA, 1998, p. 3.
5. Snow, D.M., *September 11, 2001, The New Face of War?*, Longman, New York, 2002, p. 1.
6. Lesser, I.O. et al., *Countering the New Terrorism, Implications for Strategy*, RAND, Santa Monica, CA, 1999, p. 85.
7. White, J.R., *Terrorism: An Introduction*, 4th ed., Thomson Wadsworth, Belmont, CA, 2002, pp. 23, 33, 36, 39.
8. United States Department of State Immigration and Nationality Act, Section 212 (a) (3) (B).
9. Hoffman, B., *Inside Terrorism*, Columbia University Press, New York, 1998, pp. 40, 107.
10. Gurr, T.R., Some characteristics of political terrorism in the 1960s, in *The Politics of Terrorism*, Stohl, M., Ed., Marcel Dekker, New York, 1979, pp. 25–49.
11. President, Report, The National Strategy for the Physical Protection of Critical Infrastructures and Key Assets, White House, February 2003, p. 9.
12. Able, D., *Hate Groups*, Enslow Publishers, Berkeley Heights, NJ, 2000, p. 26.
12a. O'Connor, T., Profiling Terrorists, http://faculty.ncwc.edu/toconnor/392/spy/terrorism.htm, Nov. 2002, North Carolina Wesleyan College.

12b. Harris, J.W., Domestic terrorism in the 1980's, *FBI Law Enforcement Bulletin* 56:5–13, 1987.

13. Senate Select Committee on Intelligence, The Terrorist Threat Confronting the United States, Statement for the Record of Dale L. Watson, February 6, 2002, p. 2.

14. Southern Poverty Law Center, 2001 Intelligence Report, http://www.tolerance.org/maps/hate/index.html (February 28, 2003), Hate Groups.

15. Potok, M., personal communication, March 10, 2003.

16. Perry, B., *In the Name of Hate: Understanding Hate Crimes*, Routledge, New York, 2001, pp. 138, 174.

17. MILNET, Known Domestic Terrorist Groups, http://www.milnet.com/milnet/tgp/tgpmain.htm (Oct. 25, 2002), Profiles of Domestic Terror Groups.

18. Hoffman, B., *Inside Terrorism*, Columbia University Press, New York, 1998, p. 107.

19. Southern Poverty Law Center, 2001 Intelligence Report, http://www.splcenter.org/intelligenceproject/ip-index.html (Feb. 2003, Known Active Patriot Groups in 2001).

20. MILNET, Domestic Terror: What it Holds for the Millenium, http://www.milnet.com/milnet/domestic/Dom-Terror.htm (Oct. 25, 2002), Domestic Terrorism a Definition, p. 2.

21. Uniting and Strengthening America by Providing Appropriate Tools Required to Intercept and Obstruct Terrorism (USA PATRIOT Act) Act of 2001, 107th Congress, 1st session, HR3162 (Oct. 24, 2001).

22. U.S. Senate Committees on Appropriations, Armed Services, and Select Committee on Intelligence, Threat of Terrorism to the United States, Statement for the Record, Louis J. Freeh, May 10, 2001.

23. Landau, E., *Terrorism: America's Growing Threat*, Lodestar Books (E.P. Dutton), New York, 1992, p. 45.

24. Laqueur, W., *The Age of Terrorism*, Little, Brown, Boston; New York, 1987, p. 335.

25. Council on Foreign Relations, Terrorism: Questions & Answers, http://www.cfrterrorism.org/groups/, American Militant Extremists United States, Radicals, (March 3, 2003).

26. Revell, B., A Long Path of Terror, http://www.adl.org, 1, 1, December 2002 (Feb. 20, 2003), On the Beat.

27. U.S. Justice Department, Federal Bureau of Investigation, http://www.fbi.gov/ucr/Cius_98, (Feb. 21, 2003).

28. Southern Poverty Law Center, *Hate Groups*, http://www.tolerance.org/maps/hate/index.html (March 6, 2003), Hate Group Definitions.

29. President, Report, National Strategy for Combating Terrorism, Feb. 2003, p. 6.

30. Bodansky, Y., *Bin Laden: The Man Who Declared War on America*, Forum, Rocklin, CA, 1999.

chapter three

Homeland security and analysis

The Symbionese Liberation Army (SLA) operated in the 1970s and targeted banks, initiated kidnappings, and bombed and killed law enforcement personnel, but it was seen as a revolutionary or radical group that was disgruntled with the government. Even after the final arrests, convictions, and sentencing of the remaining members in 2002 and 2003, approximately 30 years after the crime spree and killing began, they were still viewed as a fad or leftist group. They were also described as a group whose time had passed, and its members were described as criminals who were convicted and sentenced for traditional crimes. What makes this group different from members of al-Qaeda, besides al-Qaeda's international ties and size? Perhaps it was the fact that members of the SLA were citizens of the U.S. and looked and acted like the majority of other criminals or gangs.

For years, many groups such as these have operated within the country, dissatisfied with the government or the politics of the U.S. Throughout the 1960s and into the 1970s, many individuals and groups demonstrated in various ways against the U.S. and its political points of view. The war in Vietnam was frequently used as a reason for these antigovernment sentiments. Whether in the U.S. or in Europe, many factions sought to terrorize those associated with the war initiative. An example of this can be found in Germany, with the relatively small Bader-Meinhof Gang whose members had anti-Vietnam beliefs. However, much of the activity surrounding these rather small groups was seen more as a social or political nuisance rather than as terrorism. It was not until Ted Robert Gurr published the chapter "Some Characteristics of Political Terrorism" in *The Politics of Terrorism*[1] that what was taking place was shown to be more far-reaching than a mere nuisance: it was terrorism. Gurr noted that terrorist activity such as that demonstrated in the Vietnam era was conducted by very small groups and was ephemeral.

Regardless of the size of the group, terrorists and terrorism have a dramatic effect on the world, wherever the activity takes place. The victims or their family members are not concerned about the size of the group or if the group's activity was short-lived. However, they would have wanted some level of warning that an attack was imminent. Although the U.S. Government cannot provide a warning system based on intelligence for the entire world, it has been able to design and impose a system in the U.S. known as the Homeland Security Advisory System. The Homeland Security Advisory System was designed to provide a comprehensive and effective means by which to disseminate information regarding the risk of impending terrorist attacks to federal, state, and local law enforcement authorities as well as to the American public. When instituted in March 2002, the federal government initiated numerous press releases and garnered a massive amount of media attention designed to inform the public about the new advisory system. However, today many individuals in the public sector as well as in the law enforcement community still have only a vague awareness of the system and what each level on the continuum means. The following subsections are presented to ensure a standardized approach and awareness of the advisory system.

Homeland security defined

Just like defining terrorism, terrorist activity, or a terrorist, homeland security has many meanings to different people. The U.S. Federal Government defines homeland security as follows:

> Homeland security is a concerted national effort to prevent terrorist attacks within the U.S., reduce America's vulnerability to terrorism, and minimize the damage and recover from attacks that do occur.[2]

The government elaborated on each phrase in the above definition. "Concerted national effort" is based on the principles of shared responsibility and partnership with Congress, state and local governments, the private sector, and the American people. "Terrorist attacks" covers kidnappings, hijackings, shootings, conventional bombings, attacks involving chemical, biological, radiological, or nuclear weapons, cyber attacks, and any number of other forms of malicious violence. "Reduce America's vulnerability" by constantly evolving the way the government works with the private sector to identify and protect our critical infrastructure and key assets, to detect terrorist threats, and to augment our defenses. "Minimize the damage" requires our efforts to focus on the brave and dedicated public servants who are our first responders. To "recover," we must be prepared to protect and restore institutions needed to sustain economic growth and confidence, rebuild destroyed property, assist victims and their families, heal psychological wounds, and demonstrate compassion, recognizing that we cannot return to a preattack norm.

Regardless of how homeland security is defined, a terrorist threat can come from anywhere. Based on the National Strategy for Combating Terrorism report, the terrorist threat is flexible, transnational, enabled by modern technology, and characterized by loose interconnectivity within and between groups.[1a] These groups operate on three levels. The first level consists of those who operate within a single country and have a limited reach. The second level is comprised of the terrorist organizations that operate regionally. These operations transcend at least one international boundary. Organizations with global reaches constitute the third category. Their operations span multiple regions, and their reaches can be global. The U.S. is subject to attack from all three levels; therefore it is imperative that intelligence be expedited and advisories posted as soon as applicable.

Homeland security advisory system

This advisory system was instituted in March 2002 by the U.S. Federal Government to provide a level of awareness of the likelihood of potential terrorist attacks to state and local governments and ordinary citizens, regardless of their locale. The determination of each level is decided upon by high-ranking government officials based on a wide range of information and intelligence received and corroborated by a multitude of sources worldwide. Once intelligence is developed, it is verified and corroborated against multiple variables and scenarios to determine if it is credible, if there is a specific threat, or if there is a grave threat. Only then is it presented for proper advisement and color designation, following the Homeland Security Presidential Directive 3. The hierarchy used is called the Homeland Security Advisory System and is demonstrated in Figure 3.1. This system, which is used as a guide,[3] is an intelligence-driven system designed to aid law enforcement and the public in responding or preparing for a terrorist threat.

The advisory system was well publicized, but the public lacks finite understanding as to what each level represents. Outlined below is a summary of each level as posted on the Department of Homeland Security's Web site.[4]

Low condition (green)

This condition is declared when there is a low risk of terrorist attacks. Federal departments and agencies should consider the following general measures in addition to the agency-specific protective measures they develop and implement:

1. Refining and exercising, as appropriate, preplanned protective measures

Figure 3.1 Homeland Security Advisory System.

2. Ensuring that personnel receive proper training on the Homeland Security Advisory System and on specific preplanned department or agency protective measures
3. Institutionalizing a process to assure that all facilities and regulated sectors are regularly assessed for vulnerabilities to terrorist attacks, and all reasonable measures are taken to mitigate these vulnerabilities

Guarded condition (blue)

This condition is declared when there is a general risk of terrorist attacks. In addition to the protective measures taken in the previous threat condition, federal departments and agencies should consider the following general measures in addition to the agency-specific protective measures that they will develop and implement:

1. Checking communications with designated emergency response or command locations

2. Reviewing and updating emergency response procedures
3. Providing the public with any information that would strengthen its ability to act appropriately

Elevated condition (yellow)

An elevated condition is declared when there is a significant risk of terrorist attacks. In addition to the protective measures taken in the previous threat conditions, federal departments and agencies should consider the following general measures in addition to the protective measures that they will develop and implement:

1. Increasing surveillance of critical locations
2. Coordinating emergency plans, as appropriate, with nearby jurisdictions
3. Assessing whether the precise characteristics of the threat require further refinement of preplanned protective measures
4. Implementing, as appropriate, contingency and emergency response plans

High condition (orange)

A high condition is declared when there is a high risk of terrorist attacks. In addition to the protective measures taken in the previous threat conditions, federal departments and agencies should consider the following general measures in addition to the agency-specific protective measures that they will develop and implement:

1. Coordinating necessary security efforts with federal, state, and local law enforcement agencies or any National Guard or other appropriate armed forces organizations
2. Taking additional precautions at public events and possibly considering alternative venues or even cancellations
3. Preparing to execute contingency procedures, such as moving to an alternate site or dispersing their workforce
4. Restricting access to threatened facility to essential personnel only

Severe condition (red)

A severe condition reflects a severe risk of terrorist attacks. Under most circumstances, the protective measures for this condition are not intended to be sustained for substantial periods of time. In addition to the protective measures in the previous threat conditions, federal departments and agencies should also consider the following general measures in addition to the agency-specific protective measures that they will develop and implement:

1. Increasing or redirecting personnel to address critical emergency needs
2. Assigning emergency response personnel and prepositioning and mobilizing specially trained teams or resources
3. Monitoring, redirecting, or constraining transportation systems
4. Closing public and government facilities

The Homeland Security Advisory System is managed by the U.S. Attorney General in concert with the Secretary of the Department of Homeland Security. They are responsible for developing, implementing, and managing the system for the federal government based on the latest verified intelligence. A potential concern, which is not publicly addressed, regarding the system is whether the information and intelligence being used to make informed decisions are inclusive of domestic terrorist activities or are just foreign-based. Also, it is not public knowledge whether the intelligence is a derivative of local and state law enforcement information or is just from federal and military sources. Despite this, it is imperative that law enforcement agencies submit all intelligence as soon as it is developed. In addition, state and local governments have been encouraged to implement the advisory system and modify it to meet the needs of their agencies.

Use of such a system is vital to standardizing practices, approaches, and contingency plans when dealing with homeland security or terrorism risks. However, one should not become consumed with the advisory system or wait until a particular level is announced. This would be reactive, just like the system that is designed to help aid in preparing and responding. The system is full of suggestive reactionary practices that will aid any agency or its citizens in responding to threats, but law enforcement personnel are now looking to identify the threat and not just to respond. Waiting for the federal government or anyone else to initiate a threat level before doing anything would be neglect of duty. Every agency and its members are part of the solution, and analytical practices should be undertaken and be continuous, whether or not agency staff members feel they have anything to bring to the homeland security table. Regardless of the advisory level, information gathering and analysis should be continuous and should be routinely reconciled in order to paint the clearest picture. Analysis should be continuous and heightened as the advisory level is raised. Analysts must be well-rounded, look globally, and have an acute awareness of their roles and how their duties can benefit homeland security.

Homeland security and analysis

Several factors are used to assess a potential homeland security or terrorist threat. These factors include whether the threat is credible, whether it is corroborated, whether it is specific and imminent, and how grave it is. These four factors should be at the immediate crux of any form of real-time intelligence analysis being conducted. In the realm of law enforcement, the approach is often to follow a hunch or gut feeling when seeking out criminal activity or developing a trend or pattern. With homeland security, there is no such opportunity. When dealing with the traditional criminal element, there is rarely a situation that will negatively and tragically impact more people or countries than terrorism. Therefore, there is no room for anything less than credible, corroborated, timely, and well-defined information.

According to the Department of Homeland Security's White House Web site (2002), Information Analysis and Infrastructure Protection:

> The CIA will continue to gather and analyze overseas intelligence. Homeland Security will continue to require interagency coordination...[4]

Imposing vague terminology such as "require interagency coordination," reduces the chance that all law enforcement agencies will work together or in a real-time fashion. The fact that there is no mention of gathering and analyzing domestic intelligence, only overseas, is greatly disturbing and may cause law enforcement personnel to overlook potential threats to homeland security that may come about from factions in their own backyards. As alluded to in the White House's March 12, 2002, press release concerning the Homeland Security Advisory System, states and localities are encouraged to adopt and implement compatible systems. The question is, how many states and localities have adopted or implemented compatible systems? This question is not meant to be a criticism but is designed to demonstrate the need for self-initiated and documented processes and systems that will aid all parties involved in the war on terrorism. Since September 11, 2001, communication and intelligence processes were thrust into the forefront of any successful antiterrorism campaign. However, these processes vary from agency to agency. Although international or foreign-based terrorist organizations can never be overlooked, there is a great deal of information from a myriad of resources on these groups, but there is little on domestic terrorist or organized hate groups. Based on the lack of domestic intelligence coordination and communication, it is incumbent upon law enforcement personnel, analysts included, to provide real-time intelligence analysis and to effectively disseminate it and provide accurate advisories without delay.

Dealing with homeland security and terrorism analysis has been addressed up to now largely by federal law enforcement and military analysts. Even though these well-trained analysts have a lot to offer, their traditional duties and practices do not always translate easily into effective local and state law enforcement procedures. The primary reason for this is that they have two distinctly different missions. Law enforcement analysts use federal and state guidelines, and they operate in defined jurisdictional areas. Military analysts use directives, treaties, resolutions, and international laws, and they operate in an international theater. Simply put, it is crime vs. war. Therefore, it is incumbent upon law enforcement personnel to develop the best of both worlds into methods that can be readily adapted and retro-fitted in order to enhance the capabilities of analysts and investigators charged with handling homeland security issues.

One way to adapt is by developing a base from which to start. The National Strategy for Homeland Security report developed such a base. This strategy identified a strategic framework based on three national objectives that are also applicable to any agency, regardless of size. In order of priority, these are to prevent terrorist attacks within the U.S., to reduce America's vulnerability to terrorism, and to minimize the damage and recover from attacks that occur.[5] The first two objectives are those that law enforcement, particularly analysts, can be successful at obtaining. However, the third objective seems to be the focus of many lectures and training courses given to law enforcement officials. As interagency and intergovernmental coordi-nation is enhanced, the first two proactive objectives will overshadow the third, which is partially reactive. All these objectives were made slightly more attainable, in part due to legislative enhancements such as the USA PATRIOT Act.

The USA PATRIOT Act

The USA PATRIOT Act of 2001, formally known as the Uniting and Strength-ening America by Providing Appropriate Tools Required to Intercept and Obstruct Terrorism Act of 2001 from the 107th Congress, HR 3162, was established to deter and punish terrorist acts in the U.S. and around the world, and to enhance law enforcement investigatory tools.[6]

The USA PATRIOT Act of 2001 was unprecedented. National and world events surrounding September 11, 2001, were the driving force behind the evolution and passage of what has become known simply as the Patriot Act. These events were the stimuli for the possibly record-breaking pace in which this act was passed and subsequently signed by President George W. Bush on October 26, 2001. This was just one month after being initiated and being passed in the Senate by a 98-to-1 vote. This massive sweeping legislation positively impacted law enforcement agencies and their roles in combating terrorism, and it covered a broad range of topics.

Some of the topics covered by the USA PATRIOT Act include the fol-lowing:

- Enhancing domestic security against terrorism
- Enhancing surveillance procedures
- International Money Laundering Abatement and Antiterrorist Financing Act of 2001
- Protecting the border
- Removing obstacles to investigating terrorism

- Providing for victims of terrorism, public safety officers, and their families
- Increasing information sharing for critical infrastructure protection
- Strengthening criminal laws against terrorism
- Improving intelligence
- Protecting critical infrastructures

Interestingly, although the content of the act appears all-encompassing, domestic terrorism is not defined until about three-quarters of the way through the document. While this is not necessarily viewed as a negative trait, it is important that all law enforcement personnel remain cognizant of the numerous domestic-based organizations as well as the foreign-based international ones that have bases, outreaches, and supporters within the U.S. The act was a product born out of international terrorist actions. However, it is also worth noting that this act is not meant just for investigating and analyzing exotic foreign terrorist-based groups. It applies to all groups, domestic and international, and all forms of terrorism.

Passage of this act greatly improved the tools available for law enforcement. Beyond the immediate benefit of the act, which is enhanced surveillance procedures, law enforcement at all levels will reap the greatest investigative rewards from the money-laundering and financial tracking capabilities as well as the increased information sharing among agencies. The act is geared toward the one thing that no terrorist organization can do without, finances.

Importance of finances

Tracking, monitoring, and cutting off of finances are tremendously important tools in the war on terrorism. As of October 2002, an aggressive international law enforcement effort resulted in the freezing of $113 million in terrorists' assets in 500 bank accounts around the world, with much activity in Western countries, including $35 million in the U.S.[7]

The use of sleeper cells and activity associated with their efforts for financial gain has already been discussed. However, other forms of funding are used, such as nongovernment organizations (NGOs) and charitable organizations. Many of these are passed off as legitimate business ventures, but things are not always as they appear. International fundamentalist terrorists increased their use of NGOs and charitable organizations as a way to gain finances for use in their terrorist activities. NGOs are used much in the same manner as active supporters. They may offer logistical support in the forms of employment, documents, travel, and training. Uses of "fronts" by terrorist organizations (such as Hamas) in the U.S. uncovered charities, humanitarian foundations, and relief organizations that were used to raise funding in support of terrorist activities. Speaking in 1995 on the topic of protecting America, Oliver Revell stated that "Numerous front groups supporting Hamas have been established in the U.S. and several collect funds as tax exempt 501(C)(3) organizations."[8] Tremendous challenges exist for law enforcement personnel investigating terrorist fund-raising through the use of NGOs and alleged charitable humanitarian organizations. The line between legitimate and what may appear to be legitimate is often blurred.

Financing efforts by terrorist organizations have ranged from basic to sophisticated. There is probably not a financing method known that has not been tried at least once. Use of correspondent bank accounts, private bank accounts, offshore shell banks, Hawalas (see below), cash smuggling, identity theft, credit card fraud, drug trafficking, money laundering (which will be explained in further detail under enhanced analysis), and flimflams are prevalent. The terrorist's goal is to seek financial gain while remaining undetected. That is why the USA PATRIOT Act plays an important role with its emphasis on financial topics. Regardless of the form of terrorism being investigated, the PATRIOT Act opens new avenues for law enforcement. As law enforcement targets traditional financial methods, terrorists are more apt to use ancient and informal methods to move money, such as the Hawala system.

Hawala

Hawala is an ancient alternative or parallel remittance system that originated in South Asia. It is based largely on trust and extensive use of connections, such as family members and other known affiliations. It was developed in India before the introduction of traditional banking practices and is often referred to as an underground banking system. There is little documentation and record keeping. There are many motivations for using the Hawala system, including its effectiveness, efficiency, reliability, lack of bureaucracy, lack of a paper trail, and ability to evade taxes. Many transactions associated with Hawala are done in the area of import and export businesses, travel services, jewelry, and currency exchanges. Invoice manipulation can be used to cover payments. For example, if an individual owes another $10,000, a purchase of goods is arranged at $7000 and an invoice is sent for $17,000. This conceals the purchase of the goods as well as the money owed. Hawala quite often will not use any sort of negotiable instrument. Money transfers take place based on communications among members of the Hawala network.

This brief section is meant to provide an awareness of alternative forms of financial transactions that exist in the world. It is important to note that there are documented incidents of the use of Hawala in terrorist events. Further details and references on Hawala systems can be attained by law enforcement personnel through the U.S. Department of Treasury Financial Crimes Enforcement Network (FinCEN) and Interpol. Knowledge of the various methods that a group may use to conduct financial affairs is another tool that will aid law enforcement in dealing with terrorism.

Dealing with terrorism

One of the great frustrations in dealing with terrorism is the wide variety of forms that terrorist acts can take.[9] Terrorism assumes many guises, such as those noted in the previous section, e.g., political and cyber. These forms are compounded by the various types and styles of attacks beyond conventional bombings. If dealing with terrorist acts is frustrating, how are the investigative and analytical worlds to make sense of it? Traditionally, analysts and investigators have looked for common links and approaches that aided them in concluding their criminal investigations. An analyst assigned a case to monitor and gather intelligence leads and information and will utilize various analytical techniques, often through the use of sophisticated software, in order to link common variables (also known as link analysis). Analysts have criminal and statutory guidelines to assist in the pursuit of developing probable cause and securing a criminal conviction. The numerous off-the-shelf intelligence programs are designed to expedite the intelligence process and graphically illustrate interrelationships that otherwise may be overlooked. These luxuries are not as available when dealing with homeland security and terrorism. There are thousands of law enforcement agencies in the U.S., with 50 sets of varied state statutes, and much of what may be construed as a homeland security incident or terrorism becomes classified as a crime. An all-inclusive database or intelligence system that all agencies can agree upon does not exist. Whether it is a hijacking or a bombing, the first inclination of law enforcement personnel is that to treat it as a violent crime that needs immediate response and attention, not a homeland security or terrorist action. This was true until September 11, 2001. How can we be sure that everyone is on the same page and is keeping an open mind as to the potential for terrorism to strike anywhere? The answer is simply through open communication, detailed information, proactive investigations, and the use of highly trained analytical and intelligence personnel.

Enforcing cooperation between the CIA and the FBI and the Immigration and Naturalization Service (INS) is essential in dealing with terrorism.[9] This is unarguably true; however, the same premise should be enforced between municipal, county, state, and federal law enforcement agencies. All levels of response, including investigation and information gathering, are crucial pieces to the puzzle when dealing with homeland security and terrorism. After all, it is not just international terrorist organizations overseas that need to be monitored. There are many domestic-based groups actively or passively operating in everyone's own backyard. Whether an investigation is local, state, or federally based, money is one nexus that, if exposed, can bring all agencies together. International and domestic-based terrorist organizations generally have one feature in common: the need for financing. As documented in Steven Emerson's remarkable video documentary for the Public Broadcasting System (PBS) that aired in November, 1994 titled "Jihad in America," terrorist organizations, regardless of how much they despise and loath the U.S., have no problem seeking support and financial backing in the U.S. Based on this critical need, perhaps the best approach for dealing with terrorism is to track money and finances.

It can be detrimental to be one-dimensional and not to consider global approaches to homeland security and terrorist-related information. It has been demonstrated that terrorist activity can occur anywhere and at any time, but financial support is an ongoing process with many guises. This need exists and perhaps poses the greatest opportunity for law enforcement to expose and exploit in order to gain the upper hand in tracking and monitoring potential homeland security threats.

Homeland security and terrorism have received a great deal of public attention over the past couple of years. Most of the attention came from the federal government and the media. Law enforcement agencies, based on this attention, were forcefed a multitude of methods and practices for dealing with homeland security and terrorism matters. Some local and state agencies established homeland security units in an attempt to keep up with the growing concerns facing the ever-evolving world of terrorism. Traditional managers and administrators also reacted to this crisis, predictably, by having their agencies develop plans of action and contingency plans and by identifying potential targets that exist within their jurisdictions in case of an attack. However, this can be construed as nothing more than window dressing. Something near and dear to all managers is the budget, and this, perhaps, is the leading cause as to why only "window dressing" has been applied.

Agencies nationwide are continuously being asked to do more with less. Homeland security and terrorism analysis is just another opportunity to do more with less. Overnight, agencies began assigning investigative and analytical personnel to address their agencys' homeland security needs and to serve as points of contact. It has become the responsibility of these points of contact to expeditiously educate themselves in their new roles and to pass this knowledge and insight on to other personnel. Limitations were imposed on training and capital equipment purchases for numerous newly established units. Allocations were based on previously established budgets, and for many agencies the expansion of these monies is bleak. No matter what, law enforcement will have to deal with terrorism and continue to address concerns as they arise without excuses.

This has been only a cursory overview of some of the concerns facing government agencies in their attempts to deal with terrorism. The number of concerns needing to be addressed is yet to be determined, but there are some issues that can be overcome without draining the budget.

Law enforcement concerns

There are many concerns beyond budgetary to be faced by law enforcement personnel and agencies regarding homeland security and terrorism analysis. Throughout the decades, law enforcement personnel and academia have done a respectable job of educating and promoting awareness of criminal concerns across the board. There have been many models designed to standardize an array of law enforcement concerns ranging from Community-Oriented Policing (COPs) to the New York Police Department's Computerized Statistics performance-based management approach (COMPSTAT). One model that is known to virtually every sworn law enforcement person is the SARA (scan, analyze, respond, and assess) model (Figure 3.2). These components were readily understood, but before the regular use of analytical personnel law enforcement circles often joked that the "*A*"s were overlooked or forgotten.

Just as law enforcement has organized practices into a model context, the same can be done with terrorism. Also demonstrated in Figure 3.2 is the use of the SARA model as a terrorist model. Terrorists have a planning stage (target selection, analyzing, and assessing the mission), a research (reconnaissance) stage, and an execution stage (the attack). For a terrorist, use of all these stages is integrated and inseparable. Otherwise, the mission will

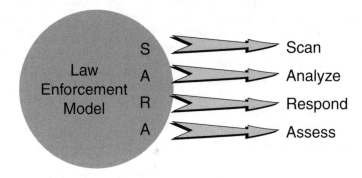

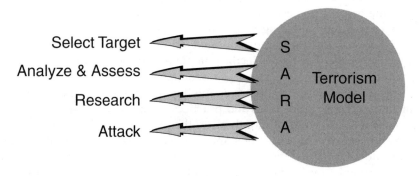

Figure 3.2 SARA and terrorism models.

fail. Terrorist activity is not designed to help anyone other than the terrorist, or the terrorist organization, in promoting their perceptions in the name of their cause. Terrorists do not randomly and spontaneously pick their targets. As history has demonstrated, terrorists are often selective in their targets, seeking to maximize the tragedy in physical and psychological terms. This requires extensive analysis and assessment. It may take years, but when they are ready they will regroup and implement their plan of action. Dealing with individuals who have the patience and capability to undertake extensive campaigns poses a new concern for law enforcement personnel used to dealing with people who commit crimes of opportunity and greed.

American law enforcement is also worried about local issues and concerns, and most police managers do not think abstractly but pride themselves on a pragmatic approach.[10] Critical thought inevitably focuses on local issues. Often overlooked are issues of displacement and how actions may impact other jurisdictions. Terrorism is viewed as too exotic for most agencies to be concerned with. This is not necessarily the fault of chiefs of police or their staffs. The political and budgetary concerns of all government entities, not just law enforcement, drives the way these businesses are run. This has led many managers and leaders to stay focused on issues specific to their jurisdictions, and when necessary on the immediate region, but seldom beyond that. This attitude permeates from the unwillingness of the constituents being served to pay for services rendered outside their jurisdictional boundaries. It is important for the law enforcement community to educate not only its personnel but also the public and government officials on the vital need to work outside any one particular jurisdiction and to work in concert with regional, state, and federal agencies on matters of homeland security and terrorism.

Sharing information and intelligence by analysts, investigators, and counterterrorism agents is essential and probably poses the greatest concern for law enforcement at all levels. Jurisdictional haggling, credit claiming, and unnecessary secrecy permeate the counterterrorist and law enforcement communities. A sense of ownership and zeal to handle a case is commendable, but when dealing with homeland security and terrorism issues there is no time to play games among agencies — time is of the essence. Interagency cooperation also fragments on jurisdictional grounds or on the perceived level of threats being exhibited and the immediacy of response needed. Most agencies have specific guidelines outlined in their policies and procedures manuals covering traditional law enforcement response and investigation but they fail to cover intelligence gathering and matters of homeland security. Procedures and practices must be demonstrated in writing and not left to word of mouth or on-the-job training. The magnitude of homeland security investigations and the need to corroborate information are dependent upon details and documentation; therefore, proven and standardized practices must be used. Once standardized practices are put into place, agencies must arrive at some sort of consensus on a database structure before developing one. Using existing systems may not suffice due to limited data fields, too many narrative fields, or lack of compatibility with other agencies. Minimum database requirements need to be established. Not every agency will have the same database software, but by following predefined requirements investigations can be enhanced and time can be saved.

Law enforcement agencies typically separate what would today be classified as terrorist into criminal, political, or mentally unstable categories, and these classifications may be too simplistic. As demonstrated earlier, terrorist behavior differs from that of ordinary street criminals. Criminal investigation techniques must be modified to reflect these differences when examining terrorist cases. Another factor to consider is how agencies and the FBI have captured data on terrorist acts in the past. The FBI has labeled the majority of domestic terrorist activities under nonterrorist headings in the Uniform Crime Reporting (UCR) system. Many incidents were investigated, classified, and reported as hate crimes, or under the routine UCR reporting classifications of Part 1, Part 2, and noncriminal. The use of the FBI's classification, hate crimes, is expressly true when dealing with domestic-based terrorist groups. This can possibly be attributed to a group's lack of leadership, infrequency of action, members being "single-event wonders," or to the hatred by some groups toward a specific segment of the population. American law enforcement officers routinely deal with significant homeland security and terrorism issues and unintentionally dismiss any correlation, referring to the incidents as routine crimes. This can be largely attributed to a lack of coordination, training, and awareness.

Coordination, training, and awareness

Paramilitary organizations such as law enforcement have long prided themselves on their expertise, training, and adaptability. Training is the foundation upon which law enforcement practices are built. From day one, officers are trained in detail on everything from report writing to firearms. However, this training is generally geared only toward handling typical street crimes, and the closest they get to terrorism—on the U.S. Army Spectrum of Conflict—is riots and disorders through Field Force or Special Event Response Team training. On the other hand, many agencies have gone to the other extreme by providing training on law enforcement response to weapons of mass destruction, the last item on the U.S. Army's Spectrum. It is commendable that training is being provided concerning weapons of mass destruction, especially to first responders, but what about the rest of the spectrum, particularly terrorism? Although there are no hard numbers to go by, it is more likely that an officer will encounter a member of any one of the hundreds of organized hate and terrorist groups before he encounters weapons of mass destruction.

How do you train between 600,000 and 700,000 American law enforcement personnel, and where do you start? You start with the basics. Many basic law enforcement training initiatives relating to terrorism are focused on response. This is indicative of being reactive, and when dealing with homeland security and terrorism one needs to be proactive. Educating on topics such as what to look for, questions to ask, identity concerns, and what homeland security and terrorism are should be emphasized. In addition to the training, many educational and reference materials available for law enforcement are geared toward response topics and some preventative scenarios. There is currently one federally funded program that since 1996 has addressed the material in between these two topics and is designed to aid with intelligence and investigations relating to domestic terrorism. However, until September 11, 2001 many agencies were probably unaware of the existence of this program, or if they were, saw no need to attend. This deficiency caused many local and state agencies to turn to training from the military and federal agencies. Cooperation such as this is commendable, but agencies need to be mindful of the inherent differences in the style, mission, and type of law enforcement being practiced.

Coordination of law enforcement activities among various agencies is something that is done daily. Agencies often work under cooperative work agreements or memorandums of understanding (MOUs) and joint regional task forces. When operating under an MOU, agencies clearly spell out the guidelines to be followed and who will be in charge. The same cannot be said for homeland security, terrorism, and some routine investigations. It is these gray areas that often lead to confusion and, more importantly, lost information or intelligence. To demonstrate this point, several general incident categories are outlined below. Information and intelligence data are often routed to specific (different) locations or agencies whose members do not necessarily share all aspects of an investigation or all information:

- Terrorist-related: Federal Bureau of Investigation (FBI)
- Bomb-related: Alcohol, Tobacco, and Firearms (ATF)
- Bomb hoaxes: Police General Investigation Units
- Biohazardous materials: Fire departments
- Arson: Fire departments, fire marshals, arson investigators, ATF
- Explosive devices or chemicals: Bomb squads
- Deaths involved: Homicide investigators
- Fugitives: U.S. Marshal's Service, FBI, County Sheriff's Office
- Miscellaneous: Gang units, robbery units, task forces, other jurisdictions, and county or state law enforcement agencies

Unless a terrorist-related event has a red flag associated with it, there is a great likelihood that the pieces of the puzzle can be scattered across multiple jurisdictions and databases.

The lack of awareness concerning homeland security, terrorism, and organized hate groups on many fronts is prevalent throughout law enforcement. Some of this is attributed to training matters and some is due to the lack of intelligence. The "I'll know it when I see it" approach will not work.

In order to have effective information gathering and analysis, all members of an organization must be on the same page. Even if an agency had investigators dedicated to information gathering and analysis, these investigators cannot be everywhere and know everything. All members in an agency are part of the solution, and in order to be of value they need to have knowledge of the matter being faced and be educated to identify what pieces of information should be gathered. Once the logistics and educational issues are addressed, agencies can then focus on gathering information.

Chapter concepts

1. Despite the brevity of the homeland security definition, each phrase is replete with meaning and can be adopted by any governmental agency.
2. The Homeland Security Advisory System consists of five levels: green, blue, yellow, orange, and red, each representing varying degrees of alert, preparation, and response.
3. The USA PATRIOT Act has many roles in the war on terrorism, particularly with respect to finances.
4. Dealing with terrorism is novel for law enforcement, and there are many new concerns being faced by agencies and government managers.
5. Government and law enforcement agencies investigating crimes must be cognizant of the need to coordinate and train their personnel, as they encounter potential terrorist and organized hate crime activities.

References

1. Stohl, M., *The Politics of Terrorism*, Stohl, M., Ed., Marcel Dekker, New York, 1979, p. 1.
1a. President, Report, The National Strategy for Combating Terrorism, White House, Feb. 2003, p. 8.
2. President, Report, The National Strategy for Homeland Security, Office of Homeland Security, July 16, 2002, p. 2.
3. Ridge, T., Gov. Ridge Announces Homeland Security Advisory System, Office of the Press Secretary, White House, March 12, 2002.
4. Department of Homeland Security, http://www.whitehouse.gov/ (Feb. 21, 2003), Homeland Security Advisory System.
5. President, Report, The National Strategy for the Physical Protection of Critical Infrastructures and Key Assets, White House, Feb. 2003, p. 1.
6. Uniting and Strengthening America by Providing Appropriate Tools Required to Intercept and Obstruct Terrorism (USA PATRIOT Act) Act of 2001, 107th Congress, 1st session, Oct. 24, 2001.

7. Congressional Research Service, Report IB95112, Terrorism, the Future, and U.S. Foreign Policy, Lee, R. and Perl, R., Issue Brief for Congress, Dec. 12, 2002, p. CRS-2.

8. Revell, O., Protecting America: law enforcement views radical Islam, March 1995, http://www.meforum.org/article/235 (March 11, 2003), *Middle East Quarterly*, p. 4.

9. Snow, D.M., *September 11, 2001, The New Face of War?*, Longman, New York, 2002, p. 11.

10. White, J.R., *Terrorism: An Introduction*, 4th ed., Thomson Wadsworth, Belmont, CA, 2002, p. 207.

chapter four

Gathering information, the key to the process

Several definitions of what constitutes the duties of an intelligence or crime analyst have been debated throughout the law enforcement profession since at least 1972. This was noted in a review of numerous job descriptions from around the United States in March 2000. Although at all levels and professions these analysts perform a wide range of tasks and skill sets, researchers consistently noted that gathering, analyzing, and disseminating crime information are among the daily duties of those they examined.

When gathering crime information for a law enforcement agency concerned with predefined jurisdictional limitations, most information is derived from one source, the offense and incident report. The inherent restriction here is that the information is limited by the fact that it must be reported. Therefore, it is reactive; and it must be written from the perspective of the responding officer, thus it is subjective. In dealing with terrorism, these restrictions must be exploited and exposed. Being proactive is a must, and in order to spawn intelligence you need as much information as possible, for without information, you will have no intelligence. There is no such thing as a bad source, only bad information. Information equals intelligence, not the other way around. Gathering or obtaining good, clean, timely, and accurate information is key.

Intelligence gathering

The primary objective of intelligence gathering "...is to deal with future danger, not to punish past crimes."[1] This rings especially true in the world of terrorism. Although you are not seeking to punish past crimes, you cannot discount their usefulness when attempting to understand the future.

Information is endless in terms of quantity. There are no limitations to the resources that can create useful and viable information. Perhaps the best source of information is that which comes from human sources. However, in law enforcement the use of undercover officers and informants is limited. The costs and risks associated with such operations are exponential. Also, many of the terrorist groups and organized hate groups are closed societies and are difficult to infiltrate. Therefore, much of the information gathered comes from traditional sources such as reports, search warrants, anonymous tips, public domain, and records management systems. This information is used to populate various investigative databases.

When investigating a crime or developing answers to ongoing patterns, series, or trends, law enforcement personnel often rely upon numerous databases and records management systems. These are used to gain information and insight to prior incidents with similar signatures or modus operandi. Police reports, field interview cards, property pawn transactions, public records, and traffic citations are some common sources of information on known criminals. Ordinary street criminals often have lengthy arrest histories and numerous encounters with law enforcement officers documented on their criminal records. Criminals do not seek to have run-ins with the law, but they do not shy away from them. Terrorists, on the other hand, go to great extremes to avoid detection. As noted in the profiles of the September 11, 2001 hijackers, other than a traffic infraction they had little if any contact with the law enforcement community. Therefore, gathering information on these individuals requires analysts to think outside the box and to identify nontraditional sources of information. One example of these sources would be purchases that perhaps an ordinary person would not make, especially if in bulk. Other sources would be the Internet, published material, court records, handouts, radio (including citizen band and ham radios), and self-published books such as *The Turner Diaries* and *Hunter* by Andrew MacDonald.

There are inherent difficulties in categorizing terrorism, which are compounded by the shaping of policy for a type of behavior that fits poorly into more familiar categories. "Terrorist acts are both crimes and forms of warfare, and in both respects are unlike what we are used to."[2] Understanding the larger possibilities, such as warfare, law enforcement will be able to make informed decisions on matters concerning data collection. When gathering information it is important to document and standardize every step of the process. This will alleviate any complications when categorizing behaviors or activities and will ensure that all participants in the process are on the same playing field.

Terrorism is different from street-level crime on many fronts. "Most crimes are the product of greed, anger, jealousy, or the desire for domination, respect, or position in a group, and not of any desire to 'improve' the state of the world or of a particular nation."[2] When gathering information or intelligence for homeland security, one must be cognizant of the differences between most crimes and terrorism. It is important to think globally and not just make decisions about collection based on jurisdictional parameters. When dealing with terrorism, most law enforcement databases are not structured to capture information from a wide array of sources. Intelligence databases, if designed for a single-use agency, should be designed with the understanding that the information may be exported for use outside the jurisdiction; otherwise, information may need to be integrated from other sources. In addition to the jurisdictional parameters placed upon an analyst and those self-imposed, other restrictions may include politics, interpretation of regulations, exotic military operations, and fear of impeding actions.

The gathering of information can be complex or rudimentary. Regardless of the degree to which an agency is willing to develop a database, there are nine basic considerations that should be captured in detail.

- Individuals
- Associates
- Relatives
- Employers
- Telephone subscribers
- Organizations, groups, or gangs
- Businesses
- Corporations
- Educational records/background

Use of these nine basic considerations for gathering detailed information on matters of homeland security, terrorism, or hate crimes will greatly aid the investigative and analytical processes, especially if the information is shared with multiple jurisdictions. This information will allow for immediate link analysis and will readily demonstrate interrelationships and associations. In order to do this in an expeditious manner, analysts often turn to their records management systems. There are some inherent problems with relying on only one system. If an agency is using an off-the-shelf records management system, it will generally be insufficient for use as a criminal intelligence database. These systems do not usually automatically collect all of the nine basic considerations. Many systems capture dispatch and self-initiated activities but more in-depth information is needed, and this will probably come from documents prepared by the first responder.

Role of the first responder

The gathering of information must start somewhere. In the field of law enforcement, information gathering is initiated when a responding officer, or first responder, is dispatched or comes upon an incident or scene. The first responder is the eyes and ears of intelligence analysis. Traditionally, the starting point for the formal process of data gathering for most law enforcement agencies is the moment that documentation begins and an offense incident report is generated. For years, officers would respond to an incident, record relevant facts, and document the incident in a manner designed to encompass all elements of the crime being investigated. The importance of detailed data gathering in a post-9/11 world cannot be limited (as a once-famous fictional television character would say, "just the facts"). Although critically important, facts are routinely centered on criminal statutes and utilized to fulfill the requirements of probable cause in order to successfully prosecute an offender. While this is extremely important and should not be overlooked, first responders need to expand their reporting repertoire to include details that may seem mundane or inconsequential to the incident being addressed. Link analysis and corroboration of information are dependent upon details, e.g., telephone numbers for cellular phones and pagers, addresses, apartment numbers, or property. If analysts and investigators cannot link similarities, only have generalities with which to work, or have to follow up on an investigation to gain details, valuable time is wasted. As the saying goes, time is money, but in homeland security and terrorism, time can save lives.

Officers must be trained in what to look for and on how to accurately portray or explain details within a police report in order for it to translate properly into databases. Human intelligence is usually the most desirable form of gathering information, but this can be extremely difficult in the world of terrorism. Officers are essentially forms of human intelligence who, if trained properly and if shortcuts are avoided, can yield leads and details that may prove beneficial in the future. Address data are crucial in just about any law enforcement database. Quite often, address data will not be verified or questioned. Knowing one's jurisdiction is something most officers have ingrained in their minds from day one. By knowing the community, officers should have an advantage over subjects and possess the insight to question addresses and information provided by them. Use of a post office box, cluster box, packing company group box, shelter, or "refused" or "unknown" as a residential address is not sufficient and will only delay investigations. Another problem is the number of reports that show addresses of occurrence as being the police department, jail, impounded lot, hospital, or as vague as Smith's Department Store on Main Street. All of these scenarios will not only delay investigations but will also negatively impact the use of analytical databases, link analysis software, and geographical information systems.

Details are the most important factor in developing quality intelligence that can be readily validated. When dealing with the typical street criminal or investigating a street crime, many investigative leads are developed through generalities such as a subject being described as a white male with a specific tattoo or mark. This is because many street criminals have encountered law enforcement officials at some point, by arrest, field interviews, pawned property transactions, or traffic stops, and law enforcement systems are laden with known subject descriptors obtained from the various encounters. Thus, criminal justice information systems are lined with a wide array of relational attributes on these suspects that, once queried, will provide numerous workable leads for investigators. The same cannot be said of potential homeland security and terrorist suspects. These suspects go through great pains to avoid law enforcement encounters and attempt to fit into the mainstream as everyday law-abiding citizens. Perhaps the greatest chance for a first responder to encounter potential suspects is through traffic crashes, traffic stops, or random calls for service, when potential suspects may only be seen as witnesses or neighbors at the time. Timothy McVeigh, the Oklahoma bomber, was initially apprehended for a traffic stop. Based on this, it is vitally important that first responders document in detail all encounters with individuals, including place of work, educational facility currently attended, phone numbers (beeper and cellular), alien card, passport, driver's license, and license plate numbers. It is equally important to document details about associates who may accompany a suspect.

First responders or road officers routinely conduct traffic stops, subject checks, and field interviews. These are golden opportunities to gather information that will dramatically enhance any homeland security database. In order for this to be effective, questions must be asked in detail. One thing an officer asks for is identification. For many officers, presentation of any form of a driver's license or state-issued identification card suffices as authentic and legitimate and causes little concern or need for further questioning. However, this is a new era in law enforcement. Officers should question all forms of identification and should look for multiple sets of documents, use of different addresses, and evidence of tampering. If other individuals are accompanying the subject, questions should be asked for the purpose of comparing intentions and knowledge of one another. Also, information obtained by examination of vehicles or residences, in accordance with applicable laws, for signs of foreign travel (i.e., photographs, maps, video cameras and tapes, airline and hotel receipts, training manuals, and radical or questionable writings), is extremely important and should be recorded in reports, as further questions may be warranted. These items are just the beginning. Many crimes can yield further links or, through the use of search warrants, can corroborate previously received information.

Crimes and incidents that may yield information or links

Just about any encounter with law enforcement may yield a link to the missing piece of the homeland security and terrorism analytical puzzle. The key is to have the opportunity to attain that piece, no matter how mundane or insignificant it may appear at the onset. Many crimes or incidents that first responders encounter provide the greatest opportunity for gathering valuable details for inclusion in their reports. The information received by first responders is fresh, and any reported scene is likely uncontaminated. In this section, several types of crimes and incidents that warrant careful review and consideration in the analytical process will be explored.

Stolen identities

One type of reported crime that can be directly associated with those in the terrorism trade is that of stolen identities (use of someone else's personal information) and issuance of fake or stolen identification papers, e.g., social security cards, drivers' licenses, passports, resident alien cards, military identification, and credit cards. Modern technology has made counterfeiting identification about as easy as desktop publishing. Identity crimes provide access to financial venues and a way to fit into the mainstream of society. Identity theft is often considered a nuisance and a crime that is a challenge to investigate. This type of crime is not one that attracts the attention of the media or that of high-ranking members of law enforcement. It is viewed as a white-collar crime that lacks the violence of homicides and home invasion robberies. However, if you analyze the potential direct and indirect relationships that are possible through this type of crime, it is not difficult to fathom the potential gains that may be realized by a terrorist. One attractive feature of identity theft is that the chances of detection and arrest are minimal. If apprehended, the time sentenced might be minor, and the crime can be carried out by street criminals or organized enterprises through technology from just about anywhere in the world. This makes it more complex for local law enforcement personnel to pursue.

False identification

Other problems related to the manufacture or sale of false or altered identification are possession of false identification and lack of supporting documentation. Incidents such as these are often encountered by first responders on traffic stops or in field interviews. Officers seldom question the identification's authenticity unless there is some obvious indicator. Although response times and minimizing the time calls are being held for dispatch are areas of concern for road patrol officers, failure to question a document's authenticity may make the critical difference. Documentation of the identification in question and responses to questions should be noted in an incident report. In the case of an arrest, impoundment of the document and making of copies, as well as notification of concerned government entities, are crucial to follow-up investigators. In the case of foreign residents, visitors, and registered aliens, identification items such as passports, alien cards, visas, airline tickets, and hotel bills are all forms of supporting documentation that should be readily accessible.

Illegal trafficking of cigarettes

One type of crime associated with aiding terrorist groups is illegal trafficking of cigarettes and smuggling of cheap cigarettes across state lines. This is done to avoid paying higher taxes and to resell them at greater profits. In the early 1990s, law enforcement personnel in the Miami, Florida area conducted operations targeting illegal cigarette sales and government-subsidized food stamps. The targets of the operations were mom-and-pop convenience stores, most of which were owned and operated by individuals of Middle Eastern descent, and were in lower-income and high-crime areas.

Allegations were raised that the profits gained from the illegal acts of the subjects were being routed to individuals in the Middle East, possibly to support fundamentalist causes. State and federal charges were eventually brought against a multitude of individuals, but charges of supporting terrorism were never brought, because this was not even considered then. Now, the climate has changed. Fast-forward 10-plus years to Charlotte, North Carolina, where nearly 20 individuals were charged with numerous crimes, some of which included smuggling cheap cigarettes to Michigan. The individuals were characterized as from a Charlotte-based cell that aided terror. At least one individual of Middle Eastern descent was found guilty of sending $3500 to the militant (terrorist) Lebanese group Hizbollah. He was also convicted on 16 separate counts and was sentenced to a series of consecutive prison terms that add up to 155 years.[3] However, these are examples of small-scale enterprises.

Misappropriation

Thefts of any magnitude should be reviewed in order to identify potential internal leakages or outright misappropriation of items that can be used for illegal activities, such as construction of explosive devices. Large-scale theft, in particular, is another type of crime that poses a potential problem. Many of these crimes take the forms of truck hijackings, cargo thefts, construction thefts, industrial thefts or losses, in-transit (airlines, shipping, and railway) thefts, and military-related crimes. The attractiveness of these crimes is twofold. The criminals are often in or go through remote areas, and there is little or no security. Whether the theft is to further a campaign of terror or to sell for financial profit, large-scale thefts provide opportunity to gain access to mass quantities of chemicals, fertilizers, explosives, fuel, technical equipment, and logistical support items and items used in the making of explosives. Items classified as explosives should pose the greatest concern. However, most law enforcement personnel are unaware of the numerous items that can be used as explosives or in developing explosives, and there should be concern that any theft of these items may be classified as theft of chemicals or merely be lost in the shuffle. In addition to thefts, mere possession of any of the explosive compound materials warrants immediate attention, but again, for what should law enforcement be looking? This question is addressed in the provisions of Section 841(d) of Title 18, United States Code (USC), and 27 CFR 55.23. The director of the ATF must publish and revise at least annually in the *Federal Register* a list of explosives determined to be within the coverage of 18 USC Chapter 40, Importation, Manufacture, Distribution, and Storage of Explosive Materials (Appendix D). Chapter 40 covers not only explosives but also blasting agents and detonators, all of which are defined as explosive materials in Section 841(C) of Title 18, USC. While the list is comprehensive, it is not all-inclusive. The fact that an explosive material may not be on the list does not mean that it is not within the coverage of the law if it otherwise meets the statutory definitions in Section 841 of Title 18, USC. Also, some chemicals may be inert, and if stolen in one jurisdiction may not receive further immediate attention. However, the counterpart to the inert chemical may be stolen in another location by other members of a group and if combined can create an explosive. That is why it is imperative that any possession or theft of any material listed on the ATF list be identified and investigated immediately.

Cargo crimes

Cargo crimes, a largely unregulated area due to lack of statutory coverage, are often documented as thefts, burglaries, or robberies. There is no precise data collection process in place within the U.S. According to the South Florida Cargo Theft Task Force, there is as much as $25 billion in cargo direct merchandise losses each year. One tractor-trailer can have between $1 and $2 million in merchandise that can be easily sold or used by the person who steals it, and if captured, the risk of being jailed for an extended period of time is likely to be less than for a bank robbery. Also, robbing a bank has a high risk factor associated with it, and for the most part, a low return, usually about a couple of thousand dollars. Analysts should be cautious when dealing with cargo crimes. Most cargo crimes are a result of tractor-trailer thefts. This seems simple, but on many occasions the tractor may be recovered in one jurisdiction and the trailer in another without the cargo. The problem is that when this takes place, the reporting agency may consider the case closed once one component is recovered, and further review or investigation is discounted.

Another consideration regarding cargo crime is what is referred to as leakage. This is the removal of property or insertion of articles, including explosives, without tampering with or removing the container's seal. There are many methods of doing this, but the two most common are by removing bolts and panels or drilling out rivets. Once access is gained, the subjects conduct the illegal act and reinstall the hardware without the knowledge of the driver, who may be picking up the trailer or container from a port. This process can also be reversed, and individuals may place items into a container outside of the country without tampering with the seal.

Cargo crimes come in several different forms and involve a wide variety of merchandise. Some items that are routinely targeted due to their high ticket value are computers and peripheral devices, cellular telephones, cigarettes, alcohol, perfume, and designer clothing. In a 1998 publication,[4] a cargo security expert noted that access to automated computer files is of serious concern because these files contain sensitive shipping information that allows criminal insiders to case entire shiploads of containers for the most lucrative cargoes. Shipments can even be electronically passed to other destinations via computers and may go undetected for weeks, especially if the shipment is transnational. This same article noted several emerging trends in cargo crimes. The first trend involves an insider who is part of the criminal conspiracy or is paid off. The second is international infiltration of cargo transportation systems. The third is fraud. Fourth is the widening intelligence information gap on cargo theft. Fifth is the stealing-to-order phenomenon, where specific items are taken in order to fill a specific request. Besides the lucrative financial advantages, cargo crimes provide an international nexus for foreign-based terrorist organizations to exploit. One area of concern cargo theft detectives focus on is seaports. This is because seaports are critical gateways for the movement of international commerce. More than 95% of our non-North American foreign trade arrives by ship. According to JayEtta Z. Hecker's testimony concerning container security in 2001, approximately 5400 ships carrying multinational crews and cargoes from around the globe made more than 60,000 U.S. port calls. More than 6 million containers (suitable for truck-trailers) enter the country annually.[5]

Suspicious vehicles

Incidents involving suspicious vehicles (especially rental vans and trucks) and suspicious persons should be immediately reviewed for consideration. Instead, these incidents are often filed away as information for future reference or "no reported" by the responding officer, due to no police action being taken. Also, civil matters such as landlord and tenant disputes or defaulting on a lease should be given consideration, particularly if they occur at strange hours or involve instances where no apparent justification is given. Reports for incidents such as those just cited should be written in great detail and include complete suspect and associate information, identification used by the suspect, actions taken by the suspect, time periods covered, vehicle information, method or form of payments made, and the existence of security monitoring videotapes, if any.

Found or abandoned property

The last type of incident that may yield leads is found or abandoned property, particularly if symbols or foreign writings are on the property. Such items often go straight to "property and evidence" rooms pending claim by the rightful owner, or they undergo some form of legal destruction. These items should not be overlooked. Property items deserving further review are computers, packages and letters, baggage, photographs and drawings, contraband, weapons, and anything labeled with foreign markings or symbols. Certain guidelines, limitations, and restrictions must be followed concerning entry of these items into a criminal intelligence database.

Gathering limitations and restrictions

Gathering intelligence information and entering it into a criminal intelligence database, whether for the purposes of homeland security, terrorism, monitoring of hate groups, or criminal enterprises, is governed by state and federal legislation. The predominant regulation in the U.S. is set forth in the 28 Code of Federal Regulation (CFR) Part 23, and is interpreted in guidelines updated and maintained by the U.S. Bureau of Justice Assistance. 28 CFR Part 23 is a guideline for law enforcement agencies operating federally funded multijurisdictional criminal intelligence systems under the Omnibus Crime Control and Safe Streets Act of 1968. It provides information for submission and entry of criminal intelligence information, security, inquiry, dissemination, and review and purging. It does not provide specific information on how standards should be implemented by individual agencies.

The CFR makes it clear that entry of information into a criminal intelligence database must be supported by reasonable suspicion. This applies to databases that will be shared with other law enforcement agencies that may be classified as criminal intelligence, intelligence case information, or similar designations. On an evidentiary scale, as shown in Figure 4.1, reasonable suspicion is just above mere suspicion (a hunch) and just below probable cause, the standard for initiating an arrest.

The federal regulation 28 CFR Part 23, 23.20 (C) defines reasonable suspicion as follows:

> Reasonable suspicion or Criminal Predicate is established when information exists which establishes sufficient facts to give a trained law enforcement or criminal investigative agency officer, investigator, or employee a basis to believe that there is a reasonable possibility that an individual or organization is involved in a definable criminal activity or enterprise.

Case law suggests that reasonable suspicion as applied in the context of whether information should be entered into a criminal intelligence database will not necessarily be the same as when applied to situations supporting the stop and frisk of a suspect. In court cases, reasonableness should be judged objectively from the perspective of a cautious and prudent law enforcement officer based on his experience and training. Additional guidance and information relating to reasonable suspicion can be found in the following court cases:

1. *Ornelas v. United States*, 517 U.S. 690, 696, 1966
2. *Illinois v. Wardlow*, 528 U.S. 119, 124, 2000
3. *U.S. v. Jimenez-Medina*, 173 F.3d 752, 756, 9th CA, 1999
4. *U.S. v. Garzon*, 119 F.3d 1146, 1451, 10th CA, 1997
5. *Jackson v. Sauls*, 206 F.3d 1156, 1165, 11th CA, 2000

Federal regulation 28 CFR 23.20(a) goes on to state that a system will only collect information on an individual if there is reasonable suspicion that

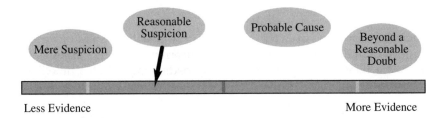

Figure 4.1 Evidentiary scale.

the individual is involved in criminal conduct or activity and if the information is relevant to that criminal conduct or activity. A 1998 policy clarification removed any ambiguity regarding information not supported by reasonable suspicion, declaring that the entry of individuals, entities, organizations, and locations that do not fall under reasonable suspicion can be included providing this is done solely for the purposes of criminal identification or is germane to the criminal suspect's activity. However, there are three requirements that must be met prior to placing such information into a criminal intelligence database:

1. Appropriate disclaimers must accompany the information, noting that it is strictly identifying information and carries no criminal connotations.
2. Identifying information may not be used as an independent basis to meet the requirement of reasonable suspicion.
3. The individual who is the criminal suspect identified by this information must meet all requirements of 28 CFR Part 23.

There is no limitation on nonintelligence information being stored on the same computer system as criminal intelligence information, provided that sufficient precautions are in place to separate the two types of information and that access is limited to appropriate personnel. Law enforcement agency personnel should be cognizant of various state public record (sunshine) laws before storing information on the same computer system. The above standards are only applicable to agencies that enter information into a multijurisdictional intelligence database, such as with task forces investigating homeland security, terrorism, and hate groups. Single-agency databases where no information is supplied outside the agency may maintain information in their agency. They would be subjected to internal policies and procedures as well as state public record laws. In either scenario, personnel should be cognizant of record-purging requirements. Some locations require that information and intelligence not currently active or without activity during a specified time period, often between 2 to 5 years, be purged.

Tips

Gathering information from tips is another gray area that should be reviewed cautiously. Limitations and restrictions concerning tips vary from state to state, but if they are entered into a multijurisdictional criminal intelligence database as enumerated above, they are subject to many of the same guidelines.

Tips are vital sources of information. They can come from a variety of sources, internal and external, such as informants, anonymous letters, tip lines such as Crime Stoppers, and online e-mails and forms, such as the one established by the FBI that allows anyone to submit information via their Web site. However, it is important to remember that tips are stand-alone pieces of information that need to be evaluated, verified, and corroborated prior to being acted upon and entered into a criminal intelligence database. Tips should be kept separate or be denoted as pending verification. Every detail of the tip, including the date and time received, caller (if known), nature of the information, and investigator assigned to followup, should be entered into a data form in order to avoid miscommunication.

Once a tip is received, it must be assigned for a timely investigative followup so that a determination of status can be made promptly. If it is determined that the information does not have lasting value, it should be removed from the database. Tip information should be reviewed every 90 to 120 days after entry to determine whether reasonable suspicion has yet been developed, thus justifying its move to the criminal intelligence database. Review processes can be continuous if warranted. However, if no real developmental activity is demonstrated on a tip, it should be purged from the system after 2 years. This will ensure that a data set remains relevant to the mission at hand and is not a conglomeration of information that can possibly result in erroneous leads or links.

Regardless whether a law enforcement agency has only an internal database, a database in which information is shared with multiple jurisdictions, or a database just for the purpose of tracking tips, there should be a written protocol to follow, as well as formal training. In addition, agencies should back up their data daily and have security measures in place to limit access and avoid being compromised.

Intelligence gathering and information interpretation

Interpretation of the information gathered is dependent upon analytical and investigative techniques used to transform it into intelligence. In a publication from the CIA, it was reported that "Major intelligence failures are usually caused by failures of analysis, not failures of collection. Relevant information is discounted, misinterpreted, ignored, rejected, or overlooked because it fails to fit a prevailing mental model or mindset."[6] Analysts and investigators need to keep open minds, be creative in approaches, and avoid assumptions that are not based on fact and corroboration.

Information that has been gathered according to the guidelines above — properly standardized, formatted, and entered into a secure criminal intelligence database — is the starting point for the intelligence interpretation phase. However, no matter what the quality of the data or the magnitude of the database, it is analytical processes that extricate the intelligence. It is essential to have an approach and to know the data. Random querying based on a mere hunch or memory is like driving with one's eyes closed. Analysts must have a hypothesis or a structured analytical problem as their roadmap, and then they can start breaking down the information into manageable or working parts. Listed below are four general "intelligence gathering and interpretation" factors.[7] These should be used as a starting point when initiating analysis concerning homeland security, terrorism, or organized hate groups:

1. *Group information* — Name(s), ideology (political or social philosophy), history of the group, and dates significant to the group (including dates on which former leaders were killed or imprisoned); publications (some groups also have a bible or manifesto that outlines activities — current, future, or hypothetical); gatherings, meetings, and rallies (often posted in periodicals or on the Internet).
2. *Financial information* — Sources of funds, proceeds from criminal activities, bank account information (domestic and foreign); the group's legal and financial supporters (generally, anyone who would write an official letter of protest or gather names on a petition for a terrorist is a legal–financial supporter, and sometimes an analysis of support will reveal links or mergers with other terrorist groups).
3.. *Personnel data* — List of past and current leaders; list of active members and former members; any personnel connections between its members and other groups of similar ideology; group structure, particularly if the organization's pattern is based on columns and cells; and the skills of all group members, e.g., weapons and electronics expertise, and explosive training. (Knowing the skills of the group is an important part of threat assessment. If the philosophy revolves around one leader, it is important to know what will occur if something happens to that leader. Often, the analysis of family background is useful to determine how radically a leader or member was raised or to identify military tenure or training.)
4.. *Locational data* — Location of group's headquarters; safe houses; training facilities owned or attended; and stash houses, where weapons and supplies may be stored. (It is important to specify the underground to which terrorists can flee. This is more difficult than determining safe havens. Terrorists also usually prefer to live in communal homes rather than alone.)

One way of conceptualizing the information is through the use of a table. Placing the above information into a table provides an at-a-glance reference for investigators and analysts to use to view the data, and provides an easy reference for future reports. This is demonstrated, based on four well-known international terrorist organizations, in Table 4.1.

Besides giving a starting point to the intelligence process, use of the four working parts will allow for sharing of the workload among agencies or personnel. Once the intelligence gathering process is initiated and completed in detail, the basic interpretation process can be undertaken. One analytical method that can be used is referred to as the "loop effect."[8] This method was initially employed as a tactical and investigative tool, but with some minor adjustments it is easily adaptable to investigations concerning terrorism and organized hate groups, as shown in Figure 4.2. The loop effect is a step process for analysts to ensure continuous follow-through, thus the "loop" reference.

Every piece of information, case, or report has a starting point, referred to as case initiation. The first two steps in the loop effect are the gathering of raw information manually and electronically. Analysts receive and categorize the information as it arrives, seeking to prioritize it according to protocols and attempting to identify items needing immediate attention. Steps one and two are the triage of analytical work.

The third step of the loop effect is also an information-gathering component, but the information gathered here comes from an investigator or an analyst asking questions and looking for initial associations and verifications. Questions asked center on the five "W"s: who, what, where, when, and why, and usually how. Once the questions are satisfactorily answered, the analyst begins his preliminary analysis, looking for pattern identification.

The fourth component of the loop effect is identification and documentation, and would also be characterized as basic analytical techniques.

These first four components, coupled with basic analytical techniques and followed by the four intelligence-gathering and interpretation parts, are only the beginning. Up to this point in the process, an analyst has undertaken massive amounts of information, striving to validate and identify patterns early on. Tentative conclusions should not be drawn until further investigation can be done to substantiate any findings and enhanced analytical steps can be initiated.

Step five consists of enhanced analysis. During this step, an analyst transforms the information and preliminary intelligence into a viable intelligence product. Relationships and associations will be elaborated upon and inferences drawn. Many variables will be examined using a wide range of analytical techniques including spatial and temporal analysis, victim, offender, and target analysis, threat and vulnerability assessments, and financial and toll record analysis. The list of techniques and tools is virtually unlimited and depends greatly on the skills, abilities, and data awareness of each analyst.

Table 4.1 Sample Intelligence Table

	Tupamaros (Uruguay)	IRA (Ireland)	ETA (Basque)	Red Brigade (Italy)
Type and History	Revolutionary; urban student radicalism	Nationalist; 2nd class treatment	Nationalist; unique language	Revolutionary; economic change
Aim	Socialist economy	United Ireland	Own nation	Societal betterment
Organiz-ation	Students organized sugar workers into cells	First tried military battalions, then cells	Shadow government, central committee	Pyramidal paired cells called brigades
Strength	Two per cell, 3000 members	Five per cell, 2000 members	700 members	800 actives, 8000 underground
Attacks	Sabotage, demonstrations	Protests, clashes, executions	Demonstrations, assassinations	Kidnapping, robbery, extortion
Social	Students and sympathizers	Average age 21, married with kids	Average age 25, middle class	Average age 27, radicalized students, criminals
Support	Ideological neo-Marxist support	Relatives and friends abroad	One-third mass support, some ideological Marxist support	Many sympathizers, Ideological Maoist support
External Aid	Cuba	Russia, U.S., PLO, others	France, Cuba, Russia, Libya, links to IRA, PLO	Czechoslovakia, links to Sicilian Mafia

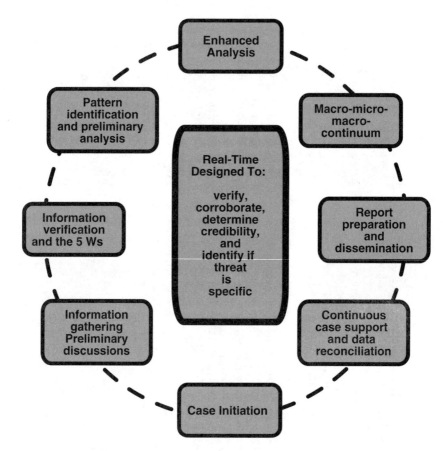

Figure 4.2 Loop effect.

Once all available resources are examined, step six will come into play: macro-micro-macro continuum, which will be explained in depth in Chapter 5. Traditionally, analysts and investigators have gathered information, reviewed it, investigated it, drew conclusions, and reacted. The macro-micro-macro continuum phase does not discount the work already performed, but as a precautionary measure it provides for a second look at the data to ensure that conclusions are consistent with the available variables and that the intelligence was corroborated.

Step seven is the end product. Analysts prepare reports, maps, and bulletins designed to aid management in making informed decisions. The final step is a given for most intelligence units: continuous case support and data reconciliation. The latter two steps will be explained in further detail in Chapter 5.

The entire loop effect is designed to work in real-time environments in order to ensure verification and corroboration, determine credibility, and identify specific threats and their severities. Once the basic requirements are fulfilled, analytical personnel are ready to begin the enhanced stage, transforming information into intelligence.

Chapter concepts

1. The gathering of information can be complex or rudimentary. Therefore, developing an understanding about the topic by everyone involved and using a standardized approach are essential.
2. There are nine basic considerations when gathering information: individuals, associates, relatives, employers, telephone subscribers, organizations, businesses, corporations, and educational records/background.
3. Thorough gathering of information is the role of the first responder. Detailed questions including the "5 Ws" need to be asked.
4. Analysts and investigators need to look beyond routine street crimes in order to identify incidents that may yield information or links to terrorist activities.
5. State and federal laws and guidelines govern intelligence-gathering limitations. When entering information into a criminal intelligence system or database, reasonable suspicion is required.

References

1. Heymann, P.B., *Terrorism and America: A Commonsense Strategy for a Democratic Society*, MIT Press, Cambridge, MA, 1998, p. 129.
2. Heymann, P.B., *Terrorism and America: A Commonsense Strategy for a Democratic Society*, MIT Press, Cambridge, MA, 1998, p. 7.
3. Associated Press, N. Carolina man gets 155 years in scheme that aided terror group, *The Miami Herald*, final edition, p. 22A.
4. Badolato, E., Current and future trends in cargo security, *Security Technol. & Design*, August 1998, pp. 15–16.
5. Hecker, J.Z., Container Security Current Efforts to Detect Nuclear Materials, New Initiatives, and Challenges, U.S. General Accounting Office, p. 2.
6. Heuer, R.J., Jr., *Psychology of Intelligence Analysis*, Center for the Study of Intelligence, Central Intelligence Agency, 1999, chap. 6, p. 1.
7. O'Connor, T., *Counterterrorism Analysis*, http://faculty.ncwc.edu/toconnor/392/spy/terrorism.htm, Intelligence Gathering and Information, Nov. 20, 2002.
8. Cooper, J., Nelson, E., and Ronczkowski, M., Tactical/investigative analysis of targeted crimes, in *Advanced Crime Mapping Topics*, National Law Enforcement and Corrections Technology Center, Denver, CO, April 2002, p. 31.

chapter five

Enhanced analysis: transforming information into intelligence

Enhanced analysis is where "the rubber meets the road." Up to this point in the analytical process, personnel have primarily been cleaning data and analyzing information using broad approaches. Transforming the information into quality intelligence requires time and skill. Whether some forms of analysis are art or science is debatable. In the case of homeland security and terrorism analysis, it is both. Methods employed by an analyst can be replicated for use on many different fronts. In addition, there are numerous scientific models and tools available for analysts that can be utilized by anyone to prove or verify information. The data should yield the same results for whoever undertakes the process.

Use of a checklist is encouraged due to the magnitude of events that can be faced by an analyst undertaking terrorism or organized hate group investigations. Too many steps are involved in the intelligence process, and information often arrives at intermittent times, making organization of the information difficult. Matrixes, link charts, time lines, and maps also play important roles in transforming information into enhanced intelligence. Whatever techniques are used to analyze the information, it is crucial to know one's criminal data and what information is available. In warfare, one needs to know the enemy, and in the analytical world one needs to know the enemy (subject or target) as well as the data. If you do not know what you have, how can you transform it into intelligence?

Analyzing: transforming information into intelligence

Philip B. Heymann pointed out in his book about international terrorism that "A primary objective of intelligence acquisition abroad is to anticipate the action of terrorist groups."[1] This is also true for domestic-based groups.

Applying this premise to the realm of law enforcement requires some adjustment. For years, analysts and investigators have spent the majority of their time focusing on linking, locating, and reacting to a suspect's action in hopes of facilitating an arrest. Forecasting and predicting a particular course of action for a suspect and responding to it is not the norm for many law enforcement managers, who usually focus on certainty, control, and the bottom line. Managers must alter their styles of operation when addressing homeland security and terrorism analysis. If law enforcement does not take the next step and anticipate the actions of terrorist groups, the results may be catastrophic.

The following is information used to develop a group's modus operandi:

- Capabilities
- History
- Statements
- Support
- Intentions/causes/motivation
- Current and future capabilities
- Vulnerabilities of the organization
- Location of operation
- Dates of meaning or significance
- Membership
- Leadership (noting there maybe a leaderless resistance)
- Threatening calls or any other messages
- Attacks
- Financing or aid

New terrorist generations learn from their predecessors. They analyze the mistakes made by former comrades who were killed or apprehended. "Press accounts, judicial indictments, courtroom testimony, and trial transcripts are meticulously culled for information on security force tactics and methods and then absorbed by surviving group members."[2] In other words, they analyze records for intelligence much like law enforcement should. Information gleaned from scrutinizing court proceedings is often overlooked or taken for granted by law enforcement personnel, partly because law enforcement has traditionally considered a case closed once a defendant has stood trial and all court matters are over. These measures can no longer be ignored if we are to completely understand and analyze terrorism. When transforming information into intelligence, one is continually trying to corroborate, advance, and reconcile data. Analysts and investigators must keep open minds when transforming information and should not discount learning from the enemy. Use of the above list, especially court-related documents and press information, will not always yield leads but these items should be monitored and routinely compared with other variables. However, do not limit yourself to media accounts and court cases in your immediate region. Terrorist organizations and organized hate groups are transnational, as represented with the list of known active patriot groups, and are located in many cities and states. Therefore a global approach is essential, where applicable. This is one aspect where law enforcement can learn from the enemy. In a terrorism training document seized in Manchester, England from a disciple of Jihad, "Military Studies in the Jihad against the Tyrants" (based on translation), also known as the al-Qaeda training manual, information sources both public and secret were detailed. It was stated that by using public sources openly and without resorting to illegal means, it was possible for an operative to gather at least 80% of the information needed about the enemy. Methods cited were newspapers, magazines, radio, and television. If terrorists believe they can get 80% of the information needed from legal sources, then law enforcement should have an advantage on the remaining 20% through quality use of criminal intelligence databases and from considering all available factors.[3]

Other factors to consider are links to common crimes, such as theft, that may have hidden variables associated with them. One such factor is the collection of necessary components used to make homemade bombs, such as fertilizer, icing sugar, and diesel fuel. "Stolen" would not normally set off bells and whistles. These are common items that anyone can purchase and possess legally, in contrast to the theft of military ordinance, such as plastic explosives or dynamite, which would immediately alarm law enforcement and initiate notifications. Whether these items are stolen separately or collectively, there is a potential for disaster. Which items might a potential terrorist seek to obtain without being detected? Although the answers to this question could be endless, analysts need to document detailed and finite descriptions of items that are located, stolen, or purchased and are in the possession of suspects. These items can then be weighed against other variables in order to develop potential links or leads.

Analytical and investigative variables

Once the form, type, classification, and modus operandi are established, there are a multitude of analytical and investigative variables to consider. These variables are used in link analysis or in charting an individual, group, or activity. Outlined below are some of the variables that should be used when corroborating information for groups and offenders. The components of a group or an organization profile listed below should also be included in terrorism and organized hate crime intelligence databases. However, these variables can be expanded upon, and an analyst should freely search narratives or miscellaneous fields. The components of an offender profile are described in *Crime Analysis: From First Report to Final Arrest*,[4] and these components are now commonplace in many analytical databases.

Components of a group or organization profile

- Culture
- Cause
- Sponsor
- Religion
- Ideology and beliefs
- Symbology, if any
- Membership
  - Make-up
  - Numbers
  - Recruitment
  - Origin
  - Prior arrests or detainments of members
- Financial
  - Make-up
  - Income generation
  - Supporters
- Hierarchy
- Chain of command
- Political position
- Target selection
- Method of attacks
- Weapons used
- Current and future capabilities
- Modus operandi
- Base of operation, e.g., local, regional, national, international, or transnational
- Prior arrest and incarceration records, if any
- Court records
- Media records
- Historical references, e.g., records, reports, and news
- Training
  - Where
  - By whom

Components of an offender profile[4]

- Age, sex, race
- Marital status
- Level of intelligence
- Sexual adjustment
- Social adjustment
- Appearance
- Employment history

- Emotional adjustment
- Work habits
- Location or residence in relation to crime scene
- Personality/characteristics
- Analysis of criminal act
- Motive
- Lifestyle
- Prior criminal history
- Sequence of events during the offense
- Mood of the offender before, during, and after the offense

When considering the use of variables, personnel are cautioned on the importance of verifying the sources and differentiating between information obtained as tips vs. actual cases. It is also imperative that the information is obtained and entered in compliance with federal, state, and local laws. Use of any of the above variables for weighting, comparing, or linking is best done with intelligence-based software, providing that the data entry methods were standardized in the database. Attempting to analyze organized groups and their supporters through manual methods and matrix charts may be possible but will only delay intelligence and investigations. No matter what methods are undertaken to analyze and use the variables, it is vitally important that personnel document their actions. Methods and variables must be documented as well as dates, times, and software used. This will allow other personnel to replicate results, if necessary, and to know if additional information was received that needs to be analyzed.

Analysts and investigators usually give the most attention to linking individuals, telephone numbers, and addresses. With terrorism and organized hate groups these variables are not always easily available or accurate, but there is one variable that drives all groups — financial. Financial considerations should weigh heavily when gathering information. Without financial backing, terrorist organizations or individuals will have difficulty in succeeding. Terrorist and organized hate groups are committed for the long haul, and as noted earlier, they often have elaborate support systems that require funding. It has been demonstrated in criminal and some terrorist cases that trailing the money will lead to the source, but this can be laborious. Money laundering plays a role in terrorism support as much as it does in ordinary criminal activity. The three stages for money laundering and several methods for completing the stages are as follows:[5]

Stages:
   a. *Placement* — Entry of bulk money into a business-based financial system
   b. *Layering* — Conduction of a series of transactions designed to conceal an audit trail
   c. *Integration* — Legitimization of illegal proceeds

Methods:

    a. Structuring (also known as "smurfing") — Possibly the most common method, many individuals deposit cash or buy bank drafts in amounts under $10,000

    b. Bank complicity — A criminally co-opted bank employee may facilitate the money laundering

    c. Currency exchanges — Allow customers to buy foreign currency that can be transported out of the country

    d. Securities' brokers — A stockbroker may take in large amounts of cash and issue securities in exchange

    e. Asset purchases with bulk cash — Big ticket items are purchased, such as automobiles and real estate, and are often registered in a friend's name

    f. Postal money orders

    g. Telegraphic or wire transfers of funds

    h. Gambling in casinos

    i. Credit cards — Credit card bills are overpaid and a high credit balance that can be turned over to cash at any time is kept

    j. Travel agencies — Cash is exchanged for travel tickets, which is a common method of moving money from one country to another

When tracking the money, it is important to be aware of the above stages and methods. However, not all currency flows through money laundering arenas, or traditional banking, or financial market systems. One such system being used legally and illegally is the Hawala remittance system that was mentioned in Chapter 3.

Web sites and other resources

Analysts and investigators must be creative and constantly look for new mediums from which to harvest information. Advances in cable and satellite television have provided international terrorist organizations, such as the Palestinian Liberation Organization (PLO), opportunities to exploit the media to their advantage and to promote their positions in the Middle East. What may be perceived as just another news broadcast or interview can yield insight to locations, individuals, and direct or indirect messages. However, this method places investigators at the whim of terrorist organizations and at the subjectivity of the news. More proactive and real-time measures are needed. The Internet is a good source of information. Organizations and membership Web sites, especially hate groups, often post their beliefs, causes, and calendars for upcoming events, propaganda, flyers, and even their manuals of operation. One can learn a great deal by viewing the world through their eyes. Figure 5.1 and Figure 5.2 are examples of flyers that groups create and distribute. The two groups with flyers depicted are the World Church of the Creator and the National Alliance. They readily

ARE YOU PREPARED
TO FIGHT THE ARAB HOLY WAR ON AMERICAN SOIL?

End Muslim Immigration Now!

World Church of the Creator
www.creator.org   Post Office Box 2002, East Peoria, IL 61611   309-699-0135

Figure 5.1 WCOTC End Muslim Immigration Now flyer.

demonstrate how concerns and topics can be conveyed to an international audience. Flyers such as these are meant to stir controversy and enlist new members. Rallies also arouse many emotions and create contention. Rallies or gatherings are held for the purposes of recruiting, promoting beliefs, and gathering attention. They may be held publicly or privately, as depicted in Figure 5.3. These venues provide valuable sources of information with uniforms and symbols (Figure 5.4) displayed. Speeches given at rallies provide additional information. Many groups utilize signs (Figure 5.5) to communicate their beliefs.

There are many Web sites associated with organized hate groups. These are promulgated by individuals and educational institutions and have a wide

COMING SOON
TO A NEIGHBORHOOD NEAR YOU

- Black savages are flooding in from Africa.
- They will spread the HIV virus to every corner of America.
- They will reproduce like cockroaches, despite being poor, uneducated, and jobless.
- They will bring murder, rape, and robbery to every community in which they are placed.

TOP LEFT: BLACK AFRICANS LINE UP TO BE TAKEN TO AMERICA. TOP RIGHT: CHILDREN LAUGH
AND PLAY AMONG THE CORPSES LEFT TO ROT IN THE STREET; A COMMON SIGHT IN AFRICA.

A campaign has been launched to bring more non-Whites to America. Recruiting
teams are being sent to Africa to persuade Blacks to move here as government-
approved immigrants.

The Jews want as many non-Whites as possible mixed in with the White population
as quickly as possible. They believe that once they have done that it will be too
difficult a task for us to unmix what they have mixed. They'll be surprised at
what we are willing to do to repair the damage they have done.

WHITE REVOLUTION: IT'S COMING TOO!

NATIONAL ALLIANCE
P.O. Box 90 • Hillsboro, WV 24946 • USA • 304-653-4600
www.natvan.com • www.natall.com

Figure 5.2 National Alliance Coming Soon flyer.

range of information and insight on activities and events that may prove
helpful to law enforcement. These sites should be viewed with some level
of skepticism, however, because their content is often skewed and subjective.
Other than a group's "official" Web site or those operated by their leadership
and members, there are two sites that are dedicated to the collection of
detailed and reliable hate crime and hate group information: Southern Poverty Law Center (SPLC) Intelligence Report (http://www.splc.org — has
resources on symbols, hate groups, attacks, legislation, and government

Figure 5.3 Florida Ku Klux Klan followers gathering at a public park.

Figure 5.4 Alleged member of a branch of the Ku Klux Klan. The military-style uniform and symbols of hate are proudly displayed and worn.

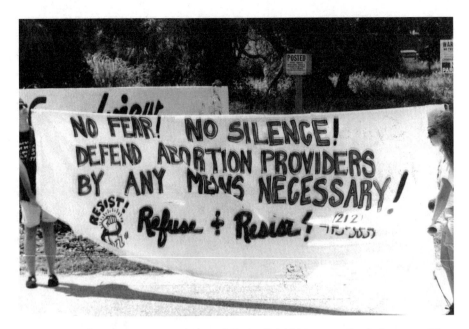

Figure 5.5 Left-wing group "Refuse and Resist," with suspected relations to a Klan faction, at a rally in Florida allegedly advocating disobedience.

resources) and the Anti-Defamation League (ADL), (http://www.adl.org — has resources directed toward law enforcement personnel and training, postings of upcoming extremist events, a terrorist attack database, and listings of extremism by state). Both of these are nonprofit organizations that also aid law enforcement. Raymond A. Franklin's "The Hate Directory" is also available on the Internet (http://www.bcpl.net/~rfrankli/hatedir.html). It provides links to a tremendous amount of Internet sites as well as servers, chat rooms, groups, and several other locations.[6] As for the SPLC and ADL, their Web sites are listed below:

There are thousands of Internet sites that can provide insight into a group or individual, as well as information geared toward law enforcement. Listed below are some of the many resources available concerning intelligence for terrorist groups or threats:

- http://www.dhs.gov — U.S. Department of Homeland Security
- http://www.fbi.gov/terrorinfo/terrorism.htm — FBI Terrorism Information
- http://www.terrorism.com — Terrorism Research Center, calendars
- http://www.1stheadlines.com — Top breaking news headlines, worldwide
- http://www.mipt.org — Significant dates, calendars
- http://www.intelbrief.com — Nonprofit intelligence brief

- http://www.whitehouse.gov/homeland — Homeland security contact listing
- http://www.state.gov/s/ct — U.S. Department of State
- http://www.nipc.gov — National Infrastructure Protection Center
- http://www.justice.gov — U.S. Department of Justice
- http://www.naco.org — National Association of Counties
- http://www.defendamerica.mil — U.S. Department of Defense News
- http://www.counterterrorism.com — Examines counterterrorism tools available to law enforcement and first responder personnel
- http://www.nlectc.org — National Law Enforcement and Corrections Technology Centers, daily terrorism update newsletter

Although it is impossible to provide an all-inclusive listing, the above sites will provide a good starting point and direction to many other online resources. If past behavior is an indication of future behavior, law enforcement personnel should routinely review the many online calendars of significant terrorist events and meaningful dates for the numerous groups all over the world. Dates of significance, anniversaries, and holidays may assist in forecasting or validating the possibility of future threats. Also, many groups or their members have published online memoirs, diaries, and books that may cite specific dates. These publications are available through various rogue Web sites and through some popular online bookstores.

Critically needed is an awareness of the various media venues available to the general public. Venues such as the Internet, shortwave radio, print media (magazines, papers, and books), and independent nonmainstream publishing companies offer an array of how-to guides that virtually anyone can purchase for $30 or less. Although some of these mediums may have a legitimate target audience, it is the quick and easy access to these items by potentially dangerous individuals that should be important to any analyst. One such example is a publishing company in Colorado that is referred to as the publisher of the "action library." This publisher is operating legally under state and federal laws. However, law enforcement should be aware of many of this publisher's publications for insight into the information they provide. There are hundreds or more of such publications of which law enforcement personnel should be aware. One such book invited the reader to tap into a unique storehouse of forbidden knowledge, with information on building weapons and explosives, opposing big government, changing one's identity, and sniping. This is just one book. Many other books are available that give instructions on forging identity documents. Numerous writings on building bombs and silencers, sniping, explosives, and ammunition are also prevalent.

These books are not necessarily written with malicious intent. Some have been written by individuals who do not have relationships with terrorist or organized hate group organizations. Some books are "how-to" manuals, recently authored, and some books are decades old, written by individuals with direct ties to terrorist and organized hate groups. One such book, a fictional publication that recently claimed revisited notoriety, was *The Turner Diaries*. After the Oklahoma City bombing and the subsequent apprehension of Timothy McVeigh, the FBI reported that McVeigh was in possession of *The Turner Diaries*. This easily obtained publication was allegedly used as a blueprint for his elicit activities. There are many eerie similarities to the bombing and the book's content, including the type of bomb used. If one person can use this writing as a blueprint for destruction, how many others are using the multitude of other books available for illegal and illicit activities? How many law enforcement personnel, including analysts, have read or are even aware of these publications?

Law enforcement personnel strive to prevent crime and identify weaknesses in their jurisdictions through analysis that may be exploited by the criminal element. This information is then used to develop operational and deployment strategies. The criminal element does not have access to this information, thus giving law enforcement the analytical advantage. However, it has access to many publications that it may use to self-train, so why should law enforcement ignore the obvious? Analytical personnel should be aware of these publications in order to gain insight into the thinking of potential terrorist-related individuals and their activities in areas such as the following:

- Robberies (financial gain)
- Gathering and making weapons and ammunition
- "Leaderless" resistance
- Cause and ideology
- How to hide out and avoid authorities
- Use of disguises
- Hideout needs (supplies)
- Making and using explosives
- Column and cell organization as well as supporters
- Symbols

Another source of published documents that may provide valuable insight for terrorists or terrorist groups is information that can be extracted from official court and criminal case documents, as described earlier. Many investigators and analysts overlook the amount of information available at the conclusion of their cases or during subsequent prosecution. Virtually every aspect of a case, including plaintiffs' and defendants' testimonies, is available for the taking. Those engaged in terrorist-related activities can easily obtain unsealed documents and use them to gain information that can have detrimental effects on future law enforcement endeavors. Analytical personnel should be aware of the availability of this information and should include a review of these documents in their post-case analysis.

An example of one such document is a how-to terrorism manual that was admitted as evidence by prosecutors during the federal trial of four men for their alleged involvement in the 1998 bombing of the U.S. Embassies in Kenya and Tanzania. This document included 18 chapters on how to operate as a terrorist. Topics that were covered in detail included counterfeiting currency and documents, communication, use of apartments, transportation, training, kidnapping and assassinations, espionage, explosives, use of poisons, and interrogations. Although this material was written for potential terrorists, law enforcement personnel can also use this information against them. In addition, law enforcement personnel should consider these publications important to future intelligence-gathering initiatives, and where applicable by law should strive to have the information sealed from public review.

Another concern for law enforcement, particularly with organized hate groups and their members, is information available from jail, prison, probation, and parole databases. Information in these systems is often overlooked, probably because many law enforcement personnel view this part of the criminal justice process as out of their hands. Stockpiles of information are waiting to be harvested in these untapped databases. Institutions capture a great deal of detailed information about inmates' activities and associations. This resource is an excellent source of information, and many correctional agencies are more than willing to share insight they may possess about these groups.

Macro–micro–macro continuum

Armed with an arsenal of databases, resources, checklists, and variables, an analyst must begin to validate inferences, probabilities, and hypotheses. In order to avoid tunnel vision on any one piece of data, analysts should employ the macro–micro–macro continuum.[7] This technique will aid analysts in reevaluating and double-checking initial results.

The first macro includes the numerous pieces of information, intelligence, and variables present in a case. It gives the big picture. Shown in Figure 5.6 are six potential sources of information that flow into the analytical resources. This includes raw computer-aided dispatch (CAD) or records management system (RMS) data that are available to local law enforcement and form the first macro step. The problem often encountered is that many data sources, with the exception of the above two, stand alone and can create delays. Therefore, use of data warehouses is encouraged where feasible.

Providing there are no database connectivity issues or data sharing restrictions, the data is then extracted, transported, transformed, and loaded into the appropriate criminal intelligence data tools. Once the data are consolidated, any number of analytical techniques can be initiated. This starts the micro step of the continuum. During this step, analysts seek to identify potential targets, relationships, associates, and supporters. The micro step

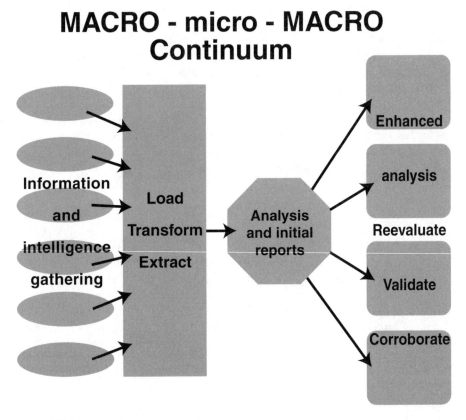

Figure 5.6 Macro–micro–macro continuum.

requires definitive answers and results. Every piece of information is scrutinized from every angle, and nothing is left out. However, this is not the end of the process. Using the results obtained after the micro step may lead to incorrect assumptions. These results must be extracted and reevaluated against the big picture in order to validate them. Caution must be exercised at the micro level, especially with terrorism groups, because of their use of sleeper cells and their widespread networks of supporters. This is why the third step, macro, is used as validation. The results from the micro stage are reevaluated and analyzed using analysis methods such as spatial, temporal, target, victim, and subject, in order to look for outcomes that may contradict the first step.

Throughout the process, analysts should continually search for one-to-many and many-to-one relationships. Too often, analysts will focus on one-to-one relationships, thus creating a potential void that leaves associations undetected. Once all three steps are performed, then the final analytical reports are completed and submitted for consideration. However, this is not the end of the analysis. The process is continuous and is never complete unless there is definitive proof to the contrary. By using the macro–micro–macro continuum, analysts will follow many of the same methods that have been used for years, but now they will be taking a step back after their initial findings and will be comparing again, with a fresh look. However, this continuum is only a technique with which to avoid errors and omissions. Analysts still must have some type of approach or method.

Analysts cannot rely upon only one method. For the purposes of verification, a minimum of two methods should be utilized. Four of the more prevalent methods used by analysts to verify leads and substantiate information are link analysis, matrix tables, timelines, and flowcharts. Three of these methods are described below.

Link analysis charts

Link analysis charts provide visual or graphical overviews of interrelationships. They are great analytical resources for long-term and complex investigations. Although there are many software packages available that provide link charts, this can be manually done with the use of virtually any computer software package that allows for the drawing of graphics. Some basic rules for developing link charts, such as the one shown in Figure 5.7, are as follows:

- When connecting relationships by using lines, it is important that only confirmed relationships be connected with solid lines and arrows to demonstrate the direction of the relationship, where applicable. When a relationship cannot be confirmed, use of a dashed line is appropriate.
- Groups or businesses are reflected through the use of a box, and in some cases individuals are drawn as individual circles within a larger circle.
- Individuals will be reflected as circles, with the appropriate annotations reflected in same.

Link charts can be drawn using link analysis pictograms, such as that shown in Figure 5.8, to reflect individuals, telecommunications, currency, and computers. Use of link charts becomes cumbersome when there are many relationships and a large organization. When this occurs, there is the likelihood that relationship lines will overlap. This is not necessarily a concern, but when there are too many the charts can be difficult to read. This can sometimes be remedied by using a curved line where the lines intersect, as if it was jumping the other line.

Association and directional matrixes

The second analytical method is the use of association and directional matrixes. An association matrix, as shown in Figure 5.9, is often used in

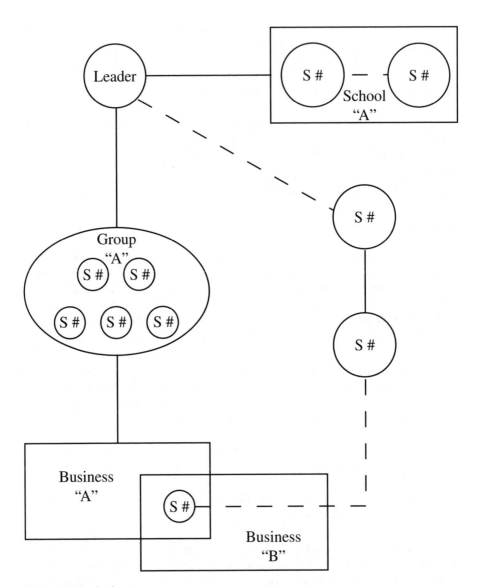

Figure 5.7 Link chart.

support of a link analysis chart. The names of individuals are entered alphabetically, with the group name on the bottom line. As associations are uncovered, criteria symbols are entered into the appropriate boxes, with a legend
identifying the symbols provided. The most commonly used symbols are
circles, shaded and unfilled, plus signs, equal signs, and checkmarks. A
directional matrix is commonly used to track the flow of goods, money, and
weapons. If there is a substantial intelligence case being worked, it may be
necessary to compile a separate chart for each commodity being monitored.
The directional matrix looks similar to an accountant's ledger and is done

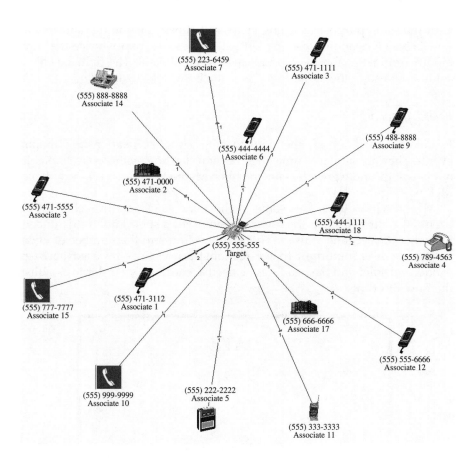

Figure 5.8 Link analysis chart using pictograms.

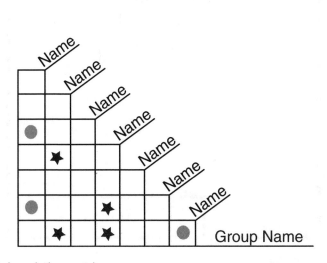

Figure 5.9 Association matrix.

with the same purpose as a link chart, but shows commodity and money flow between relationships. The left axis represents from whence the commodity originates, and the top indicates where it went. The right axis has a column reflecting the "total from" and the bottom a "total to."

Event flowcharts

Event flowcharts are another tool to help visualize relationships among events. They are similar to time lines. Several charting methods are available, but two of the more prevalent are the Birch Method (Figure 5.10), and Mercer Method (Figure 5.11).[5]

The Birch Method uses some of the same rules as a link chart. If an event is confirmed, then the box is drawn with a solid line. If it is unconfirmed, a dashed line is used. There are no limits to the number of event boxes, but it is important that directional arrow lines be used between events and solid and dashed lines be used accordingly in order to establish the flow of events.

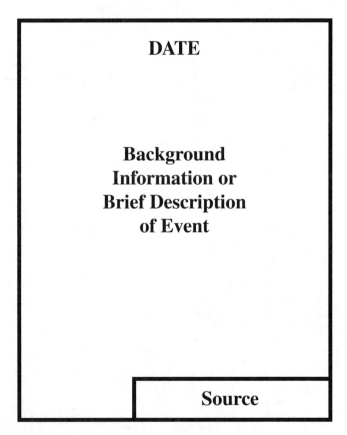

Figure 5.10 Birch Method event chart.

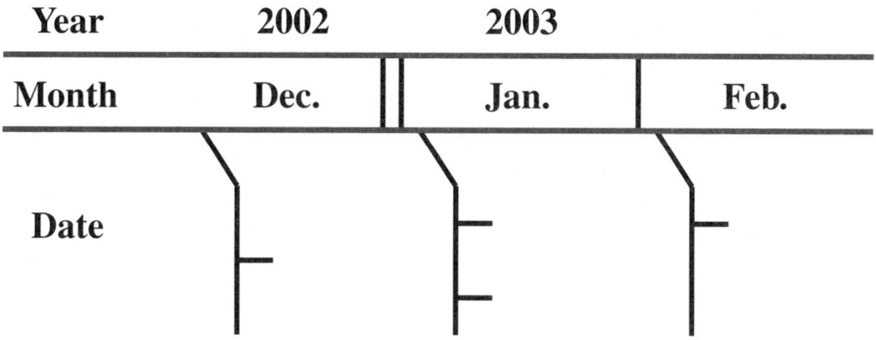

Year	2002	2003	
Month	Dec.	Jan.	Feb.

Figure 5.11 Mercer Method event chart.

The Mercer Method places the year on the top line, the applicable months on the second line, and the years separated on the month line, using two vertical lines. A diagonal line is then drawn from the month down and is connected to a vertical line, with the dates on the left and a brief description on the right. As with the other charts, an unconfirmed connection is marked with a dashed line and a confirmed connection with a solid line. If an event date is unknown, the month span can be specified (such as March to July) and the unknown date marked with a question mark.

Use of either of the above two methods will greatly enhance the understanding of any intelligence case. Personal preference will usually dictate the method used. Once the final diagram is generated, it should be reviewed by someone who was not directly involved in its production. This is important because an analyst can become too close to a case, and relationships may be taken for granted or overlooked.

Heuer's analysis of competing hypotheses (ACH)

Another assessment method is Heuer's 1999 Analysis of Competing Hypotheses (ACH). ACH is an 8-step procedural tool used to enhance judgment on important issues and to minimize common analytical pitfalls, as listed below:[8]

1. Identify the possible hypotheses to be considered. Use a group of analysts with different perspectives to brainstorm the possibilities.
2. Make a list of significant evidence and arguments for and against each hypothesis.
3. Prepare a matrix with hypotheses across the top and evidence down the side. Analyze the "diagnosticity" of the evidence and arguments — that is, identify the items that are most helpful in judging the relative likelihood of the hypotheses.
4. Refine the matrix. Reconsider the hypotheses, and delete evidence and arguments that have no diagnostic value.

5. Draw tentative conclusions about the relative likelihood of each hypothesis. Proceed by trying to disprove the hypotheses rather than prove them.
6. Analyze how sensitive your conclusion is to a few critical items of evidence. Consider the consequences for your analysis if that evidence were wrong, misleading, or subject to different interpretation.
7. Report conclusions. Discuss the relative likelihood of all the hypotheses, not just the most likely one.
8. Identify milestones for future observation that may indicate that events are taking a different course than expected.

Heuer's list is comprehensive. It also complements two methods already discussed, the macro–micro–macro continuum and the loop effect, by demonstrating a consistent approach to tackling complex issues.

Use of any one of these methods alone or together will greatly enhance the quality of a report as well as aid in threat and vulnerability assessments.

Assessing the threat

Terrorists are strategic actors. They choose their targets based on the weaknesses they see in the victim's defenses and preparedness. This is where threat assessments come into play. Government agencies have used threat assessment models and reports to identify sources and potential threats for many years. Assessments also assist with identifying the likelihood of the threat's occurrence. Assessments should emphasize well-documented events in terms of dangers or opportunities that exist due to a terrorist or organized hate group against an agency's interests. Agencies have a tremendous need to detect and intercept security threats that may impact their jurisdiction. However, gathering information and analyzing it solely based on individuals or groups creates a void. The void is the target that may be threatened. These threats should be measured against venues within a jurisdiction by law enforcement agencies using a set of predefined standards to ensure that all communities are evaluated in like terms.

In a post-September 11, 2001, International Association of Chiefs of Police (IACP) Project Response report, a team of law enforcement experts identified a four-level standardized system for locating and measuring community risk. The four tiers of the risk system are:[9]

1. First Priority Level — Fatal (functions that upon failure could result in death, severe financial loss, or legal liability)
2. Second Priority Level — Critical (functions that would be difficult to do without for any length of time)
3. Third Priority Level — Important (functions that are not critical to an agency)

4. Fourth Priority Level — Routine (functions that are not strategically important and that, if they fail, would only be an inconvenience)

The IACP four-tier system is more of a criticality assessment rather than a threat assessment but should be included as part of a threat assessment. According to a U.S. General Accounting Office publication:[10]

> A criticality assessment is a process designed to systematically identify and evaluate important assets and infrastructure in terms of various factors, such as the mission and significance of a target. For example, nuclear power plants, key bridges, and major computer networks might be identified as "critical" in terms of their importance to national security, economic activity, and public safety.

Criticality assessments or the IACP's four-tier system should be used to bolster a threat assessment because they provide a basis for identifying which assets and structures are the most likely to be at risk.

The purpose of a threat assessment is to evaluate the likelihood of terrorist activity against a given asset or location. It is a support tool for making decisions concerning how to establish and prioritize security program requirements, planning, and resource allocations. Raymond J. Decker, Director of Defense Capabilities and Management, stated, "A threat assessment identifies and evaluates each threat on the basis of various factors, including capability, intention, and lethality of an attack."[11] For several years, the Department of Defense has been utilizing threat assessments in its antiterrorism program for its military installations.

Threat assessment approaches involve many factors, but three of the most common are a terrorist group's intentions, past activities, and capabilities. These factors are detected throughout the analytical and investigative processes and should be applied when developing threat assessments.

Threat assessment models are designed to be generic in nature unless specific details dictate otherwise. They are not based on worst-case scenarios, as are vulnerability assessments. It is impossible to develop a model for every feasible threat scenario or group, but threat assessments provide a foundation from which to build. Developing a threat assessment model requires knowledge and survey of the jurisdiction or region in order to identify potential threats or areas of concern.

Threat assessment reports usually begin with an introduction, a description of the geographical area being considered, and a list of reporting or participating agencies. This is followed by the report body, and the report usually concludes with related activities, a synopsis, and a forecast. The following layout is suggested for regular assessments in matters of homeland security. It should be followed by the completed site survey in the body's text:

- List identified targeted groups, members (suspects), and incidents.
- Report results from checking Web sites and publications; report target and suspect analyses.
- Initiate link analysis.
- Provide link charts and matrixes; sort based on numerous variables.
- Provide results of reviewing against other link charts and older data.
- Report data search results on victims, suspects, groups, and targets (based on findings).
- Identify specific details: groups, members, targets, and geographical limitations.
- Verify leads and information (should be done at all steps).
- Report results of site file reviews and visits.
- Determine posture of the sites' physical security status.
- Report results of briefings conducted (should be done at all steps, as needed).
- Identify all splinter groups.
- Identify all supporter groups (active and passive).
- Identify financial links.
- Continually update all links and information without delay.
- Perform final analysis review of all available data.

Threats or terrorist activities do not occur overnight. They are often elaborate and well financed and are planned months or years in advance. This is to the advantage of law enforcement. The chances of gaining information or insight to a group are enhanced by time and by attending the following types of gatherings and investigating the following propaganda for potential threat indicators:

- Public demonstrations
- Meetings, rallies
- Unrest at colleges and public speeches advocating violence
- Training
- Antigovernment posters and leaflets
- Publications and CDs
- Phone threats

Evaluation and assessments should be continuous. Because threat assessments are invaluable decision-making tools, they need to be updated at least annually. Threats can change and new threats emerge; failure to reconcile assessment data can produce invalid information. While assessments are key decision-making support tools, it is important to understand that they might not properly capture emerging terrorist threats.

Vulnerability assessment

Vulnerability assessments help provide in-depth analyses into the inner workings of a facility or designated site in order to identify components that may be at risk for attack. The following is The U.S. General Accounting Office's working definition of a vulnerability assessment:[12]

> A vulnerability assessment is a process that identifies weaknesses in physical structures, personnel protection systems, processes, or other areas that may be exploited by terrorists and may suggest options to eliminate or mitigate those weaknesses.

Vulnerability assessments are related to a current period of time and should be performed at least annually. All possible "what if" and worst-case scenarios should be researched. The "what if" scenarios involve security, design, engineering, mitigation, response, and damage buffers. Once an assessment is initiated and the site to be protected is identified, the perimeter of the identified target should be expanded to ensure that all possible ingresses and egresses are secured.

Typically, vulnerability assessments are conducted by teams of skilled experts. Areas such as engineering, security, finance, and information systems are generally beyond the scope of law enforcement personnel. Therefore, the experts and those with an intimate working knowledge of the site will conduct the assessment. The level of protection needed should be determined, and the site in question should be evaluated against different threat levels. Some factors to consider when determining threat levels are: national security, critical infrastructures, on- and off-site hazards, proximity to population centers, and adequacy of the site's existing preparedness plans. These factors will help law enforcement personnel make key management and deployment decisions should the need arise.

Government facilities are not the only facilities that should have vulnerability assessments performed annually. Many private-sector facilities could be attractive targets for terrorists and organized hate groups. Therefore, law enforcement officials should try to get copies of private industry assessments, especially for high-risk-style businesses such as power plants, natural gas facilities, and schools. Conducting an assessment is only one part of the process. Any identified exposures should be addressed and rectified before conclusion of the assessment or within a specific time-frame.

With the information from threat and vulnerability assessments, law enforcement managers and government officials will be armed with sufficient information to make judgments concerning risks of terrorist attacks. Threat and vulnerability assessments can be expedited and made readily available through the use of spatial analysis geographic information systems

(GIS). Examples of how GIS can aid law enforcement are shown in Figure 5.12, Figure 5.13, and Figure 5.14. These figures can be used to demonstrate the vulnerability of a dirty bomb in an urban setting. Figure 5.12 is a bird's eye view of a metropolis before the scenario begins. A 1000-lb conventional high-explosive device contained in a sport utility vehicle and laced with powdered and liquid radioactive waste is detonated in an intersection. Figure 5.13 shows the fallout pattern of the device 1 hour after detonation, demonstrating the vulnerability of numerous buildings within close proximity to the blast site, which will help law enforcement to evacuate and quarantine the area. Figure 5.14 reveals the extent radiation levels can reach within the blast area. Using the results of GIS modeling algorithms such as these, it is possible to conduct detailed vulnerability assessments that go beyond the mere recognition of a building or specific target. Analysts are thus able to immediately assist homeland security plans with command center and staging area logistics, establishment of perimeters, and model contamination of soil and groundwater.

Figure 5.12 Bird's-eye view. (Courtesy of Dan Helms, Bair Software Research and Consulting, 2003.)

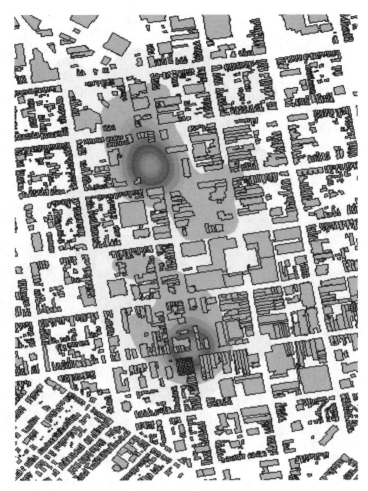

Figure 5.13 Fallout pattern. (Courtesy of Dan Helms, Bair Software Research and Consulting, 2003.)

Spatial referencing and its use in homeland security analysis

Geography and space are substantial variables to consider in analysis, threat assessment, response, recovery, and investigation. GIS can provide decision makers with the data needed to confront a wide variety of threats including disasters, sabotage, and terrorist attacks. Mapping, or spatial referencing, of terrorist threats and capabilities, current and future, is done with specific facilities and vulnerable targets. This allows authorities to determine the organizations that pose the greatest threats and the facilities and sectors that are at greatest risk. It also allows planners, managers, and policy makers to develop thresholds for preemptive or protective action through the use of attribute data via what are referred to as layers. Layers of data in geographical software allow the user to paint a picture in a wide variety of patterns

Figure 5.14 Radiation levels. (Courtesy of Dan Helms, Bair Software Research and Consulting, 2003.)

by activating one layer against another in order to visualize and identify important factors that may otherwise go undetected.

Spatial analysis, although growing in popularity with the analytical community in the form of crime mapping, is often bypassed by agencies due to the perceived complexity of operation and associated costs. This may be why law enforcement and military personnel rely so heavily on tabular data and matrixes. Although the military uses satellite imagery as well as other forms of spatial referencing, the law enforcement community lags behind. In recent years this has started to change, partly due to numerous federal agencies such as the National Law Enforcement and Correction Technology Centers, and several private corporations that have offered funding and training for GIS. The law enforcement community has also begun to reap the benefits of spatial analysis through the recent use of affordable and user-friendly desktop GIS. However, personnel need to understand GIS.

According to the Federal Interagency Coordinating Committee on Digital Cartography, GIS is "A system of computer hardware, software, and procedures designed to support the capture, management, manipulation, analysis and display of spatially referenced data for solving complex planning and management problems."[11] The latter part of the definition, solving complex planning and management problems, is appropriate when dealing with homeland security and terrorism, because terrorism is complex and poses a variety of management problems for law enforcement managers.

Through the use of GIS, law enforcement and government agencies can share information on several different platforms. This is particularly important when analyzing data from locales outside traditional jurisdictional boundaries. With GIS, law enforcement personnel are capable of mapping incidents or potential targets at various levels, from statewide (small scale) to street level (large scale). Virtually the only restriction placed on this capability would be the projection, or real-world reference, at which the base map data are displayed, but this is easily transformed via most desktop GIS applications. Issues such as not having a neighboring jurisdiction's base map can be easily rectified through the use of free resources such as the U.S. Census Bureau's Topologically Integrated Geographic Encoding and Referencing (TIGER) files. These files provide a wide variety of geographical layers available on the Internet that when downloaded (and projected if needed) can enhance analysts' abilities to visualize areas with which they are unfamiliar. In addition, there are many Internet sites and resources, some free and some fee-based, that show new ways to view intelligence and the world. This is just the beginning. GIS has an extensive range of applications, some of which have been used for decades and are just now being discovered by the law enforcement community.

Range of GIS uses

The range of uses and benefits of GIS are exponential. Beyond the previous obvious use of enhanced information sharing, GIS offers an integrated analysis for law enforcement personnel. The ability to map a city's infrastructure against a wide range of potential homeland or security targets will enable personnel to make informed decisions based on the whole picture.

GIS can assist in homeland security analysis through many facets. First are detection, deterrence, and identification. It is essential that all potential at-risk locations be identified and properly referenced on a map. This allows an analyst or first responder to visually detect other potential indirect targets, thus enhancing the likelihood of deterring future attacks. Additionally, first responders would be able to instantly identify a potential field of fire if a gunman or sniper were to open fire from any given location. This capability would also be helpful during the evidence collection process, because it would limit the search area.

The second facet is preparing and planning. Law enforcement personnel, regardless of assignment, are trained in planning and preparing for the worst-case scenario. This is particularly important in homeland security. Proper preparation and planning are crucial at all levels. Through the use of GIS, all personnel involved in a plan of action can gain a multidimensional view of various layers of data. By developing layers that account for the "what if" scenarios, analysts will be able to readily call upon and visualize a variety of data without interfering with any one aspect of an operation.

The remaining three facets are resource deployment, response and evacuation, and recovery. All are critical to any emergency preparedness plan, but they can easily go unnoticed by an analyst not looking at the global picture. Deployment and evacuation are two facets that pose perhaps the greatest concern for local and state law enforcement agencies. Deployment scenarios, depending on the seriousness of the operation or incident, are something for which most agencies have contingency plans. These usually occur during civil disorders or demonstrations, but they are adjustable to fit most plans. In addition to basic deployment planning and monitoring, GIS software will enable managers to estimate response times of field units.

Evacuations add a new dimension, because most agencies do not have control over civilians and outside parties. Evacuation plans are often established when a particular segment of the population is affected, as with natural disasters or nuclear accidents. These plans are frequently used by emergency operation command centers that have a specific criterion for evacuation and predefined locations to which to send evacuees. In a terrorist situation, law enforcement does not have the luxury of dictating all of the evacuation or deployment criteria. The use of real-time spatial data can greatly enhance an ad hoc plan of action.

The Federal Geographic Data Committee (FGDC), a 19-member interagency committee composed of representatives from the executive office of the President and cabinet-level and independent agencies, posted a document entitled "Homeland Security and Geographic Information Systems" on their Web site, detailing how GIS and mapping technology can save lives and protect property in a post-September 11, 2001 America. They cited several uses for GIS within homeland security, some of which have been described above, and expanded upon the topic.

According to the FGDC, the following characteristics that make up geographic information technologies, combined with appropriate sets of geospatial information, constitute an invaluable tool for handling, displaying, and analyzing information involved in every aspect of homeland security. Outlined below are the characteristics, as cited by the FGDC:[13]

> *Detection*: Geospatial information provides the spatial and temporal backdrop upon which effective and efficient threat analysis is accomplished. By linking and analyzing temporally and spatially associated

information in real time, patterns may be detected that lead to timely identification of likely modalities and targets.

Preparedness: Emergency planners and responders must often depend on geospatial information to accomplish their mission. Current, accurate information that is readily available is crucial to ensuring the readiness of teams to respond. Geospatial information access and interoperability standards are essential elements, as they support the means for the Nation's response units to react to terrorist attacks, natural disasters, and other emergencies.

Prevention: Geospatial information provides a means to detect and analyze patterns regarding terrorist threats and possible attacks. This information, coupled with information about borders, waters, and airspace, in turn, may lead to disruption of terrorists' plans or prevention or interdiction of their attacks.

Protection: Geospatial information is an important component in the analysis of critical infrastructure vulnerabilities and in the use of decision support technologies such as visualization and simulation to anticipate and protect against cascading effects of an attack on one system as it relates to other interdependent systems.

Response and recovery: Geospatial information is used by many organizations in response to and recovery from natural disasters. Similarly, this information is invaluable for emergency response services of all kinds, as well as for carrying out long-term recovery operations. The Federal Response Plan, developed by 26 federal agencies and the Red Cross, identifies overall responsibilities and the concept of operations for presidential declared disasters. A number of emergency support functions are identified, with the Federal Emergency Management Agency (FEMA) in the lead for coordinating response to natural disasters and the federal wildland agencies responsible for coordinating response to wildland fires.

These are examples of the potential that can be achieved with the use of GIS. GIS is a relatively new tool for many law enforcement agencies that are just beginning to discover and harness the power of these systems. Powerful GISs are now available that quickly render one to several layers of digital geospatial data into map-like products. These systems can facilitate near-realtime performance of a wide range of relevant geospatial analyses. They can also be used to access and process digital geospatial data virtually anywhere because digital data, unlike analog data, can be instantly transmitted. This ability will be of great benefit during preparation and planning stages.

Preparation and planning

Use of GIS in homeland security is dependent upon good, clean, accurate, and timely data. The two fundamental components to using GIS are incident data and base map data. Clean incident data, particularly addresses, are extremely important and are one of the leading reasons that information does not get geocoded or mapped. That is why it is essential that all participants have a complete understanding of the importance of standardized data. The second component of GIS is the quality of the base map used by the analyst. Analysts often have to work with layers of data that are maintained and updated by independent contractors or other departments. These can contribute to the learning curve associated with mastering the use of GIS-based programs. No matter who is charged with maintaining or updating the numerous GIS layers, updates must be done consistently and with a sense of urgency. Changes need to be shared with all end users, either through word of mouth, or preferably through formal means such as metadata (data about the data). The National Spatial Data Infrastructure (NSDI) is a working example of compiling metadata to facilitate integration of data and support decision making. The NSDI is a network of federal, state, and local geospatial information databases that provide metadata for all information holdings to make information easier to find and to use.

Effective planning and analysis require that officials anticipate the future while remaining cognizant of the past. When assessing and evaluating potential hazards and risks spatially, the integration of historical incidents against current issues may provide a vision for the future. Terrorists often seek to learn from those they consider to have achieved some level of success with their tactics. Their continuous review of historical material, such as writings and court material, is designed to assist them in developing future plans of attack. Law enforcement must not overlook the same tactic of learning from the past, locally and nationally.

GIS linking

In the field of GIS, three words are commonly mentioned: points, lines, and polygons. Points are often referred to as dots or pins. They are known to law enforcement as the locations of crimes, but they can also be residential locations and potential targets. Lines usually represent street center lines, roadways, and property lines. Polygons are often used to depict building footprints, land use and zoning, and jurisdictional boundaries. Perhaps one of the greatest benefits of GIS is the capability to link images, documents, data tables, building floor plans, operational plans, points of contact, and guidelines through a process known as hot linking. Hot linking provides a valuable tool for all law enforcement officials. It allows for the use of the full power of technology by incorporating a mechanism designed to reduce or eliminate manual efforts and multiple sources of data within one single project or file. Once information is plotted within GIS and saved as a project, law enforcement officials have a venue in which they can link a wide array of documents and images. The end user can simply point and click on a map location in order to gain access to all of the linked items.

Additional benefits of GIS

Additional benefits to be gained from GIS include the ability to anticipate and visualize fields of view that may be available to field commanders as well as the ability to see other possible points of interest and dispersion patterns for chemical and toxic plumes. The latter are critical aspects of the planning stage, when anticipating and developing evacuation models, as well as when developing deployment strategies that ensure the safety of all first responders. Figure 5.15 shows a hypothetical scenario of a chemical plant along a waterway and possibly within 5 miles of residential areas. In this scenario, responding officers and managers would be able to readily identify areas affected by toxic plumes through use of the 1- and 3-mile buffers. This would include the water and railways that may otherwise go undetected, because they might be perceived as barriers but toxic plumes do not recognize such barriers. The ability to identify potential exposure areas is one facet. Another is the ability to identify potential targets that terrorists and organized hate groups may seek out.

Identifying potential targets

GIS is a powerful tool that allows for more than a one-dimensional view. It can depict orthophotography images, satellite images, three-dimensional (3D) modeling (as demonstrated in Figure 5.16), and elevations. However, before enhanced models or projects are built, law enforcement personnel should consider all potential targets and vulnerable areas. Although no list can be all-inclusive, the following list of potential targets and vulnerable areas may be used for review, analysis, and geographical consideration when developing and conducting spatial analysis for the purposes of homeland security and terrorism initiatives. Figures in parentheses are approximate for the entire U.S. as reported in The National Strategy for the Physical Protection of Critical Infrastructures and Key Assets:[15]

- Utilities, above ground and underground
- Water treatment (1800 federal reservoirs and 1600 municipal waste-water facilities)
- Well fields (water and oil)
- Oil and gas
- Energy and nuclear (104 commercial nuclear power plants)
- Government buildings (3000 government owned and operated)
- Government officials
- Informational resources/infrastructure
- Landmarks (5800 historic buildings)
- Skyscrapers (460)
- Transportation: land, air, and sea (5000 airports, 120,000 miles of railway, 300 inland/coastal ports, 590,000 highway bridges)

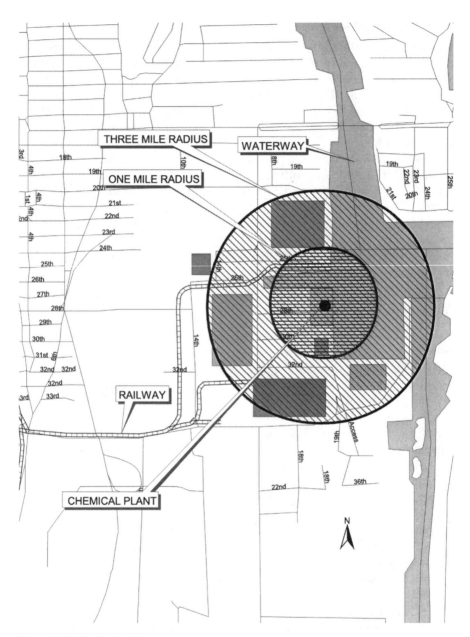

Figure 5.15 Radius buffers.

- Banking and financial institutions (26,600 FDIC-insured institutions)
- Schools
- Military bases or personnel
- Private-sector defense contractors

Figure 5.16 Three-dimensional modeling of a target. (Courtesy of Dan Helms, National Law Enforcement and Corrections Technology Center — Rocky Mountain Region, Crime Mapping and Analysis Program.)

- Law enforcement buildings or personnel
- International corporations
- Shopping areas
- Sports arenas
- Sporting events
- Special or symbolic events
- Media spectacles
- Annual special events, e.g., boat and automobile shows, art festivals
- Symbols of capitalism
- Judicial facilities
- Items associated with dates of significance
- Cellular telephone tower sites
- Agriculture (1,920,000 farms)
- Postal and shipping sites (137 million delivery sites)
- Chemical industry (66,000 chemical plants)
- Pipelines (2 million miles of pipeline)
- Public health and emergency services (5800 registered hospitals)
- Religious institutions
- Air- and seaports

- Bridges and dams (80,000 dams)
- Amusement parks

When identifying potential targets, law enforcement agencies need to coordinate with other government entities or private-sector groups that work directly with the areas of concern. Protection of infrastructures and assets "... requires coordinated action on the part of federal, state, and local governments; the private sector; and concerned citizens across the country."[15] The lion's share of these assets are owned and operated by the private sector. An example of this coordination would be the identification of a water-pumping station. A law enforcement agency may see the need to identify and secure only the pumping station, but an employee of the water department may have additional concerns, such as the need for electricity to operate the pump, which may be overlooked and lead to extensive flooding.

Mass transit systems are targets that present a challenge for law enforcement. Bus and rail systems are mobile, cover an enormous area, and travel through densely populated regions. This makes them attractive soft targets due to their accessibility and often unsecured nature. For this reason, buses have been popular targets for terrorist groups for years in such places as Israel. In the U.S. it would be virtually impossible to guard and secure every bus and rail system with law enforcement personnel. GIS can help fill the void by identifying potential weaknesses or high risk areas that may appear attractive to potential terrorists. Soft government targets such as mass transit may be selected for acts of sabotage or violence in response to government actions such as war. However, soft targets are not always chosen. Hard targets are also selected for the impact that will be felt by the victim country.

Terrorists often select targets in order to make a statement. In addition, they want to minimize exposure and maximize casualties. Security measures at a facility or site should not be used as a variable when deciding whether or not to identify a location. Terrorists are not fearful of maximum security, as shown by the bombings of the Khobar Towers in Saudi Arabia, the U.S.S. Cole in Yemen, and embassies throughout the world. Once identified, maps, just like any other intelligence product, are of little value if they are not disseminated and used.

Dissemination of intelligence

Intelligence has no value if it is not disseminated. No matter how good the analysis and intelligence are, if management and other government officials do not review, consider, and respond to it with open minds and in a timely manner, it will be of no use. We will only hear, after the fact, anecdotal testimonials of warnings that were made but ignored. Past history demonstrates this to be true, as illustrated by three devastating events in the history of the U.S.: the bombing of Pearl Harbor (December 7, 1941), the World Trade Center attack (September 11, 2001), and the Columbia Shuttle disaster (February 1, 2003). The signs, and possibly some documentation, were allegedly present. Information was gathered and reviewed but not acted upon. This demonstrates the need for accurate, timely, and verifiable intelligence. Information should not be ignored because it lacks any of these three conditions (accurate, timely, and verifiable) but an open mind to all possible scenarios must be kept.

In November, 2001 the U.S. Attorney General reported that sharing of information with all government employees is critical in order to prevent and disrupt terrorist acts. Many law enforcement agencies traditionally disseminated intelligence information based on "need" to certain segments of the force. With homeland security, everyone shares in the need for information. There are some instances when intelligence must be restricted, but on many occasions there is no reason for these constraints.

In the Antiterrorism Act of 1996, the FBI was the agency charged with gathering terrorist information. During the same year, the FBI Counterterrorism Center was established to combat terrorism on three fronts: international, domestic, and countermeasures relating to both. Joint task forces also play a role in the nation's response to terrorism. As of 2003, FBI Director Mueller reported that there were 56 Joint Terrorism Task Forces (JTTFs) in operation within the U.S.[6] The JTTFs are the conduits used by many local and state law enforcement agencies to introduce the information or intelligence that they harvest. Questions remain whether they will be the sole conduits or if regional-level task forces should be used much like a chain-of-command. There are two other avenues for disseminating information, and it will depend on the state as to which, if any, are utilized. They are offices of statewide intelligence and designated state homeland security units. On the White House Web site a map with a link to a contact name, telephone number, or e-mail address for each state and territory in the Union is provided. This information has been compiled into a reference list in Appendix F.

Commonly used analytical reports

Regardless of the venue, it is critical that information be reported and disseminated immediately. Many styles of analytical reports have been commonly used in the past several years. There is no need to reinvent the wheel just because it now deals with terrorism or organized hate, and analysts should stay with proven methods.

Outlined below are various types of analytical reports. Each has a place in the analytical world and should be applied accordingly:

- Assessments – Threat and vulnerability assessments are two of the more common.

- Briefings — These reports are not case studies, but rather are designed to provide a summary overview of the case in question. They are usually delivered to command staff members and address only the basic facts.
- Bulletins — These short reports are often in the form of "be on the lookout" (BOLO), identifying areas of concern and wanted subjects. They are direct and concise.
- Chronological reports — These are commonly referred to as timelines and include confirmed and unconfirmed information, noted accordingly.
- Commodity flowcharts — These are used to track the flow of currency and goods. A separate chart is often done for each item.
- Event flowcharts — These charts come in different styles, two of which were described earlier, and are used to visually depict a series of events or occurrences. Only a summary of the event is noted.
- Frequency distribution lists — Uses a table of numbers, indicating the number of event occurrences. These events are often analyzed and weighted with respect to a case.
- Link analysis — This method is used to identify and establish interrelationships among activities, events, individuals, corporations, finances, and telephone records by visual means.
- Maps — These are also referred to as spatial analysis, spatial referencing, and geographic distribution analysis. The potential use of geographical information is virtually endless and includes the use of orthophotography and satellite imagery.
- Matrix charts — These charts are used to identify connections or relationships among people and organizations using a series of grids and symbols.
- Net worth analysis —Also referred to as financial analysis reports. These documents show the financial affairs of the target in question as well as its assets and expenses.
- Profiles — These are comprehensive reports on an individual, group, or corporation, and include virtually every aspect of their existence, including behavior.
- Statistical reports — These reports are often used for comparative purposes and aid management in identifying shifts in activity.
- Strategic reports — These reports are often used to monitor, track, and project long-range activities.
- Tactical reports — These reports are designed to meet the immediate needs of a case and are used by management in developing operational and deployment strategies.
- Telephone and toll record analysis — These reports are often done with the assistance of complex computer programs that establish links, track incoming and outgoing calls, and aid in identifying locations.

- Warnings — These are used to forecast or predict the occurrences of future behavior based on validated, corroborated, and threat analysis information.

One report being produced by the federal government is the *FBI Intelligence Bulletin*. According to FBI Director Robert Mueller, "a new *FBI Intelligence Bulletin* is sent to more than 17,000 law enforcement agencies virtually every week."[16] The question that should be posed to members of an agency is how many people have seen this bulletin or even know it exists? It is commendable that a bulletin is being prepared and disseminated, but if it is not reaching personnel beyond the command staff, how much value is there in producing it? The FBI has done its part. A check of several personnel working in analytical units in a large metropolitan area revealed that no one had ever seen this document or even knew of its existence. These are the employees who will be asked to analyze matters surrounding homeland security. Dissemination practices have to be direct, concise, and reach those in the trenches.

Special requests for dissemination, such as "for internal use only" or "in-house distribution" should be avoided. Once a document is disbursed, it is no longer under the sender's control. It must be assumed that every document will end up in court, be subject to public record laws, or innocently distributed out of the sender's intended circle. There is also the chance that the information may be leaked to individuals without clearance.

When preparing a report questions should be answered, not created. The reader of the document should be able to clearly understand the content of the report and not need to return to the preparer for further clarification. Documents should include the preparer's name or initials, date prepared, source or sources of the data used to compile the report, a document identification number, and if there have been any revisions these should also be noted. For every document there should be supporting documents. Analysts must log requests as they come in, document actions taken, and maintain copies of all analytical subproducts (queries). When compiling these records, it is important to maintain their true form as they evolve. Storage of these records, whether manual or electronic, is an issue dependent on public record laws of a jurisdiction. In some locales, storing records on a local unsecured personal computer may subject the entire case to public review. This can lead to the leakage of intelligence through completely legal means. Caution has to be used at every step. Nothing should be taken for granted.

Dissemination of the report is what the analyst is working toward. Therefore, it is important that the proper personnel be on the receiving end. Within an agency, the two most common methods of dissemination are photostatic copies or electronic mail (e-mail). Use of e-mail poses a whole new set of concerns. When distributing documents via e-mail, the size of the document is important. If it is difficult for the recipient to access the information, they may delete it. Another consideration is the use of electronic tracking and expirations. Electronic tracking provides assurance that the document was received and opened. Intelligence reports should never be typed directly into an e-mail. Analysts should prepare an independent document and insert it as an attachment. This will aid in diverting improper viewing. Expiration dates should be established when disseminating information electronically. These help ensure that information is reviewed in a timely manner and that information is not reviewed for possible action after it is no longer valid.

Chapter concepts

1. Information is transformed into intelligence. It is important to use various sources in order to develop a group's modus operandi, e.g., capabilities, history, statements, and intentions, causes, and motivations.
2. When investigating terrorist and organized hate groups, it is essential that the components of a group or organization profile and the components of an offender profile be analyzed thoroughly.
3. Various nontraditional resources for analytical consideration are available. When analyzing these resources, tunnel vision can be avoided through the use of the macro–micro–macro continuum.
4. The role of threat and vulnerability assessments in homeland security is discussed. These assessments need to be current and conducted via partnering with the private sector.
5. Valuable insight can be gained through the use of spatial referencing and analysis and through identifying potential targets.
6. Commonly used analytical reports are described. The ways intelligence is disseminated are discussed.

References

1. Heymann, P.B., *Terrorism and America: A Commonsense Strategy for a Democratic Society*, MIT Press, Cambridge, MA, 1998, p. 25.
2. Hoffman, B., Countering the new terrorism, in *Terrorism Trends and Prospects*, Lesser, I.O., Ed., RAND, Santa Monica, CA, 1999, p. 25.
3. The Smoking Gun, Bin Laden's Terrorism Bible, http://thesmokinggun.com/archive/jihadmanual.html, Terrorism 101: A How-To Guide (Feb. 27, 2003).
4. Gottlieb, S., Arenberg, S., and Singh, R., *Crime Analysis: from First Report to Final Analysis*, Alpha Publishing, Montclair, CA, 1994, p. 59.
5. Sweeney, W.J., *Intelligence Analyst's Source Book*, Alpha Group Center, May 2002, photocopy.
6. Franklin, R.A., The Hate Directory: Hate Groups on the Internet, http://www.bcpl.net/~rfrankli/hatedir.html, Jan. 15, 2003, Release 7.1.
7. Cooper, J., Nelson, E., and Ronczkowski, M., Tactical/investigative analysis of targeted crimes, in *Advanced Crime Mapping Topics*, National Law Enforcement and Corrections Technology Center, Denver, CO, 2002, p. 32.

8. Heuer, R.J., Jr., *Psychology of Intelligence Analysis*, Center for the Study of Intelligence, Central Intelligence Agency, 1999, chap. 8, p. 2.

9. International Association of Chiefs of Police Project Response, Leading from the Front: Law Enforcement's Role in Combating and Preparing for Domestic Terrorism, IACP, Alexandria, http://www.theiacp.org, Feb. 28, 2003, p. 8.

10. United States General Accounting Office, Homeland Security Key Elements of a Risk Management Approach, Decker, R.J., Oct. 12, 2001, p. 6.

11. United States General Accounting Office, Homeland Security Key Elements of a Risk Management Approach, Decker, R.J., Oct. 12, 2001, p. 3.

12. United States General Accounting Office, Homeland Security Key Elements of a Risk Management Approach, Decker, R.J., Oct. 12, 2001, p. 5.

13. Federal Interagency Coordinating Committee on Digital Cartography, Geographic Information Systems, 1988.

14. Federal Geographic Data Committee, Homeland Security and Geographic Information Systems, http://www.fgdc.gov/publications/homeland.html, Mar. 12, 2003.

15. President, Report, The National Strategy for The Physical Protection of Critical Infrastructures and Key Assets, White House, Feb. 2003, p. vii.

16. Mueller, R.S., III, Teamwork is our future, *The Police Chief*, Jan. 2003, p. 8.

chapter six

What the future may hold

Law enforcement is heading for uncharted waters. Beyond dealing with criminal activity and enforcing state statutes, law enforcement personnel are at the time of this writing in the throes of war with a frontline that has no defined latitude or longitude. The enemy is often faceless and leaderless. What will the future hold? Although no one person or group can predict the future, one certainty is that technology will be at the forefront. Another certainty is that international and domestic terrorist groups are here to stay, but they will no longer be treated as two distinct factions. There are no boundaries with terrorists or organized hate groups. Law enforcement has embarked on a new frontier that cannot be disregarded and appears to be endless. Times have changed and so must law enforcement.

Chances are that the greatest terrorist impact will come from technology or science, such as cyber- or bioterrorism, rather than from conventional bombs. No matter what the source of the impact is, agencies are cautioned against a simplistic approach. History has demonstrated that most terrorist attacks are events that are planned, often over the course of months and years. Therefore, we must use extreme caution when gathering information and must avoid overlooking any seemingly harmless aspect of situations or events presented. The smallest, seemingly meaningless, communication, transmission, purchase, or inquiry could be the missing component that links events. Agencies should take this information into account as well as all the categories mentioned in previous chapters when developing their database structures. Relegating minor items to a "comments" section or omitting them altogether may have adverse effects in the future. Also, database managers should include information on the various forms of terrorism, especially cyber and biological.

Foreign-based terrorist influence

The influence of foreign-based terrorist organizations is here to stay, and al-Qaeda is not the only one. Appendix D lists many other groups in the world that are full of hate and have no limitations in their pursuit of fulfilling their beliefs. Many groups have had a presence, a following, or have conducted business in the U.S. for decades. According to the U.S. State Department's designated foreign terrorist organization list for 2002, four groups have a confirmed presence in the U.S.:

- *al-Qaeda*, Arabic for "the base" (worldwide), an Islamic extremist organization that opposes "non-Islamic" regimes and that has been linked to bombings throughout the world against U.S. government interests
- *Al-Gama'A Al-Islamiyya* (Egypt), an Islamic extremist group responsible for attacks on tourists in Egypt
- *Hizbollah* (Lebanon), an Islamic extremist group linked to the Iranian government and responsible for suicide truck bombings against U.S. interests
- *Kahane Chai* (Israel and the West Bank), a Jewish extremist group seeking to continue the founder's rejectionist agenda

Hamas, a Palestinian fundamentalist group, an offshoot of the Muslim Brethren that came into existence in 1987, is another group with an alleged presence in the United States.

In addition to the deep-seated concern of the groups with confirmed presences in the U.S., seven countries have been designated as being sponsors of terrorism: Cuba, Iran, Iraq, Libya, Sudan, North Korea, and Syria. The potential for terrorist activities that threaten the security of the U.S., its nationals, or allied nations, is greatly enhanced because of the states that sponsor terrorism. However, these countries cannot be handled by local or state law enforcement. This mission falls on the federal government and the military. The role of law enforcement is to provide detailed local information and intelligence to the appropriate authorities on domestic-related matters and on those that involve international groups. Cyber-activity is one component that will likely play key roles in future foreign-based terrorist endeavors and will be handled largely by law enforcement. The cyberworld provides a way for faceless operatives within terrorist organizations to attack key infrastructure systems from virtually anywhere in the world.

Cyberterrorism

The U.S. infrastructure is fragile, even though it is perceived as secure. For every precaution in place, it is likely that there is an individual or group trying to compromise or access the system.

Technology growth has expanded the opportunities for penetrating vital commercial and financial computer systems and for disabling a national computer infrastructure. This can be characterized as a cyber or technical

Pearl Harbor. Cyberterrorism will probably not have a body count associated with it, but it can cripple a nation, put corporations out of business, and cause huge financial loss. An example of financial loss was demonstrated in a survey of 611 companies doing business on the Internet in 2001. Results indicated that 83% of the companies experienced security breaches and 62% said there was some type of financial loss, with average damages of $47.8 million, compared to $26.6 million in 1999.[1] This is a drop in the bucket compared to the potential for disaster if a place like the stock market were targeted.

The information listed above is for one country, the United States. A 2001 Dartmouth College Institute for Security Technology Studies report[1] reviewed four international cases. It demonstrated the correlation between conflict among countries and the rise in the number of Web site defacements that were experienced by one or both of the countries involved in physical conflicts.

The first case study examined the Pakistan/India/Kashmir region conflict. Pakistani hacker groups allegedly defaced hundreds of Indian Web sites between 1999 and the summer of 2001. By the end of summer in 2001, India experienced a 107% increase in the number of attacks compared to the entire year of 2000.

The second case study reviewed data from the Israel/Palestinian conflict. A strong connection was realized between Web site defacements and key physical events between February 2000 and April 2001. It was evident that during the height of sustained violence there was a dramatic spike in the number of cyber attacks in the form of Web defacements, denial of service, and use of worms and Trojan horses.

The third case reviewed was the Former Republic of Yugoslavia (FRY) and NATO conflict in Kosovo. During a NATO bombing campaign, hackers allegedly employed by the FRY military began a ping saturation campaign to keep legitimate users from accessing data, and was directed to servers hosting NATO's Web site and electronic mail traffic.

The final case study involved the U.S. and China spy plane incident. After a mid-air collision on April 1, 2001 between a U.S. spy plane and a Chinese fighter aircraft, an online campaign of mutual cyber attacks and defacements took place on both sides. Between April and May of that year, over 1000 U.S. sites experienced denial of service attacks and defacements. Sites attacked included the White House, the Department of Energy, and the U.S. Air Force.

Although just four case studies were reviewed, there is strong evidence supporting the connection between events and cyber attacks. For law enforcement, this is another point to consider when identifying patterns or trends.

Defining cyberterrorism

Just as with every other component of terrorism, a working definition is needed for cyberterrorism. One of the first recognized working definitions came from the U.S. Air Force in the late 1970s. The problem associated with this definition was that it was broad-based and encompassed virtually anything dealing with information. Cyberterrorism was defined as "The use of information and information systems as weapons in a conflict where information and information systems are targets."[2]

Over time the above definition, although not incorrect, has been modified. The National Defense Agency expanded upon the U.S. Air Force's definition and can be readily modified to fit the needs of most law enforcement agencies. They define cyberterrorism as "Any action to deny, exploit, corrupt or destroy the enemy's information and its functions; protecting ourselves against those actions; and exploiting our own military information functions."[2] Although this definition mentions enemy and military information functions and war-like terms, it is just as applicable to law enforcement now that it is part of the war effort. Regardless of the definition, law enforcement must remain cognizant of local, state, and federal laws governing cyber crimes.

Spectrum of cyber conflict

The spectrum of cyber conflict can be used to help understand the scale of activity associated with the cyberworld. Few agencies routinely deal with incidents of cyber crimes. This, coupled with the in-depth knowledge needed to investigate crimes of this magnitude, has greatly limited proactive investigations concerning cyber crimes. Much of what is publicly mentioned about proactive cyber crime investigations is centered on child pornography and sexual predators.

Tracking violations of law or computer intrusions currently rests with law enforcement, but this is not seen as a priority. Much of the information and evidence collection is done after the fact and is often left up to local law enforcement officials, or perhaps the FBI in the case of a large investigation. Unlike in the U.S. Army's Spectrum of Conflict, the military or Department of Defense (DOD) is not likely to participate in such actions. This is because many of the occurrences are of a domestic nature, and the traditional war-fighting military is prohibited from performing these duties. Its role is to provide national defense and to operate in an international theater.

Distinguishing between the two separate domains, domestic and international, requires coordination of the military and law enforcement, because cyber warfare provides for the ability to attack infrastructures vital to the national security from within or from outside the country. This is ironic, considering that the DOD has been the victim of numerous intrusion attempts since 1994. The total number of network attacks reported in 1994 throughout the DOD was 225. By 1999, the total reported events escalated to just over 22,000 and this number was anticipated to reach 24,000 by the end of 2001.[3] Examples of some of these attacks can be found in Figure 6.1, Figure 6.2, and Figure 6.3. Information shown in Figure 6.1 is from the U.S. Army Web site from the year 2000, that was hacked by a 16-year-old from

```
connecting to terrorist HQ...
connection established...
receiving...
receiving...
receiving...
done...
processing...
processing...
processing...
processing... [damn we should buy a PentiumII]
processing...
done...
reading messages:
'We are the TERRORIST'S OF THE NEW AGE, we owned 95% of US military systems, you have no chance. Don't try to do anything stupid cause we're
gonna blow up these computer. Here are our demands:
1. MILK - 10 gallons...
2. CHOCOLATE - 20 boxes...
3. CARS - 2 MERCEDES GTR
4. GIRLS - Lot of them
5. MONEY - 'bout 666 million dollars should be enough
6. A COW & SHEEP - don't ask me why
7. A Pentium II processor cause this one is damn slow.
If you don't sent us these items right now, we're gonna erase all your files.
Greetings to: P s i c O S i s, Diablo and the rest of Pentaguard, Fu Manchu:2, and every terrorist of the new age. WE WILL WIN !!!
logging out...
```

Figure 6.1   Army (hacked Web screen). (Courtesy of Sergeant Sean Holtz.)

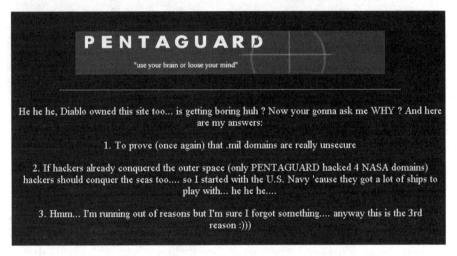

Figure 6.2 Navy (hacked Web screen). (Courtesy of Sergeant Sean Holtz.)

Poland who referred to himself as "Terrorist of the New Age." It was reported that the Army's Web site was "pinged" three times per second in 1999. Figure 6.2 shows the result of a hack in 1999 by a 17-year-old from England into the U.S. Navy Web site. Navy personnel reported that their Web site experienced a hack attempt every 23 seconds in 1999. Figure 6.3 shows a hack into the official Pentagon Web site.[4] Cyber vulnerability of the Armed Services "… is magnified by the fact that 95 percent of all U.S. military traffic moves over civilian telecommunications and computer systems."[5]

It has been stated that "Internet users now number 120 million — 70 million of them in the United States. An estimated 1 billion people — one-sixth of humanity — will be on-line by 2005, two-thirds of them abroad."[6] These staggering figures demonstrate the tremendous tasks ahead for law enforcement. Even though the number of attacks is dwarfed by the

Figure 6.3 Pentagon (hacked Web screen). (Courtesy of Sergeant Sean Holtz.)

number of potential users, law enforcement must remain vigilant when investigating cyber attacks because just one computer hard drive can contain over 50 million pages of data.

One of the primary cyber crimes that exists and receives little media attention is often referred to as hacking. In 1998, the vulnerability of infrastructure systems was highlighted in an investigation into a Department of Energy laboratory that was shut down for a few weeks due to a breach of its systems by a hacker. Most hackers are thrill-seeking individuals driven to outdo each other with their unique abilities and who generally will not damage data or systems. They will make it known that they gained access and will leave their electronic signature or cyber tag. A cyberterrorist, on the other hand, will try to avoid detection through the use of a Trojan horse and phreaking. This enables them to completely eliminate target records or systems while remaining anonymous and avoiding detection.

The spectrum of cyber conflict was discussed in a report prepared by a commanding member of the U.S. Air Force in 2001, and law enforcement's role was explained in detail. It was noted that the spectrum consists of "… various forms of cyber attack such as hacking, hacktivism (a form of computer-based civil disobedience), espionage, terrorism, and information warfare."[3] The level of escalation as it relates to the spectrum that was detailed in the report is demonstrated in Figure 6.4. A dashed vertical line divides the spectrum in order to differentiate between unintentional and intentional

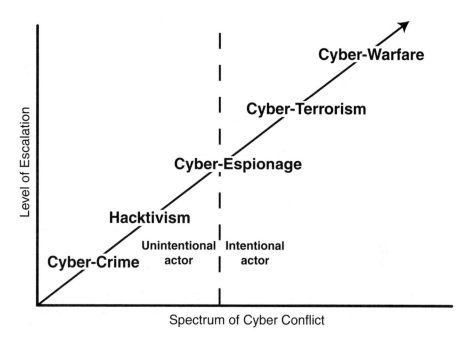

Figure 6.4 Spectrum of Cyber Conflict.

actors. The activity to the left of this line is seen as that of individuals who may be largely unaware or do not truly understand the international ramifications of their actions. Activity to the right of the dashed line is viewed as that of people with motive and intention to inflict damage on national security interests.

Cyber crime on the spectrum is first on the level of escalation and is sometimes referred to as illegal exploration or hacking. Much of this activity comes in the form of illegal access into a company or government network system. Some hackers start out as outsiders who use various password attacks in order to gain access as a user of the network. Many begin as insiders, in the form of disgruntled or former employees. They will use known weaknesses in the system to gain further access as an administrator or super user. Once these privileges are attained, a hacker then can read or alter files, control a system, and insert a rogue code such as a virus to damage the infrastructure.

Hacktivism, the second step on the spectrum, is described as a form of electronic disobedience. The goal is to draw attention to a particular issue, such as human rights or political beliefs, by engaging in actions that are unusual in order to attract media attention. The motivation of a person committing an act of hacktivism differs from that of a hacker in that hactivism represents a political motivation.

The next step on the spectrum is intentional actions in the form of cyber espionage. This may appear to be hacking, but in reality the mission of a cyber espionage attack is to avoid detection and to gather as much information as possible from the targeted system. With the ability to attack through cyber means, terrorist organizations have a new arena in which to commit their acts and to gather valuable information about those they see as the enemy. Many organizations, especially organized hate groups, are technologically savvy. They know how to use the systems to spread their messages, recruit, and attain illicit funds. The ability to commit acts of terrorism through nonlethal means, such as access to information and intelligence and infrastructures, can cause detrimental effects on the general populous.

Reaching government infrastructures through cyberterrorism leaves only one step on the spectrum, cyber warfare. Cyber warfare is an intentional act designed to affect national security. It is an intensified extension of cyberterrorism.

No matter what level of the spectrum is used, law enforcement will be involved. However, military involvement will generally be limited to acts ranging from cyber espionage to cyber warfare, providing a third country is involved.

One way the law enforcement community may become involved is by being a victim of cyber crimes or hacking. For example, several agencies, including the Los Angeles Police Department, U.S. Department of Justice (DOJ), and the CIA were directly victimized in the past several years. Figure 6.5 illustrates an attack to the CIA Web site. Figure 6.6 is from the DOJ site, showing a symbol used by several organized hate groups. Hackers as well as terrorists are resilient, and no single government agency is immune to attack.

In order to enhance cyber security, law enforcement will need to partner with private-sector corporations. More than 80% of all information systems in this country are owned by the private sector.[7] Any solutions for improving cyber security will require joint initiatives between government and private entities.

Bioterrorism and weapons of mass destruction (WMD)

Biological and chemical weapons and their uses are receiving a great deal of media attention. Attaining or making these WMD takes some level of expertise. Relatively few places in the world (approximately 17 states) have the people with the skills necessary to develop a biological weapon or possess the radioactive material necessary to develop a nuclear weapon.[8] Although opportunities appear limited and results unpredictable, chemical and biological materials should not be overlooked. A report by the CSIS in 2000, referring to biological agents such as anthrax and plague, noted that "Ounce for ounce, the lethality of these agents is many times that of chemical agents or nuclear weapons."[5] There are five general categories of WMD that can be used by analysts tracking materials and investigative leads:

Figure 6.5 CIA (hacked Web screen). (Courtesy of Sergeant Sean Holtz.)

Figure 6.6 DOJ (hacked Web screen). (Courtesy of Sergeant Sean Holtz.)

1. Biological
2. Chemical
3. Explosive
4. Incendiary
5. Nuclear

WMD that fall into these categories come in many deadly forms and devices. In the U.S., Title 18 of the U.S. Code covers the legislative description for many of the destructive devices used as WMD. A synopsis of what Title 18 encompasses is listed below.

- Poison gas
- Any weapon involving a disease organism
- Any weapon designed to release radiation or radioactivity at a level dangerous to human life
- Any destructive device as defined in Section 921 of this Title

The destructive devices as defined in Section 921 of Title 18 U.S.C. are as follows:

- Any explosive, incendiary, or poison gas:
  - Bomb
  - Grenade
  - Rocket having a propellant charge of more than four ounces
  - Missile having an explosive or incendiary charge of more than one-quarter ounce
  - Mine
  - Device similar to any of the devices described in the preceding clauses
- Any type of weapon (other than a shotgun or a shotgun shell) which may be readily converted to expel a projectile … with a bore of more than one-half inch in diameter
- Any combination of parts … from which a destructive device can be assembled

FBI data reveals over 10,000 bombings resulting in 355 deaths and over 3000 injuries between 1990 and 1995. Based on FBI data calculations, approximately 70% of domestic terrorist incidents involve some type of explosives. Analysts need to be aware that explosive devices can be comprised of a wide variety of materials. A comprehensive list of explosive materials as listed by the ATF that should be added to all databases is provided in Appendix E.

The number of chemical, biological, and nuclear attack incidents are not as startling as those of conventional explosives mentioned above. The Center for Non-Proliferation Studies, in a 2000 CSIS report, showed that in 1999 there were 175 reports of chemical, biological, and nuclear terrorism, 104 of which occurred in the U.S. This was a dramatic increase over the database findings in February, 2000 of a total of 687 incidents since 1900.[9] Definitive numbers are difficult to attain. The Center uses the media as its source of information, and it was noted that apparent increases might be attributed to hoaxes and different reporting methods. Regardless of the true numbers, there definitely appears to be an increase in the use or the perceived use of these agents.

There are numerous biological agents that can be employed by terrorists. The U.S. Army Medical Research Institute of Infectious Diseases lists the following diseases and biological toxins as potentially suitable for introduction into the population by deliberate dispersal:[10]

1. Bacterial infections — anthrax, cholera, plague, tularemia, and "Q" fever
2. Viruses — smallpox, Venezuelan equine encephalitis, and viral hemorrhagic fevers
3. Biological toxins — botulinum, staphylococcal enterotoxin B, *ricin*, and T-2 Mycotoxins

Chemical agents have been used in warfare for years, even by law enforcement in the form of riot-control agents. The following are among the commonly employed chemical agents:[10]

1. Nerve agents — Sarin (GB)
2. Vesicants — Mustard gas (HD, H), Lewisite (L)
3. Lung-damaging agents — Phosgene
4. Cyanide
5. Riot-control agents — CS and CN

Methods of exposure to the biological and chemical agents mentioned above include the following:

1. Absorption (through the skin)
2. Ingestion (swallowing or eating)
3. Inhalation (breathing)
4. Injection (usually through a hypodermic syringe)

The above chemical and biological concerns are critical components for analyzing materials and data, but a greater concern exists for the first responder. It is one thing to analyze information about WMD, but it is the first responders of the world who will encounter, usually unsuspectingly, chemical and biological agents. Therefore it is essential that information be made immediately available to them as it is discovered, and that they be properly trained in all aspects of this extremely dangerous situation.

Many how-to documents are available, some covering chemical and biological agents. In the previously mentioned terrorism training manual document seized in Manchester, England, "Military Studies in the Jihad against the Tyrants," several poisons were described in detail. Included in this compendium was information on extracts or derivatives of herbal and plant products that can be used to make substances such as ricin. Also included was the weight of each item needed, and symptoms that can result from exposure. One method of poisoning that was mentioned in this manual, which law enforcement personnel, especially those investigating deaths, should be aware of, is of poisoning from eating intentionally spoiled food. The method of spoiling food is explained in detail, including the symptoms and their timeline, and how to "cook" the poison. It is virtually a cookbook on the topic. The fact that this has been put into writing and made available to the general public means that law enforcement must consider it a method of bioterrorism.

The past, present, and future

The focus of this book has been on circumstances surrounding the U.S., but like many other subjects, law enforcement topics are applicable to other locales and nations. Past events have demonstrated the violence and hatred associated with terrorist and organized hate groups and have proved that rogue extremists know no borders. Thousands of events have taken place throughout the world over the past three centuries from which the law enforcement community can learn. Successful planning for the future requires an understanding of recent and distant past events. An example of this can be found in a 1999 Library of Congress Federal Research Division report that studied and analyzed terrorists and their organizations.[11] Events that were examined included the 1998 U.S. cruise missile attack against an al-Qaeda camp in Afghanistan, the use of nuclear suitcase bombs, and the bombing of one or more airliners with timebombs. Spectacular retaliation methods against Americans were proposed. Apparently, there were signs or some indicators present that elaborate methods of destruction existed, or these assumptions could not have been made 2 years before the deadly World Trade Center attack.

Current international terrorist threats against the U.S. and other countries can be divided into three categories:

1. State sponsors of terrorism
2. Formal terrorist organizations
3. Loosely affiliated rogue extremists

These three categories have been addressed in some manner throughout this book. Even though there is tremendous concern regarding international or foreign-based terrorists, law enforcement must also remain aware of the numerous domestic-based terrorist and organized hate groups. The greatest danger at present is the mixture of international and domestic terrorism. Hate and terrorism have no borders. Future considerations should be directed toward opening lines of communication and sharing data.

Plans for the future are evolving. The chances of having a national law enforcement database have been viewed as remote for years, but this is changing. If agencies are struggling simply to standardize methods and data entry within their own jurisdictions, can data be managed and overseen on a national level?

This is one question being answered today. U.S. Attorney General John Ashcroft unveiled the Gateway Information Sharing Project, a pilot program that integrates investigative data from federal, state, and local law enforcement agencies into one database. It will ultimately be accessible to all agencies participating via secure Internet. This program is the result of cooperation between numerous Illinois and Missouri local, county, and state agencies, the FBI, the U.S. Attorneys' offices of the Southern District of Illinois, and the Eastern District of Missouri St. Louis Joint Terrorism Task Force.

No matter what the future holds, the three components that cannot be overlooked are quality personnel, experience, and training. Training is probably the primary key to the future. The most important things to keep in mind are an understanding of the topic being analyzed, knowing what is being accomplished, and continually honing skills. Groups such as professional trade associations, private consultants, educators, and peers provide the best venues for future development.

Chapter concepts

1. Many foreign-based groups in the world are full of hate and are limitless in their pursuit of fulfilling their beliefs. Their influence is and will continue to be felt in the U.S.
2. Cyberterrorism is one way that foreign-based terrorists will extend their reaches into other countries, and this will primarily be handled by law enforcement.
3. The spectrum of cyber conflict demonstrates the five levels that law enforcement will face: cyber crime, hacktivism, cyber espionage, cyber warfare, and cyberterrorism.
4. Weapons of Mass Destruction include biological, chemical, explosive, incendiary, and nuclear devices. Chemical agents pose significant threats, and exposure is caused by absorption, ingestion, inhalation, and injection.
5. Current international terrorist threats against the U.S., as well as other countries, can be divided into three distinct categories: state sponsors of terrorism, formal terrorist organizations, and loosely affiliated rogue extremists.

References

1. Vatis, M.A., Cyber attacks during the war on terrorism: a predictive analysis, Institute for Security Technology Studies, Dartmouth College, Hanover, N.H., Sept. 22, 2001, pp. 5–9.
2. Holtz, S., *Cyber Terrorism*, Florida Atlantic University, Davie (Feb. 19, 2003), photocopy.
3. Adkins, B.N., *The Spectrum of Cyber Conflict from Hacking to Information Warfare: What is Law Enforcement's Role?*, U.S. Air Force, April 2001, pp. vii, 1–2.
4. Holtz, S., Cyber Terrorism, Miami-Dade Police Department, Miami (Mar. 14, 2003), presentation.
5. Cilluffo, F. et al., *Defending America in the 21st Century: New Challenges, New Organizations, and New Policies*, CSIS, Washington, D.C., 2000, pp. 3–4.
6. Webster, W., and de Borchgrave, A., *Cybercrime ... Cyberterrorism ... Cyberwarfare ... : Averting an Electronic Waterloo*, CSIS, Washington, D.C., 1998, p. 3. http://www.csis.org/pubs/cyberfor.html (Feb. 28, 2003).
7. RAND, Third Annual Report to the President and the Congress of the Advisory Panel to Assess Domestic Response Capabilities for Terrorism Involving Weapons of Mass Destruction, Dec. 15, 2001, http://www.rand.org/nsrd/terrpanel (Feb. 28, 2003), p. 41.
8. Heymann, P. B., Dealing with terrorism: an overview, http://mit-press.mit.edu/journals/pdf/isec_26_03_24_0.pdf, *Int. Security*, 26, 3, Winter 2001/02, MIT (Feb. 14, 2003), p. 24.
9. Cordesman, A.H., *Defending America: Redefining the Conceptual Borders of Homeland Defense*, CSIS, Washington, D.C., 2000, p. 66.
10. IACP Project Response Team, Leading from the front: project response terrorism, International Association of Chiefs of Police, Alexandria, VA, p. 6.
11. Library of Congress Federal Research Division, The sociology and psychology of terrorism: who becomes a terrorist and why? http://www.loc.gov/rr/frd/terrorism.htm, Sept. 1999 (Mar. 7, 2003), pp. 1–53.

chapter seven

Conclusion

Many analysts began as clerical help and secretaries, working in back rooms and performing only administrative functions. Times have changed. They are now sought after and hired in large numbers. Their positions have come full circle and they are now recognized as professional and vital to many law enforcement organizations. International professional trade associations such as the International Association of Crime Analysts (IACA) and the International Association of Law Enforcement Intelligence Analysts (IALEIA) have made great strides in the preceding decade in the areas of training and sharing of practices, but one component, national certification, still eludes the associations. However, certification looms on the horizon and will greatly standardize practices of analysts worldwide.

Information access is another analytical area that has been addressed by some agencies. Analysts should be granted access to all pertinent case information. If analysts are restricted, the quality and type of intelligence obtained will be deficient. Communication is consistently mentioned as the number one key to successful intelligence. Limiting an analyst is essentially the same as censoring him. Proactively working together and sharing information is the answer to addressing future incidents and combating issues that threaten homeland security worldwide.

The modern era of terrorism has a relatively short but devastating past. As noted earlier, the federal government has undertaken initiatives toward terrorism since at least 1972. In 1985, President Ronald Reagan gave a speech on terrorism in Chicago, Illinois. He noted that if there is no reaction to terrorism, it will spread like a cancer. He was right, and now the cancer has reached our shores. During that same period the FBI and CIA created high-tech state-of-the-art antiterrorism centers with the focus on cogent intelligence. The federal government has established numerous intelligence centers throughout the U.S. since 1985, but not all focus on terrorism. Many were established in high drug-trafficking areas, and others in remote locales. How many are interconnected and share information? As learned in a post 9/11 world, the FBI and CIA collected in-depth intelligence on many groups but were prohibited by law from exchanging it. President Reagan's speech is similar to the same rhetoric that is voiced now that the terrorist scourge has hit home. The same "importance of intelligence and communication" speeches from nearly 20 years ago are being replayed now. This is supported by the conclusions drawn in the 2000 CSIS working group reports on homeland defense, that "U.S. homeland defense which efforts have been reactive, disjointed, and focused on post facto consequence management."[1]

Technology is one way to overcome this. However, in order for technology to be effective there must be a set of national standards for each agency to follow. Law enforcement agencies are going to continue to purchase records management and CAD systems and develop proprietary databases designed to fit their needs and budgets, but with national standards the sharing of intelligence and data would be greatly enhanced. By establishing national standards, a designated agency such as the Department of Homeland Security has the opportunity to warehouse data from agencies throughout the nation. This could be achieved with little difficulty and minimal data conversion. The problem now being faced is that there are nearly 18,000 law enforcement agencies capturing data in 18,000 different formats. If we are ever to see continuous and effective sharing of information and intelligence, there must be national standards. Federal committees have been established in the arena of GIS. Effective standards, formal and informal, designed for use by programmers, cartographers, and analysts utilizing GIS, have made the sharing of GIS information routine among a wide variety of local, state, and federal agencies.

One method to effectively address information and intelligence sharing is by streamlining the process and consolidating resources into a "one-stop shop." The reorganization of the federal government's agencies under the Department of Homeland Security was perhaps the first step toward achieving this. One way to achieve a "one-stop shop" is to establish a national homeland security clearinghouse. Use of clearinghouses has proved to be an effective tool in law enforcement. In South Florida, a county-wide robbery clearinghouse was established 10 years ago to analyze and process information on nearly 10,000 robbery cases from over 30 different agencies. Since its inception, the clearinghouse has assisted in increasing the clearance rate well above the national average and decreasing the incidence of robbery. With the use of clearinghouses, detectives no longer have to rely on personal contacts and traveling around the county to check multiple databases. They have come to rely on the clearinghouse as their sole source of information and intelligence for coordinating countywide robbery-related events. By establishing a national homeland security clearinghouse, agencies throughout the country would be able to standardize practices, expedite the intelligence process, and rely on a single source rather than pass information through a wide range of local, county, state, and federal agencies, or individuals.

The public focus is still on excellent intelligence and information sharing, but little has been done to enhance the capabilities of routine law enforcement on this front. All the intelligence in the world cannot always prevent a tragedy. Only the proactive moves of those in charge, armed with quality intelligence, can help control possible future events. The U.S. intelligence machine is primarily geared toward threats from foreign attacks. That is where law enforcement comes in. Federal agents and the military cannot be everywhere, but with the entire law enforcement community working together for a common goal, the combined effort and force will be able to deter the actions of terrorist organizations. In order for law enforcement to help in the war on terrorism, it must have an understanding of the mission at hand. Terrorism has been around for years. It may not be possible to eliminate it completely, but through comprehensive and thorough law enforcement it can be controlled. Help prevent future catastrophic events and play an essential role in the war on terrorism. Success and victory in the war on terrorism will be achieved by working together.

Reference

1. Cilluffo, F. et al., *Defending America in the 21st Century: New Challenges, New Organizations, and New Policies*, CSIS, Washington, D.C., 2000, p. 9.

Domestic-based terrorist organizations

Information comes from Jonathan R. White, *Terrorism: An Introduction*, Wadsworth Publishing, Florence, KY, MILNET Web site (http://www.milnet.com), SPLC Web site (http://www.splcenter.org), ADL Web site (http://www.adl.org) and the individual groups' Web sites.

1. **American Coalition for Life Activists**: Based in Oregon; founded by Andrew Burnett, a long-time antiabortionist activist whose group endorses the justifiable homicide of abortion clinic doctors
2. **Animal Liberation Front**: Support groups are based throughout North America; in 1993, the group reportedly planted arson or incendiary devices in four Chicago stores; based on its Web site, it does not condone violence, and membership only carries out direct action by whatever means necessary
3. **Army of God**: Highly militant antiabortion movement that believes God has given them the duty to kill abortionists; it allegedly claimed responsibility for a number of abortion clinic bombings in Georgia and Alabama; financially affiliated with Glory to Jesus Ministries in Virginia
4. **Aryan Nation** (aka **Aryan Republican Army** and **Aryan National Alliance**): Base of operation is located in Hayden Lake, Idaho; categorized as white supremacists, Christian Identity group; founded by Richard Butler in the mid-1970s; believe that it is its duty to populate the country with member's progeny through polygamy; allegedly seek to overthrow the American government using bank robberies as an end to their means; ideology follows Christian Identity, neo-Nazi, and paramilitary
5. **Branch Davidians**: Thought to be an extinct operation; during their height of operation, they had bases of operation in Utah and Texas; considered by some to be a form of a cult, they are primarily firearms protestors

6. **Christian Identity Movement**: Chapters are in approximately 18 states with an estimated 31 groups; alleged members were convicted of conspiracy to manufacture explosives; they are considered to be antiabortion and antibanking, and they depict Jews as biologically descended from Satan

7. **Colorado First Light Infantry**: Alleged members were charged with possessing and manufacturing illegal firearms; group publicly supports Timothy McVeigh's actions and the Oklahoma City bombing on April 19, 1995

8. **Colorado Militia**: Based in Aurora, Colorado; professed goals are those of weapons rights

9. **Citizens of the Republic of Idaho**: Based in St. Maries, Idaho; founded by Hari Heath; members do not believe in the bureaucracy of the U.S. courts and government; therefore, they created their own; considered to be relatively docile

10. **Covenant** (aka **Sword and Arm of the Lord**): Christian Identity group started in 1971 by James Ellison on the Arkansas/Missouri state line; based in Arkansas; considered to be a violent white supremacist group with close ties to members of the Ku Klux Klan

11. **Earth Liberation Front (ELF)** (aka **North American ELF**): Alleged members were linked to attacks against the U.S. Forest Service, logging companies, and bioengineering corporations; group is categorized as ecological activists

12. **Evan Mecham Eco-Terrorist International Conspiracy (EMETIC)**: Formed in 1985; satirically uses the name of an Arizona governor; the group is known for spiking trees and various forms of sabotage

13. **Freeman**: Based in Montana; group members believe the U.S. legal system is not valid; supports an internal separatist government; alleged members were convicted for fraud and robbery; categorized as a right-wing group

14. **Ku Klux Klan**: Categorized as a white supremacy group established during the Civil War era, December 1865; the group is primarily active in the South but allegedly has membership in approximately 28 different states, with an estimated membership base of 5500 to 6000 in just over 100 different groups. Subgroups go by various names including Invisible Empire, Knights of the Klu Klux Klan, United Klans of America, and the National Knights of the Ku Klux Klan

15. **Los Macheteros**: Marxist–Leninist group formed in 1976, but emerged publicly in 1978; it wants Puerto Rico to be an independent nation; name translation means "machete wielders" or "cane cutters;" Puerto Rican revolutionary group based in Puerto Rico and operating in several Northeastern states including New York; members allegedly detonated explosives in New York and committed homicides; members are also known for their many publicly claimed

robberies in the early 1980s, including one for $7.1 million in Connecticut

16. **Michigan Militia**: Formed in April 1994 by a firearm store owner named Norman Olson and real-estate agent Ray Southwell; categorized as a large weapons rights, survivalist, and militant antigovernment organization; no major illegal activity was directly traced to this group's membership; membership was reported as high as 12,000

17. **Militia of Montana (MOM)**: Founded in February 1994 by John, David, and Randy Trochmann; categorized as a weapons rights and militant antigovernment organization; encourages members to arm themselves with guns and knives; no major illegal activity has been directly traced to this group's membership; paramilitary militia

18. **Mountaineer Militia**: Based in West Virginia; categorized as paramilitary, antigovernment, and weapons rights organization; alleged leader was convicted in August 1997 for conspiracy to engage in the manufacture of explosives

19. **National Alliance**: Founded by William Pierce, author of *The Turner Diaries*, in Hillsboro (Mill Point), West Virginia in 1974; categorized as a white supremacist and neo-Nazi organization; Leader is Erich Gliebe

20. **North American Militia of Southwestern Michigan**: Categorized as a paramilitary, antigovernment, and weapons rights organization

21. **Patriot's Council**: Based in Minnesota; categorized as a violent antigovernment and tax protest organization; the group allegedly created ricin, a toxic nerve agent

22. **Phineas Priesthood**: Inspired by the book *The Vigilantes of Christendom* by Richard Hoskins; group membership opposes homosexuality, abortions, and interracial marriages; members have allegedly committed bank robberies and abortion clinic bombings.

23. **Posse Comitatus**: Founded by Henry Beach in the early 1970s; name is Latin for power of the county; categorized as anti-Semitic and as a white supremacist organization; chapters were established in almost every state of the union and have had ties with the Arizona Patriots

24. **Reclaim the Seeds**: Categorized as an antibiotechnology organization; members allegedly claimed responsibility for a 2000 attack on crops at Seminis Vegetable Seeds Research Center and Davis campus of the University of California

25. **Republic of Texas**: Based in the Davis Mountains in West Texas; alleged leader is Richard McLaren; the organization contends that Texas was illegally annexed into the union in 1845 and that it remains an independent nation

26. **Southern California Minuteman**: Group is allegedly against the influx of illegal aliens into the U.S. from Mexico and has used snipers to control them

27. **The Order** (aka **The New Order**): Based in Oregon, Illinois, and Michigan; founded by the late Robert Mathews; categorized as a right-wing, white supremacist, neo-Nazi, racist, and anti-Semitic group; followed by and affiliated with such groups as the Silent Brotherhood and Strike Force II

28. **Viper Militia**: Based in Arizona; categorized as a paramilitary and antigovernment organization; allegedly had ties with Timothy McVeigh; trained to make illegal weapons and construct and detonate fertilizer bombs

29. **World Church of the Creator**: Founded in 1973 and headquartered in Riverton, Wyoming; also based in East Peoria, Illinois; alleged leader is Matt Hale; categorized as a white supremacist group

appendix b

Known active "Patriot" groups in the United States as of 2001

The Southern Poverty Law Center's Intelligence Project identified 158 "Patriot" groups that were active in 2001. Of these groups, 73 were militias, two were "common-law courts," and the remainder fit into a variety of categories, such as publishers, ministries, and citizens' groups. Generally, Patriot groups define themselves as opposed to the "New World Order" or advocate or adhere to extreme antigovernment doctrines. Groups listed here are not implied to advocate or engage in violence or other criminal activities, or be racist. The list was compiled from field reports, Patriot publications, the Internet, law enforcement sources, and news reports. Groups are identified by the city, county, or region where they are located. Within states, groups are listed alphabetically by place of origin.

Alabama
Alabama Committee to Get US Out of the United Nations, Birmingham

Alaska
Jefferson Party, Anchorage

Arizona
American Patriot Friends Network, Glendale
Sovereign Citizen Resource Center, Thatcher
Arizona Free Citizen's Militia, Tucson

Arkansas
Militia of Washington County, Fayetteville
Arkansas State Militia, Franklin County
Constitution Party, North Little Rock

California
California Militia, Brea

John Birch Society, Brea
State Citizens Service Center Research Headquarters, Canoga Park
Truth Radio, Delano
John Birch Society, Fountain Valley
Free Enterprise Society, Fresno
Second Amendment Committee, Hanford
John Birch Society, Laguna Hills
John Birch Society, Mission Viejo
John Birch Society, Newport Beach
John Birch Society, Oceanside
Southern California High Desert Militia, Oceanside
John Birch Society, Orange
John Birch Society, Riverside
John Birch Society, Santa Ana
Truth In Taxation, Studio City
Freedom Law School, Tustin

Colorado
American Freedom Network, Johnstown

Connecticut
Connecticut 51st Militia,Terryville

District of Columbia
American Free Press, Washington

Florida
Constitutional Guardians of America, Boca Raton
Citizens for Better Government, Gainesville
Constitution Party, Jupiter

Georgia
Militia of Georgia, Lawrenceville
Constitution Party, Woodstock

Idaho
Sons of Liberty, Boise
Police against the New World Order, Kamiah

Illinois
Illinois State Militia, Addison
Southern Illinois Patriots League, Benton
Constitution Party, Springfield

Indiana
Old Paths Baptist Church, Campbellsburg
NORFED, Evansville
Indianapolis Baptist Temple, Indianapolis
Indiana Militia Corps 2nd Brigade, Northeast Indiana
Indiana Militia Corps 1st Brigade, Northwest Indiana
Indiana State Militia 14th Regiment, Owen County
Indiana Militia Corps 5th Brigade, Pendleton

Constitution Party, Shoals
Indiana Militia Corps 4th Brigade, Southeast Indiana
Indiana Militia Corps 3rd Brigade, Southwest Indiana

Iowa

Constitution Party, Randall

Kansas

Constitution Party, Wichita

Kentucky

Take Back Kentucky, Clarkson
Free Kentucky, Lebanon
Constitution Party, Louisville
Kentucky State Militia, Nicholasville
Kentucky Mountain Rangers, Smilax
Kentucky State Militia 9th Battalion, Western Kentucky

Louisiana

Common Law Defense Fund, Lafayette

Maine

Maine Militia, Belfast
Constitution Party, Spruce Head

Maryland

Southern Sons of Liberty, Citizens Militia of Maryland, Baltimore
Constitution Party, Taneytown
Save A Patriot Fellowship, Westminster

Michigan

Proclaim Liberty Ministry, Adrian
Michigan Militia Corps Wolverines, 3rd Division, Benzonia
Southern Michigan Regional Militia, Burton
St. Clair County Militia, Capac
Southern Michigan Regional Militia, Capac
Justice Pro Se, Dearborn
Michigan Militia, Detroit
Southern Michigan Regional Militia, Fowlerville
Michigan Militia Corps Wolverines, Kalamazoo
Southern Michigan Regional Militia, Monroe County
Michigan Militia, Inc., Redford
Southern Michigan Regional Militia, St. Clair
Lawful Path, Tustin

Minnesota

Minnesota Militia, St. Cloud
Constitution Party, St. Paul

Missouri

Missouri 51st Militia, Grain Valley
7th Missouri Militia, Granby

2nd Missouri Militia, Tuscumbia

Montana
Project 7, Kalispell
Militia of Montana, Noxon

Nevada
Center For Action, Sandy Valley

New Jersey
Constitution Party, Palmyra
New Jersey Committee of Safety, Shamong
New Jersey Militia, Trenton

New Mexico
New Mexico Liberty Corps, Albuquerque

New York
New York Patriot Militia, Slate Hill

North Carolina
United America Party, Zebulon

North Dakota
Constitution Party, Casselton

Ohio
Right Way L.A.W., Akron
Ohio Unorganized Militia Assistance and Advisory Committee, Ashtabula County
Ohio Unorganized Militia Assistance and Advisory Committee, Champaign County
True Blue Freedom, Cincinnati
Ohio Unorganized Militia, Columbiana County
Central Ohio Unorganized Militia, Columbus County
Ohio Unorganized Militia Assistance Advisory Committee, Darke County,
Ohio Unorganized Militia Assistance and Advisory Committee, Delaware County
Central Ohio Unorganized Militia, Franklin County
E Pluribus Unum, Grove City
Ohio Unorganized Militia Assistance and Advisory Committee, Lebanon
Central Ohio Unorganized Militia, Madison County
Ohio Unorganized Militia Assistance and Advisory Committee, Montgomery
Ohio Unorganized Militia Assistance and Advisory Committee, Portage County
Ohio Unorganized Militia Assistance and Advisory Committee, Westerville

Oklahoma
Present Truth Ministry, Panama

Oregon
Emissary Publications, Clackamas
Southern Oregon Militia, Eagle Point
Freedom Bound International, Klamath Falls
Constitution Party, Portland
Embassy of Heaven, Stayton

Pennsylvania
American Nationalist Union, Allison Park
Pennsylvania 1st Unorganized Militia, Harrisburg
Constitution Party National Office, Lancaster

South Carolina
AWARE Group, Greenville
Constitution Party, Greenville

Tennessee
Militia of East Tennessee, Knox County
Constitution Party, Germantown

Texas
Texas Unified Field Forces, Alto
People's Court of Common Law, Arlington
13th Texas Infantry Regiment, Austin
Constitution Society, Austin
John Birch Society, Austin
Living Truth Ministries, Austin
Constitution Party, Brenham
13th Texas Infantry Regiment, Bryan
Buffalo Creek Press, Cleburne
13th Texas Infantry Regiment, Conroe
Citizens for Legal Reform, Dallas
Republic of Texas, Dallas
Texas Unified Field Forces, Duncanville
Republic of Texas, Fort Worth
Texas Unified Field Forces, Grimes County
Texas Unified Field Forces, Harleton
Texas Unified Field Forces, Harris County
Texas Unified Field Forces, Hill County
Republic of Texas, Houston
Texas Unified Field Forces, Hunt County
Texas Unified Field Forces, Huntington
Texas Unified Field Forces, Jackson County
Texas Unified Field Forces, Neches
Texas Unified Field Forces, Potter County

Texas Unified Field Forces, Red Rock
13th Texas Infantry Regiment, San Antonio
American Opinion Bookstore, San Antonio
Texas Unified Field Forces, Tom Green County
Republic of Texas, Victoria
Church of God Evangelistic Association, Waxahachie
Republic of Texas. White Oak

Vermont

Constitution Party, Quechee

Virginia

Virginia Citizens Militia, Roanoke
Constitution Party, Vienna

Washington

Yakima County Militia, Yakima County
Jural Society, Ellensburg
Constitution Party, Tacoma

Wisconsin

John Birch Society, Appleton
Constitution Party, Watertown

appendix c

Symbols of hate

White supremacists and other extremists have long been fond of signs, symbols, logos, and emblems, the meanings of which are not always obvious to the uninformed observer. Reproduced here with permission are some of the most popular symbols in current use on the Internet or in extremist publications, as displayed on the Southern Poverty Law Center's Web site (http://www.splcenter.org):

Ku Klux Klan Blood Drop

The blood drop is one of the Ku Klux Klan's best-known symbols. For Klan members, the drop represents the blood that Jesus Christ shed on the cross as a sacrifice for the White race.

The Night Rider

This depiction of the traditional robed Klansman on horseback signifies the Ku Klux Klan. Night riders originated in Ohio in the 1920s as a group of black-robed Klan terrorists who specialized in violent attacks on blacks and others.

ZOG

Zionist Occupied Government, a phrase used by anti-Semitic and white supremacist groups to denote the federal government. These groups believe the government is secretly controlled by Jews.

Nazi Swastika

Adopted in 1935 as the official emblem of Germany's Nazi Party, the swastika is now widely used by neo-Nazi, skinhead, and other white supremacist groups. Dozens of variations on the swastika are common.

War Skins

This logo, incorporating a skull and crossbones, is used by the skinhead followers of the neo-Nazi group White Aryan Resistance (W.A.R.).

Celtic Cross

Originally a symbol for the Celts of ancient Ireland and Scotland, the Celtic cross was adopted by many American white supremacist groups. In modern times, it was first used by the far-right National Front in England.

Thunderbolt

This is a Nazi symbol signifying the Schutzstaffel (SS), the elite military arm of Adolf Hitler's Third Reich. The SS supervised Nazi Germany's network of death camps.

National Alliance Life Rune

This is the official symbol of the neo-Nazi National Alliance, based in Hillsboro, West Virginia. Originally, it was a character from a Runic alphabet that signified life, creation, birth, rebirth, and renewal. Several Runic alphabets were used by the Germanic peoples between the 3rd and 13th centuries.

White Pride World Wide

Some groups incorporated this white supremacist slogan into the Celtic cross.

W.A.R. Swastika

The symbol used by the neo-Nazi group White Aryan Resistance (W.A.R.) incorporates the California-based group's acronym into a Nazi swastika.

Aryan Nations

This symbol is used by the neo-Nazi Aryan Nations, based in Hayden Lake, Idaho.

Crossed Hammers

Crossed hammers signify the many skinhead groups that use the word "hammer" as part of their names. Such groups exist in Australia, Europe, and the United States, and many incorporate the crossed hammers into their own symbols.

Three-Bladed Swastika

This is a variation of the traditional swastika of Nazi Germany that is popular among some skinhead and other white supremacist groups. It also has been used by some South African extremist groups.

Skinhead Skull and Crossbones

Many skinhead groups use variations of this symbol, which incorporates the Celtic cross into a skull and crossbones.

Two forms of text labeling are also common and are listed below:

14 Words

This is shorthand for a slogan coined by David Lane, an imprisoned member of The Order, or Silent Brotherhood: "We must secure the existence of our people and a future for White children." The Order was a revolutionary neo-Nazi group responsible for the theft of millions of dollars in armored car heists and the murder of a Jewish radio talk show host in the 1980s.

88

This number, widely used by neo-Nazis and others, is shorthand for "Heil Hitler." H is the eighth letter of the alphabet, and so the abbreviation H.H. is translated as 88.

appendix d

Foreign-based terrorist organizations

The organization details listed here are from the U.S. Department of State publication "Patterns of Global Terrorism 2001," Annual Report, published May 21, 2002, in Washington, D.C. These are not the only foreign-based terrorist organizations in existence; they are just the predominant and most active ones.

Abu Nidal Organization (ANO)

Other names

Fatah Revolutionary Council
Arab Revolutionary Brigades
Black September
Revolutionary Organization of Socialist Muslims

Description

International terrorist organization led by Sabri al-Banna. Split from the PLO in 1974. The group is made up of various functional committees, including political, military, and financial.

Activities

The group has carried out terrorist attacks in 20 countries, killing or injuring almost 900 persons. Targets include the United States, United Kingdom, France, Israel, moderate Palestinians, the PLO, and various Arab countries. Major attacks included the Rome and Vienna airports in December 1985, the Neve Shalom synagogue in Istanbul, the Pan Am flight 73 hijacking in Karachi in September 1986, and the City of Poros day-excursion ship attack in Greece in July 1988. The group is suspected of assassinating PLO deputy chief Abu Iyad and PLO security Chief Abu Hul in Tunis in January 1991. ANO assassinated a Jordanian diplomat in Lebanon in January 1994 and was linked to the killing of the PLO representative there. The ANO has not attacked Western targets since the late 1980s.

Strength

A few hundred, plus a limited overseas support structure.

Location/area of operation

Al-Banna relocated to Iraq in December 1998, where the group maintains a presence. It has an operational presence in Lebanon in the Bekaa Valley and has several Palestinian refugee camps in coastal areas of Lebanon. It also has a limited presence in Sudan and Syria, among others, although financial problems and internal disorganization reduced the group's activities and capabilities. Authorities shut down the ANO's operations in Libya and Egypt in 1999. ANO has demonstrated the ability to operate over a wide area, including the Middle East, Asia, and Europe.

External aid

Has received considerable support, including safe havens, training, logistical assistance, and financial aid from Iraq, Libya, and Syria (until 1987), in addition to close support for selected operations.

Abu Sayyaf Group (ASG)

Description

The ASG is the most violent of the Islamic separatist groups operating in the southern Philippines. Some ASG leaders studied or worked in the Middle East and allegedly fought in Afghanistan during the Soviet war. The group split from the Moro National Liberation Front in the early 1990s under the leadership of Abdurajak Abubakar Janjalani, who was killed in a clash with Philippine police on December 18, 1998. His younger brother, Khadaffy Janjalani, replaced him as the nominal leader of the group, which is composed of several semiautonomous factions.

Activities

The ASG engages in kidnappings for ransom, bombings, assassinations, and extortion. Although from time to time it claims that its motivation is to promote an independent Islamic state in western Mindanao and the Sulu Archipelago, areas in the southern Philippines heavily populated by Muslims, the ASG now appears to use terror mainly for financial profit. The group's first large-scale action was a raid on the town of Ipil in Mindanao in April 1995. In April of 2000, an ASG faction kidnapped 21 persons, including 10 foreign tourists, from a resort in Malaysia. Separately in 2000, the group abducted several foreign journalists, three Malaysians, and a U.S. citizen. On May 27, 2001 the ASG kidnapped 3 U.S. citizens and 17 Filipinos from a tourist resort in Palawan, Philippines. Several of the hostages, including one U.S. citizen, were murdered.

Strength

The ASG is believed to have a few hundred core fighters, and at least 1000 individuals motivated by the prospect of receiving ransom payments for foreign hostages allegedly joined the group in 2000–2001.

Location/area of operation

The ASG was founded in Basilan Province and mainly operates there and in the neighboring provinces of Sulu and Tawi-Tawi in the Sulu Archipelago. It also operates in the Zamboanga Peninsula, and members occasionally travel to Manila and other parts of the country. The group expanded its operations to Malaysia in 2000 when it abducted foreigners from a tourist resort.

External aid

The ASG is largely self-financed through ransom and extortion. The group may receive support from Islamic extremists in the Middle East and South Asia. Libya publicly paid millions of dollars for the release of the foreign hostages seized from Malaysia in 2000.

al-Aqsa Martyrs Brigade

Description

The al-Aqsa Martyrs Brigade comprises an unknown number of small cells of Fatah-affiliated activists who emerged at the outset of the current Intifadah to attack Israeli targets. It aims to drive the Israeli military and settlers from the West Bank, Gaza Strip, and Jerusalem and to establish a Palestinian state.

Activities

The al-Aqsa Martyrs Brigade has carried out shootings and suicide operations against Israeli military personnel and civilians and killed Palestinians
whom the group believed were collaborating with Israel. At least five U.S.
citizens, four of them dual Israeli–U.S. citizens, were killed in these attacks.
The group probably did not attack them because of their U.S. citizenship. In
January 2002, the group claimed responsibility for the first suicide bombing
carried out by a female.

Strength

Unknown.

Location/area of operation

The al-Aqsa Martyrs Brigade operates mainly in the West Bank and claimed
attacks inside Israel and the Gaza Strip.

External aid

Unknown.

Armed Islamic Group (GIA)

Description

An Islamic extremist group, the GIA aims to overthrow the secular Algerian
regime and replace it with an Islamic state. The GIA began its violent activities in early 1992 after Algiers voided the victory of the Islamic Salvation
Front (FIS) — the largest Islamic party — in the first round of legislative
elections in December 1991.

Activities

The GIA is responsible for frequent attacks against civilians, journalists, and
foreign residents. In the last several years the GIA conducted a terrorist
campaign of civilian massacres, sometimes wiping out entire villages in its
Area of Operations and frequently killing hundreds of civilians. Since
announcing its terrorist campaign against foreigners living in Algeria in
September 1993, the GIA killed more than 100 expatriate men and women
— mostly Europeans — in the country. The GIA uses assassinations and
bombings, including car bombs, and is known to kidnap victims and slit
their throats. The GIA hijacked an Air France flight to Algiers in December

1994. In late 1999, several GIA members were convicted by a French court for conducting a series of bombings in France in 1995.

Strength

Precise numbers are unknown — probably around 200.

Location/area of operation

Algeria and France.

External aid

Algerian expatriates and GSPC members abroad, many of whom reside in Western Europe, provide financial and logistical support. In addition, the Algerian Government has accused Iran and Sudan of supporting Algerian extremists.

'Asbat al-ansar

Description

'Asbat al-Ansar — the Partisans' League — is a Lebanon-based, Sunni extremist group composed primarily of Palestinians, which is associated with Osama Bin Ladin. The group follows an extremist interpretation of Islam that justifies violence against civilian targets to achieve political ends. Some of those goals include overthrowing the Lebanese Government and thwarting perceived anti-Islamic influences in the country.

Activities

'Asbat al-Ansar has carried out several terrorist attacks in Lebanon since it first emerged in the early 1990s. The group carried out assassinations of Lebanese religious leaders and bombed several nightclubs, theaters, and liquor stores in the mid-1990s. The group raised its operational profile in the year 2000 with two dramatic attacks against Lebanese and international targets. The group was involved in clashes in northern Lebanon in late December 1999, and carried out a rocket-propelled grenade attack on the Russian Embassy in Beirut in January 2000.

Strength

The group commands about 300 hundred fighters in Lebanon.

Location/area of operation

The group's primary base of operations is the 'Ayn al-Hilwah Palestinian refugee camp near Sidon in southern Lebanon.

External aid

The group probably receives money through international Sunni extremist networks and Bin Ladin's al-Qaida network.

Aum Supreme Truth (Aum)

Other names

Aum Shinrikyo

Description

A cult established in 1987 by Shoko Asahara, the Aum aimed to take over Japan and then the world. Approved as a religious entity in 1989 under Japanese law, the cult ran candidates in a Japanese parliamentary election in 1990. Over time, the cult began to emphasize the imminence of the end of the world and stated that the U.S. would initiate Armageddon by starting World War III with Japan. The Japanese government revoked its recognition of the Aum as a religious organization in October 1995, but in 1997 a government panel decided not to invoke the Anti-Subversive Law against the cult, which would have outlawed them. A 1999 law gave the Japanese government authorization to continue police surveillance of the cult due to concerns that Aum might launch future terrorist attacks. Under the leadership of Fumihiro Joyu, the Aum changed its name to Aleph in January, 2000 and claimed to have rejected the violent and apocalyptic teachings of its founder. (Joyu took formal control of the organization early in 2002 and remains its leader.)

Activities

On March 20, 1995, Aum members simultaneously released the chemical nerve agent sarin on several Tokyo subway trains, killing 12 persons and injuring up to 6000. The group was responsible for other mysterious chemical accidents in Japan in 1994. Its efforts to conduct attacks using biological agents have been unsuccessful. Japanese police arrested Asahara in May, 1995, and he remained on trial facing charges in 13 crimes, including seven counts of murder, at the end of 2001. Legal analysts say it will take several more years to conclude the trial. Since 1997, the cult has continued to recruit new members, engage in commercial enterprise, and acquire property, although it scaled back these activities significantly in 2001 in response to public outcry. The cult maintains an Internet home page. In July 2001, Russian authorities arrested a group of Russian Aum followers who planned to set off bombs near the Imperial Palace in Tokyo as part of an operation to free Asahara from jail and then smuggle him to Russia.

Strength

The Aum's current membership is estimated at 1500 to 2000 persons. At the time of the Tokyo subway attack, the group claimed to have 9000 members in Japan and up to 40,000 worldwide.

Location/area of operation

The Aum's principal membership is located only in Japan, but a residual branch comprising an unknown number of followers surfaced in Russia.

External aid

None.

al-Gama'a al-Islamiyya

Other names

Islamic Group (IG)

Description

Egypt's largest militant group; has been active since the late 1970s. The group appears to be loosely organized, with an external wing with supporters in several countries worldwide. The group issued a cease-fire in March 1999 but its spiritual leader, Shaykh Umar Abd al-Rahman, sentenced to life in prison in January 1996 for his involvement in the 1993 World Trade Center bombing and incarcerated in the U.S., rescinded his support for the cease-fire in June, 2000. The Gama'a has not conducted an attack inside Egypt since August, 1998. A senior member signed Osama Bin Ladin's fatwa in February, 1998 calling for attacks against the U.S. The group unofficially split into two factions: one that supports the cease-fire led by Mustafa Hamza, and one led by Rifa'i Taha Musa, calling for a return to armed operations. Taha Musa in early 2001 published a book in which he attempted to justify terrorist attacks that would cause mass casualties. Musa disappeared several months thereafter, and there are conflicting reports as to his current whereabouts. The group's primary goal is to overthrow the Egyptian Government and replace it with an Islamic state, but disaffected IG members, such as those potentially inspired by Taha Musa or Abd al-Rahman, may be interested in carrying out attacks against U.S. and Israeli interests.

Activities

The group conducted armed attacks against Egyptian security and other government officials, Coptic Christians, and Egyptian opponents of Islamic extremism before the cease-fire. From 1993 until the cease-fire, al-Gama'a launched attacks on tourists in Egypt, most notably the attack in November 1997 at Luxor that killed 58 foreign tourists. Also, the group claimed responsibility for the attempt in June 1995 to assassinate Egyptian President Hosni Mubarak in Addis Ababa, Ethiopia. The Gama'a never specifically attacked a U.S. citizen or facility but has threatened U.S. interests.

Strength

Unknown — but at its peak, the IG probably commanded several thousand hard-core members and a like number of sympathizers. The 1999 cease-fire and security crackdowns following the attack in Luxor, Egypt in 1997, and more recently security efforts following September 11, probably resulted in a substantial decrease in the group's numbers.

Location/area of operation

The IG operates mainly in the Al-Minya, Asyu't, Qina, and Sohaj Governorates of southern Egypt. The group also appears to have support in Cairo, Alexandria, and other urban locations, particularly among unemployed graduates and students. It has a worldwide presence, including in the United Kingdom, Afghanistan, Yemen, and Austria.

External aid

Unknown — but the Egyptian government believes that Iran, Bin Ladin, and Afghan militant groups support the organization. The group may also obtain some funding through various Islamic nongovernmental organizations.

Euzkadi Ta Askatasuna (ETA)

Other names

Basque Fatherland and Liberty

Description

ETA was founded in 1959 with the aim of establishing an independent homeland based on Marxist principles in the northern Spanish Provinces of Vizcaya, Guipuzcoa, Alava, and Navarra, and the southwestern French Provinces of Labourd, Basse-Navarra, and Soule.

Activities

The group is primarily involved in bombings and assassinations of Spanish government officials, security and military forces, politicians, and judicial figures. ETA finances its activities through kidnappings, robberies, and extortion. The group killed more than 800 persons and injured hundreds of others since it began lethal attacks in the early 1960s. In November 1999, ETA broke its "unilateral and indefinite" cease-fire and began an assassination and bombing campaign that killed 38 individuals and wounded scores more by the end of 2001.

Strength

Unknown — the ETA may have hundreds of members, plus supporters.

Location/area of operation

The group operates primarily in the Basque autonomous regions of northern Spain and southwestern France, but also bombed Spanish and French interests elsewhere.

External Aid

The ETA has received training at various times in the past in Libya, Lebanon, and Nicaragua. Some ETA members allegedly received sanctuary in Cuba, while others reside in South America.

Hamas (Islamic Resistance Movement)

Description

Formed in late 1987 as an outgrowth of the Palestinian branch of the Muslim Brotherhood. Various Hamas elements used political and violent means, including terrorism, to pursue the goal of establishing an Islamic Palestinian state in place of Israel. Hamas is loosely structured, with some elements working clandestinely and others working openly through mosques and social service institutions to recruit members, raise money, organize activities, and distribute propaganda. Hamas strength is concentrated in the Gaza Strip and a few areas of the West Bank. Hamas has also engaged in peaceful political activity, such as running candidates in West Bank Chamber of Commerce elections.

Activities

Hamas activists, especially those in the Izz el-Din al-Qassam Brigades, have conducted many attacks — including large-scale suicide bombings — against Israeli civilian and military targets. In the early 1990s they also targeted Fatah rivals and began a practice of targeting suspected Palestinian collaborators, which continues. There was increased operational activity in 2001 during the Intifadah. Numerous attacks against Israeli government interests were claimed. The group has not targeted U.S. interests and continues to confine its attacks to Israelis inside Israel and the territories.

Strength

There are an unknown number of hardcore members and tens of thousands of supporters and sympathizers.

Location/area of operation

The group operates primarily on the West Bank, Gaza Strip, and Israel. In August 1999, Jordanian authorities closed the group's political bureau offices in Amman, arrested its leaders, and prohibited the group from operating on Jordanian territory. Hamas leaders are also present in other parts of the Middle East, including Syria, Lebanon, and Iran.

External aid

The group receives funding from Palestinian expatriates, Iran, and private benefactors in Saudi Arabia and other moderate Arab states. Some fundraising and propaganda activities take place in Western Europe and North America.

Harakat ul-Mujahidin (HUM)

Description

The HUM is an Islamic militant group based in Pakistan that operates primarily in Kashmir. It is politically aligned with the radical political party, Jamiat-i Ulema-i Islam Fazlur Rehman faction (JUI-F). Long-time leader of the group, Fazlur Rehman Khalil, stepped down as HUM emir in mid-February, 2000, turning the reins over to the popular Kashmiri commander and his second-in-command, Farooq Kashmiri. Khalil, who was linked to Bin Ladin and signed his fatwa in February 1998 calling for attacks on U.S. and Western interests, assumed the position of HUM Secretary General. HUM operated terrorist training camps in eastern Afghanistan until Coalition airstrikes destroyed them during fall 2001.

Activities

The group conducted a number of operations against Indian troops and civilian targets in Kashmir. It is linked to the Kashmiri militant group al-Faran that kidnapped five Western tourists in Kashmir in July, 1995: one was killed in August, 1995 and the other four reportedly were killed in December of the same year. The HUM is responsible for the hijacking of an Indian airliner on December 24, 1999, which resulted in the release of Masood Azhar — an important leader in the former Harakat ul-Ansar imprisoned by the Indians in 1994 — and Ahmad Omar Sheikh, who was arrested for the abduction/murder in January–February, 2001 of U.S. journalist Daniel Pearl.

Strength

The HUM has several thousand armed supporters located in Azad Kashmir, Pakistan, and India's southern Kashmir and Doda regions. Supporters are mostly Pakistanis and Kashmiris and also include Afghans and Arab veterans of the Afghan war. Supporters use light and heavy machine guns, assault rifles, mortars, explosives, and rockets. HUM lost a significant share of its membership in defections to the Jaish-e-Mohammed (JEM) in 2000.

Location/area of operation

Although based in Muzaffarabad, Rawalpindi and several other towns in Pakistan, members conduct insurgent and terrorist activities primarily in Kashmir. The HUM trained its militants in Afghanistan and Pakistan.

External aid

The group collects donations from Saudi Arabia and other Gulf and Islamic states, as well as from Pakistanis and Kashmiris. The HUM's financial collection methods also include soliciting donations from magazine ads and pamphlets. The sources and amount of HUM's military funding are unknown. In anticipation of asset seizures by the Pakistani Government, the HUM withdrew funds from bank accounts and invested in legal businesses, such as commodity trading, real estate, and production of consumer goods. Its fundraising in Pakistan was constrained since the government clamped down on extremist groups and froze terrorist assets.

Hizballah (Party of God)

Other names

> Islamic Jihad
> Revolutionary Justice Organization
> Organization of the Oppressed on Earth
> Islamic Jihad for the Liberation of Palestine

Description

Formed in 1982 in response to the Israeli invasion of Lebanon, this Lebanon-based radical Shi'a group takes its ideological inspiration from the Iranian revolution and the teachings of the Ayatollah Khomeini. The Majlis al-Shura, or Consultative Council, is the group's highest governing body and is led by Secretary General Hassan Nasrallah. Hizballah formally advocates ultimate establishment of Islamic rule in Lebanon and liberation of all occupied Arab lands, including Jerusalem. It expressed as a goal the elimination of Israel. The group expressed its unwillingness to work within the confines of Lebanon's established political system; however, this stance changed with the party's decision in 1992 to participate in parliamentary elections. Although closely allied with and often directed by Iran, the group may have conducted operations that were not approved by Tehran. While Hizballah does not share the Syrian regime's secular orientation, the group has been a strong tactical ally in helping Syria to advance its political objectives in the region.

Activities

The group is known or suspected to have been involved in numerous anti-U.S. terrorist attacks, including the suicide truck bombings of the U.S.

Embassy in Beirut April, 1983, the U.S. Marine barracks in Beirut in October, 1983, and the U.S. Embassy annex in Beirut in September, 1984. Three members of Hizballah, 'Imad Mughniyah, Hasan Izz-al-Din, and Ali Atwa, are on the FBI's list of 22 Most Wanted Terrorists for the 1985 hijacking of TWA Flight 847, during which a U.S. Navy diver was murdered. Elements of the group were responsible for the kidnapping and detention of U.S. and other Western hostages in Lebanon. The group also attacked the Israeli Embassy in Argentina in 1992 and is suspect in the 1994 bombing of the Israeli cultural center in Buenos Aires. In fall, 2000 it captured three Israeli soldiers in the Shabaa Farms and kidnapped an Israeli noncombatant whom it may have lured to Lebanon under false pretenses.

Strength

There are several thousand supporters and a few hundred terrorist operatives.

Location/area of operation

The group operates in the Bekaa Valley, the southern suburbs of Beirut, and southern Lebanon. It has established cells in Europe, Africa, South America, North America, and Asia.

External aid

The group receives substantial amounts of financial, training, weapons, explosives, political, diplomatic, and organizational aid from Iran and received diplomatic, political, and logistical support from Syria.

Islamic Movement of Uzbekistan (IMU)

Description

This is a coalition of Islamic militants from Uzbekistan and other Central Asian states opposed to Uzbekistani President Islom Karimov's secular regime. Before the counterterrorism coalition began operations in Afghanistan in October, 2001, the IMU's primary goal was the establishment of an Islamic state in Uzbekistan. If IMU political and ideological leader Tohir Yoldashev survives the counterterrorism campaign and can regroup the organization, however, he might widen the IMU's targets to include all those he perceives as fighting Islam. The group's propaganda has always included anti-Western and anti-Israeli rhetoric.

Activities

The IMU primarily targeted Uzbekistani interests before October, 2001 and is believed to have been responsible for five car bombs in Tashkent in February, 1999. Militants also took foreigners hostage in 1999 and 2000, including four U.S. citizens who were mountain climbing in August, 2000, and four Japanese geologists and eight Kyrgyzstani soldiers in August, 1999. Since October the Coalition captured, killed, and dispersed many of the militants who remained in Afghanistan to fight with the Taliban and al-Qaeda, severely degrading the IMU's ability to attack Uzbekistani or Coalition interests in the near term. IMU military leader Juma Namangani apparently was killed during an air strike in November. At year's end, Yoldashev remained at large.

Strength

Militants probably number under 2000.

Location/area of operation

Militants are scattered throughout South Asia and Tajikistan. The area of operations includes Afghanistan, Iran, Kyrgyzstan, Pakistan, Tajikistan, and Uzbekistan.

External aid

The Coalition has support from other Islamic extremist groups and patrons in the Middle East and Central and South Asia. IMU leadership broadcasts statements over Iranian radio.

Jaish-e-Mohammed (JEM)

Other names

Army of Mohammed

Description

The Jaish-e-Mohammed (JEM) is an Islamic extremist group based in Pakistan that was formed by Masood Azhar upon his release from prison in India in early 2000. The group's aim is to unite Kashmir with Pakistan. It is politically aligned with the radical political party, Jamiat-i Ulema-i Islam

Fazlur Rehman faction (JUI-F). The U.S. announced the addition of JEM to the U.S. Treasury Department's Office of Foreign Asset Control's (OFAC) list (which includes organizations that are believed to support terrorist groups and have assets in U.S. jurisdiction that can be frozen or controlled) in October and the Foreign Terrorist Organization list in December. The group was banned and its assets were frozen by the Pakistani Government in January, 2002.

Activities

The JEM's leader, Masood Azhar, was released from Indian imprisonment in December, 1999 in exchange for 155 hijacked Indian Airlines hostages. The 1994 HUA kidnappings by Omar Sheikh of U.S. and British nationals in New Delhi and the July 1995 HUA/Al Faran kidnappings of Westerners in Kashmir were two of several previous HUA efforts to free Azhar. The JEM on October 1, 2001, claimed responsibility for a suicide attack on the Jammu and Kashmir legislative assembly building in Srinagar that killed at least 31 persons, but later denied the claim. The Indian government publicly implicated the JEM along with Lashkar-e-Tayyiba for the December 13, 2001, attack on the Indian Parliament that killed 9 and injured 18.

Strength

The JEM has several hundred armed supporters located in Azad Kashmir, Pakistan and in India's southern Kashmir and Doda regions, including a large cadre of former HUM members. Supporters are mostly Pakistanis and Kashmiris and also Afghans and Arab veterans of the Afghan war. The group uses light and heavy machine guns, assault rifles, mortars, improvised explosive devices, and rocket grenades.

Location/area of operation

The group is based in Peshawar and Muzaffarabad, but members conduct terrorist activities primarily in Kashmir. The JEM maintained training camps in Afghanistan until the fall of 2001.

External aid

Most of the JEM's cadre and material resources were drawn from the militant groups Harakat ul-Jihad al-Islami (HUJI) and the Harakat ul-Mujahedin (HUM). The JEM had close ties to Afghan Arabs and the Taliban. Osama Bin Ladin is suspected of providing funding to the JEM. The JEM also collects funds through donation requests in magazines and pamphlets. In anticipation of asset seizures by the Pakistani government, the JEM withdrew funds from bank accounts and invested in legal businesses such as commodity trading, real estate, and production of consumer goods.

al-Jihad

Other names

> Egyptian Islamic Jihad
> Islamic Jihad
> Jihad Group

Description

This is an Egyptian Islamic extremist group active since the late 1970s. al-Jihad merged with Bin Ladin's al-Qaeda organization in June, 2001 but may retain some capability to conduct independent operations. The group continues to suffer setbacks worldwide, especially after the September 11, 2001 attacks. The primary goals are to overthrow the Egyptian government and replace it with an Islamic state and attack U.S. and Israeli interests in Egypt and abroad.

Activities

The al-Jihad specializes in armed attacks against high-level Egyptian government personnel, including cabinet ministers, and car bombings against official U.S. and Egyptian facilities. The original Jihad was responsible for the assassination in 1981 of Egyptian President Anwar Sadat. They claimed responsibility for the attempted assassinations of interior minister Hassan al-Alfi in August, 1993 and prime minister Atef Sedky in November, 1993. The al-Jihad has not conducted an attack inside Egypt since 1993 and has never targeted foreign tourists there. In 1995 the group was responsible for the Egyptian Embassy bombing in Islamabad; in 1998, a planned attack against the U.S. Embassy in Albania was thwarted.

Strength

Not known but probably has several hundred hard-core members.

Location/area of operation

The al-Jihad operates in the Cairo area but most of its network is outside Egypt, including Yemen, Afghanistan, Pakistan, Lebanon, and the United Kingdom, and its activities for several years have been centered outside Egypt.

External aid

Unknown, but the Egyptian government claims that Iran supports the al-Jihad. Its merger with al-Qaeda boosts Bin Ladin's support for the group. The group may obtain some funding through various Islamic nongovernmental organizations, cover businesses, and criminal acts.

Jemaah Islamiya Organization (JI)

Description

Jemaah Islamiya is an Islamic extremist group with cells operating throughout Southeast Asia. Recently arrested JI members in Singapore, Malaysia, and the Philippines revealed links with al-Qaeda. The JI's stated goal is to create an Islamic state comprising Malaysia, Singapore, Indonesia, and the southern Philippines. Three Indonesian extremists, one of whom is in custody in Malaysia, are the reported leaders of the organization.

Activities

The JI began developing plans in 1997 to target U.S. interests in Singapore, and in 1999 conducted videotaped casings of potential U.S. targets in preparation for multiple attacks in Singapore. A cell in Singapore acquired 4 tons of ammonium nitrate, which has not yet been found.

In December 2001, Singapore authorities arrested 15 Jemaah Islamiyah members, some of whom had trained in al-Qaeda camps in Afghanistan, who planned to attack the U.S. and Israeli Embassies and British and Australian diplomatic buildings in Singapore. Additionally, the Singapore police discovered forged immigration stamps, bomb-making materials, and al-Qaeda-related material in several suspects' homes.

Strength

Exact numbers are unknown, but press reports approximate that the Malaysian cells may comprise 200 members.

Location/area of operation

The JI has cells in Singapore and Malaysia. Press reports indicate the JI is also present in Indonesia and possibly the Philippines.

External aid

Largely unknown, probably self-financed; possible al-Qaeda support.

Kach and Kahane Chai

Description

Their stated goal is to restore the biblical state of Israel. Kach (founded by radical Israeli-American rabbi Meir Kahane) and its offshoot Kahane Chai, which means "Kahane Lives," (founded by Meir Kahane's son Binyamin following his father's assassination in the U.S.) were declared to be terrorist organizations in March, 1994 by the Israeli Cabinet under the 1948 Terrorism Law. This followed the groups' statements in support of Dr. Baruch Goldstein's attack in February, 1994 on the al-Ibrahimi Mosque — Goldstein was affiliated with Kach — and their verbal attacks on the Israeli government. Palestinian gunmen killed Binyamin Kahane and his wife in a drive-by shooting in December, 2000 in the West Bank.

Activities

The groups organize protests against the Israeli Government and harass and threaten Palestinians in Hebron and the West Bank. They have threatened to attack Arabs, Palestinians, and Israeli government officials. The groups vowed revenge for the death of Binyamin Kahane and his wife.

Strength

Unknown.

Location/area of operation

These groups have Israel and West Bank settlements, particularly at Qiryat Arba' in Hebron.

External aid

They receive support from sympathizers in the U.S. and Europe.

Kurdistan Workers Party (PKK)

Description

This party was founded in 1974 as a Marxist–Leninist insurgent group primarily composed of Turkish Kurds. The group's goal is to establish an independent Kurdish state in southeastern Turkey, where the population is predominantly Kurdish. In the early 1990s the PKK moved beyond rural-based insurgent activities to include urban terrorism. Turkish authorities captured Chairman Abdullah Ocalan in Kenya in early 1999; the Turkish State Security Court subsequently sentenced him to death. In August, 1999, Ocalan announced a "peace initiative," ordering members to refrain from violence and withdraw from Turkey and requesting dialogue with Ankara on Kurdish issues. At a PKK Congress in January 2000, members supported Ocalan's initiative and claimed the group now would use only political means to achieve its new goal, improved rights for Kurds in Turkey.

Activities

The group's primary targets have been Turkish government security forces in Turkey. The group conducted attacks on Turkish diplomatic and commercial facilities in dozens of West European cities in 1993 and again in spring, 1995. In an attempt to damage Turkey's tourist industry, the PKK bombed tourist sites and hotels and kidnapped foreign tourists in the early to mid-1990s.

Strength

PKK has approximately 4000 to 5000 members, most of whom currently are located in northern Iraq. The group also has thousands of sympathizers in Turkey and Europe.

Location/area of operation

PKK operates in Turkey, Europe, and the Middle East.

External aid

The PKK received safe haven and modest aid from Syria, Iraq, and Iran. Damascus generally upheld its September, 2000 antiterror agreement with Ankara, pledging not to support the PKK.

Lashkar-e-Tayyiba (LT)

Other names

Army of the Righteous

Description

The LT is the armed wing of the Pakistan-based religious organization, Markaz-ud-Dawa-wal-Irshad (MDI) — a Sunni anti-U.S. missionary organization formed in 1989. The LT is led by Abdul Wahid Kashmiri and is one of the three largest and best-trained groups fighting in Kashmir against India; it is not connected to a political party. In October 2001 the U.S. announced the addition of the LT to the U.S. Treasury Department's Office of Foreign Asset Control's (OFAC) list — which includes organizations that are believed to support terrorist groups and have assets in U.S. jurisdiction that can be frozen or controlled. The group was banned, and its assets were frozen by the Pakistani government in January 2002.

Activities

The LT has conducted a number of operations against Indian troops and civilian targets in Kashmir since 1993. The LT claimed responsibility for numerous attacks in 2001, including a January attack on Srinagar airport that killed five Indians along with six militants, an attack on a police station in Srinagar that killed at least eight officers and wounded several others, and an attack in April against Indian border security forces that left at least four dead. The Indian government publicly implicated the LT along with JEM for the December 13, 2001, attack on the Indian Parliament building.

Strength

The LT has several hundred members in Azad Kashmir, Pakistan, and in India's southern Kashmir and Doda regions. Almost all LT cadres are foreigners — mostly Pakistanis from seminaries across the country and Afghan veterans of the Afghan wars. Goup members use assault rifles, light and heavy machine guns, mortars, explosives, and rocket-propelled grenades.

Location/area of operation

The LT was based in Muridke (near Lahore) and Muzaffarabad. The LT trains its militants in mobile training camps across Pakistan-administered Kashmir and trained in Afghanistan until fall, 2001.

External aid

The group collects donations from the Pakistani community in the Persian Gulf and United Kingdom, Islamic NGOs, and Pakistani and Kashmiri businessmen. The LT also maintains a Web site (under the name of its parent organization Jamaat ud-Daawa), through which it solicits funds and provides information on the group's activities. The amount of LT funding is unknown. The LT maintains ties to religious and military groups around the world, ranging from the Philippines to the Middle East and Chechnya through the MDI fraternal network. In anticipation of asset seizures by the Pakistani Government, the LT withdrew funds from bank accounts and invested in legal businesses such as commodity trading, real estate, and production of consumer goods.

Lashkar i Jhangvi

Description

This group is a military wing of the Sipah-i-Sahaba-i-Pakistan, a Sunni-Deobandi terrorist outfit. Lashkar i Jhangvi means "army of Jhang," a region in Pakistan. Lashkar i Jhangvi (LJ) is an extremist organization that emerged in 1997.

Activities

While LJ initially directed most of its attacks against the Pakistani Shia Muslim community, it also claimed responsibility for the 1997 killing of four U.S. oil workers in Karachi. Lashkar i Jhangvi also attempted to assassinate then-Pakistani prime minister Nawaz Sharif in 1999. The group is also responsible for the January, 2002 kidnapping and killing of U.S. journalist Daniel Pearl and a March, 2002 bus bombing that killed 15 people, including 11 French technicians. Lashkar I Jhangvi have been tied to the Islamabad Protestant church bombing in Karachi March, 2002 in which two U.S. citizens were killed. In July, 2002 Pakistani police arrested four Lashkar i Jhangvi members for the church attack.

Strength

Membership numbers are unknown. LJ has ties to al-Qaeda and the Taliban and received sanctuary from the Taliban in Afghanistan for its activity in Pakistan.

Location/area of operation

Afghanistan and Pakistan.

External aid

Unknown.

Liberation Tigers of Tamil Eelam (LTTE)

Other known front organizations

World Tamil Association (WTA)
World Tamil Movement (WTM)
Federation of Associations of Canadian Tamils (FACT)
The Ellalan Force
The Sangillan Force

Description

Founded in 1976, the LTTE is the most powerful Tamil group in Sri Lanka and uses overt and illegal methods to raise funds, acquire weapons, and publicize its cause of establishing an independent Tamil state. The LTTE began its armed conflict with the Sri Lankan Government in 1983 and relies on a guerrilla strategy that includes the use of terrorist tactics.

Activities

The Tigers integrated a battlefield insurgent strategy with a terrorist program that targets not only key personnel in the countryside but also senior Sri Lankan political and military leaders in Colombo and other urban centers. The Tigers are notorious for their cadre of suicide bombers, the Black Tigers. Political assassinations and bombings are commonplace. The LTTE refrained from targeting foreign diplomatic and commercial establishments.

Strength

The group's exact strength is unknown, but the LTTE is estimated to have 8000 to 10,000 armed combatants in Sri Lanka, with a core of trained fighters of approximately 3000 to 6000. The LTTE also has a significant overseas support structure for fundraising, weapons procurement, and propaganda activities.

Location/area of operation

The Tigers control most of the northern and eastern coastal areas of Sri Lanka but have conducted operations throughout the island. Headquartered in northern Sri Lanka, LTTE leader Velupillai Prabhakaran established an extensive network of checkpoints and informants to keep track of any outsiders who enter the group's area of control.

External aid

The LTTE's overt organizations support Tamil separatism by lobbying foreign governments and the United Nations. The LTTE also uses its international contacts to procure weapons, communications, and any other equipment and supplies it needs. The LTTE exploits large Tamil communities in North America, Europe, and Asia to obtain funds and supplies for its fighters in Sri Lanka, often through false claims or extortion.

Mujahedin-e Khalq Organization (MEK or MKO)

Other names

> National Liberation Army of Iran (NLA, the militant wing of the MEK)
> People's Mujahedin of Iran (PMOI)
> National Council of Resistance (NCR)
> Muslim Iranian Student's Society (front organization used to garner financial support)

Description

The MEK philosophy mixes Marxism and Islam. Formed in the 1960s, the organization was expelled from Iran after the Islamic Revolution in 1979, and its primary support now comes from the Iraqi regime of Saddam Hussein. Its history is studded with anti-Western attacks as well as terrorist attacks on the interests of the clerical regime in Iran and abroad. The MEK now advocates a secular Iranian regime.

Activities

The MEK worldwide campaign against the Iranian government stresses propaganda and occasionally uses terrorist violence. During the 1970s, the MEK killed several U.S. military personnel and U.S. civilians working on defense projects in Tehran. It supported the takeover in 1979 of the U.S. Embassy in Tehran. In 1981, the MEK planted bombs in the head office of the Islamic Republic Party and the Premier's office, killing some 70 high-ranking Iranian officials, including chief justice Ayatollah Mohammad Beheshti, President Mohammad-Ali Rajaei, and Premier Mohammad-Javad Bahonar. In 1991, it assisted the government of Iraq in suppressing the Shia and Kurdish uprisings in northern and southern Iraq. Since then, the MEK continues to perform internal security services for the government of Iraq. In April 1992, it conducted attacks on Iranian embassies in 13 different countries, demonstrating the group's ability to mount large-scale operations overseas. In recent years, the MEK targeted key military officers and assassinated the deputy chief of the Armed Forces General Staff in April 1999. In April 2000, the MEK attempted to assassinate the commander of the Nasr Headquarters — the interagency board responsible for coordinating policies on Iraq. The normal pace of anti-Iranian operations increased during the "Operation Great Bahman" in February 2000, when the group launched a dozen attacks against Iran. In 2000 and 2001, the MEK was involved regularly in mortar attacks and hit-and-run raids on Iranian military and law enforcement units and government buildings near the Iran–Iraq border. Since the end of the Iran–Iraq War, tactics along the border garnered few military gains and have become commonplace. MEK insurgent activities in Tehran constitute the biggest security concern for the Iranian leadership. In February, 2000, for example, the MEK attacked the leadership complex in Tehran that houses the offices of the Supreme Leader and President.

Strength

The MEK has several thousand fighters, located on bases scattered throughout Iraq, and armed with tanks, infantry fighting vehicles, and artillery. The MEK also has an overseas support structure. Most of the fighters are organized in the MEK's National Liberation Army (NLA).

Location/area of operation

In the 1980s the MEK's leaders were forced by Iranian security forces to flee to France. Since resettling in Iraq in 1987, the group conducted internal security operations in support of the government of Iraq. In the mid 1980s, the group did not mount terrorist operations in Iran at a level similar to its activities in the 1970s, but by the 1990s, the MEK claimed credit for an increasing number of operations in Iran.

External aid

Beyond support from Iraq, the MEK uses front organizations to solicit contributions from expatriate Iranian communities.

National Liberation Army (ELN) — Colombia

Description

The ELN is a Marxist insurgent group formed in 1965 by urban intellectuals inspired by Fidel Castro and Che Guevara. The group began a dialogue with Colombian officials in 1999 following a campaign of mass kidnappings — each involving at least one U.S. citizen — to demonstrate its strength and continuing viability and force the Pastrana administration to negotiate. Peace talks between Bogotá and the ELN, started in 1999, continued sporadically through 2001 until Bogota broke them off in August. Talks resumed in Havana, Cuba, by year's end.

Activities

ELN activities include kidnapping, hijacking, bombing, extortion, and guerrilla war. The group has modest conventional military capability. It annually conducts hundreds of kidnappings for ransom, often targeting foreign employees of large corporations, especially in the petroleum industry. It frequently assaults the energy infrastructure, and has inflicted major damage on pipelines and the electric distribution network.

Strength

The ELN has approximately 3000 to 5000 armed combatants and an unknown number of active supporters.

Location/area of operation

ELN members can mostly be found in rural and mountainous areas of north, northeast, and southwest Colombia and Venezuela border regions.

External aid

Cuba provides some medical care and political consultation.

Palestine Islamic Jihad (PIJ)

Description

The PIJ originated among militant Palestinians in the Gaza Strip during the 1970s. The PIJ-Shiqaqi faction, currently led by Ramadan Shallah in Damascus, is most active. The group is committed to the creation of an Islamic Palestinian state and the destruction of Israel through holy war. It also opposes moderate Arab governments that it believes were tainted by Western secularism.

Activities

PIJ activists conducted many attacks, including large-scale suicide bombings against Israeli civilian and military targets. The group increased its operational activity in 2001 during the Intifadah, claiming numerous attacks against Israeli interests. The group has not targeted U.S. interests and continues to confine its attacks to Israelis inside Israel and the territories.

Strength

Unknown.

Location/area of operation

The group is located and operates primarily in Israel, the West Bank and Gaza Strip, and other parts of the Middle East including Lebanon and Syria, where the leadership is based.

External aid

The PIJ receives financial assistance from Iran and limited logistic assistance from Syria.

Palestine Liberation Front (PLF)

Description

The PLF broke away from the PFLP-GC in the mid-1970s. It later split again into pro-PLO, pro-Syrian, and pro-Libyan factions. The pro-PLO faction is led by Muhammad Abbas (Abu Abbas), who became a member of the PLO Executive Committee in 1984 but left it in 1991.

Activities

The Abu Abbas-led faction is known for aerial attacks against Israel. Abbas's group also was responsible for the attack in 1985 on the cruise ship Achille Lauro and the murder of U.S. citizen Leon Klinghoffer. A warrant for Abu Abbas's arrest is outstanding in Italy.

Strength

Unknown.

Location/area of operation

The PLO faction was based in Tunisia until the Achille Lauro attack. Now it is based in Iraq.

External aid

The group receives support mainly from Iraq. In the past, it received support from Libya.

Popular Front for the Liberation of Palestine (PFLP)

Description

The PFLP is a Marxist–Leninist group founded in 1967 by George Habash as a member of the PLO. He joined the Alliance of Palestinian Forces (APF) to oppose the Declaration of Principles signed in 1993 and suspended participation in the PLO. He then broke away from the APF, along with the DFLP, in 1996 over ideological differences. Then, he took part in meetings with Arafat's Fatah party and PLO representatives in 1999 to discuss national unity and the reinvigoration of the PLO but continues to oppose current negotiations with Israel.

Activities

The PFLP committed numerous international terrorist attacks during the 1970s. Since 1978, the group has conducted attacks against Israeli or moderate Arab targets, including killing a settler and her son in December 1996. The PFLP stepped up operational activity in 2001, highlighted by the shooting death of the Israeli Tourism Minister in October to retaliate for Israel's killing of the PFLP leader in August.

Strength

The group has approximately 800 members.

Location/area of operation

Syria, Lebanon, Israel, West Bank, and Gaza Strip.

External aid

The PFLP receives safe haven and some logistic assistance from Syria.

Popular Front for the Liberation of Palestine–General Command (PFLP–GC)

Description

The PFLP–GC split from the PFLP in 1968, claiming it wanted to focus more on fighting and less on politics. The group is violently opposed to Arafat's PLO. Led by Ahmad Jabril, a former captain in the Syrian Army, the PFLP-GC is closely tied to Syria and Iran.

Activities

The group carried out dozens of attacks in Europe and the Middle East during 1970 to 1980. The PFLP-GC is known for cross-border terrorist attacks into Israel using unusual means, such as hot-air balloons and motorized hang gliders. The primary focus now is on guerrilla operations in southern Lebanon, small-scale attacks in Israel, West Bank, and Gaza Strip.

Strength

Several hundred.

Location/area of operation

The PFLP-GC is headquartered in Damascus with bases in Lebanon.

External aid

The group receives support from Syria and financial support from Iran.

al-Qaeda

Description

al-Qaeda was established by Osama Bin Ladin in the late 1980s to bring together Arabs who fought in Afghanistan against the Soviet Union. The group helped finance, recruit, transport, and train Sunni Islamic extremists for the Afghan resistance. The group's current goal is to establish a pan-Islamic Caliphate throughout the world by working with allied Islamic extremist groups to overthrow regimes it deems "non-Islamic" and expel Westerners and non-Muslims from Muslim countries. al-Qaeda issued a statement under the banner of "The World Islamic Front for Jihad Against the Jews and Crusaders" in February, 1998, saying it was the duty of all Muslims to kill U.S.

citizens — civilian or military — and their allies everywhere. The group merged with Egyptian Islamic Jihad (Al-Jihad) in June, 2001.

Activities

On September 11, 2001, 19 al-Qaeda suicide attackers hijacked and crashed four U.S. commercial jets, two into the World Trade Center in New York City, one into the Pentagon near Washington, D.C., and a fourth into a field in Shanksville, Pennsylvania, leaving about 3000 individuals dead or missing. The October 12, 2000 attack on the USS Cole in the port of Aden, Yemen, killing 17 U.S. Navy members and injuring another 39 was conducted by al-Qaeda. The group also conducted the bombings in August, 1998 of the U.S. Embassies in Nairobi, Kenya, and Dar es Salaam, Tanzania that killed at least 301 individuals and injured more than 5000 others. The group claims to have shot down U.S. helicopters and killed U.S. servicemen in Somalia in 1993 and to have conducted three bombings that targeted U.S. troops in Aden, Yemen, in December 1992.

Al-Qaeda is linked to the following plans that were not carried out: to assassinate Pope John Paul II during his visit to Manila in late 1994, to kill President Clinton during a visit to the Philippines in early 1995, to conduct the midair bombing of a dozen U.S. trans-Pacific flights in 1995, and to set off a bomb at Los Angeles International Airport in 1999. Al-Qaeda also plotted to carry out terrorist operations against U.S. and Israeli tourists visiting Jordan for millennial celebrations in late 1999. (Jordanian authorities thwarted the planned attacks and put 28 suspects on trial.) In December, 2001, suspected al-Qaeda associate Richard Colvin Reid attempted to ignite a shoe bomb on a transatlantic flight from Paris to Miami.

Strength

Al-Qaeda may have several thousand members and associates. The group also serves as a focal point or umbrella organization for a worldwide network that includes many Sunni Islamic extremist groups, some members of al-Gama'a al-Islamiyya, the Islamic Movement of Uzbekistan, and the Harakat ul-Mujahidin.

Location/area of operation

Al-Qaeda has cells worldwide and is reinforced by its ties to Sunni extremist networks. Coalition attacks on Afghanistan since October 2001 dismantled the Taliban — al-Qaeda's protectors — and led to the capture, death, or dispersal of al-Qaeda operatives. Some al-Qaeda members at large probably will attempt to carry out future attacks against U.S. interests.

External aid

Osama Bin Ladin, member of a billionaire family that owns the Bin Ladin Group construction empire, is said to have inherited tens of millions of dollars that he uses to help finance the group. Al-Qaeda also maintains money-making front businesses, solicits donations from like-minded supporters, and illicitly siphons funds from donations to Muslim charitable organizations. U.S. efforts to block al-Qaeda funding have hampered al-Qaeda's ability to obtain money.

Real IRA (RIRA)

Other names

True IRA

Description

Formed in early 1998 as clandestine armed wing of the 32-County Sovereignty Movement, the RIRA is a "political pressure group" dedicated to removing British forces from Northern Ireland and unifying Ireland. The 32-County Sovereignty Movement opposed Sinn Fein's adoption in September 1997 of the Mitchell principles of democracy and nonviolence and opposed the amendment in December, 1999 of Articles 2 and 3 of the Irish Constitution, which laid claim to Northern Ireland. Michael "Mickey" McKevitt, who left the IRA to protest its cease-fire, leads the group; Bernadette Sands-McKevitt, his wife, is a founder–member of the 32-County Sovereignity Movement, the political wing of the RIRA.

Activities

The RIRA conducts bombings, assassinations, and robberies. Many Real IRA members are former IRA members who left that organization following the IRA cease-fire, and they bring to RIRA a wealth of experience in terrorist tactics and bomb making. Targets include British military and police in Northern Ireland and Northern Ireland Protestant communities. RIRA is linked to and understood to be responsible for the car bomb attack in Omagh, Northern Ireland on August 15, 1998, that killed 29 and injured 220 persons. The group began to observe a cease-fire following Omagh, but in 2000 and 2001 resumed attacks in Northern Ireland and on the U.K. mainland against targets such as MI6 headquarters and the BBC.

Strength

The group has 100 to 200 activists plus possible limited support from IRA hardliners dissatisfied with the IRA cease-fire and other republican sympathizers. British and Irish authorities arrested at least 40 members in the spring and summer of 2001 including leader McKevitt, who is currently in prison in the Irish Republic awaiting trial for being a member of a terrorist organization and directing terrorist attacks.

Location/area of operation

Northern Ireland, Irish Republic, and Great Britain.

External aid

RIRA is suspected of receiving funds from sympathizers in the U.S. and of attempting to buy weapons from U.S. gun dealers. RIRA also is reported to have purchased sophisticated weapons from the Balkans. Three Irish nationals associated with RIRA were extradited from Slovenia to the United Kingdom and are awaiting trial on weapons procurement charges.

Revolutionary Armed Forces of Colombia (FARC)

Description

Established in 1964 as the military wing of the Colombian Communist Party, the FARC is Colombia's oldest, largest, most capable, and best-equipped Marxist insurgency. The FARC is governed by a secretariat, led by septuagenarian Manuel Marulanda, aka "Tirofijo," and six others, including senior military commander Jorge Briceno, aka "Mono Jojoy." The group was organized along military lines and includes several urban fronts. In 2001, the group continued a slow-moving peace negotiation process with the Pastrana Administration that gained the group several concessions, including a demilitarized zone used as a venue for negotiations.

Activities

The FARC is responsible for bombings, murders, kidnapping, extortion, hijacking, as well as guerrilla and conventional military action against Colombian political, military, and economic targets. In March, 1999 the FARC executed three U.S. Indian rights activists on Venezuelan territory after it kidnapped them in Colombia. Foreign citizens are often targets of FARC kidnapping for ransom. FARC has well-documented ties to narcotics traffickers, principally through the provision of armed protection.

Strength

FARC has approximately 9000 to 12,000 armed combatants and an unknown number of supporters, mostly in rural areas.

Location/area of operation

FARC operates in Colombia with some activities — extortion, kidnapping, logistics, and R&R — and in Venezuela, Panama, and Ecuador.

External aid

Cuba provides some medical care and political consultation.

Revolutionary Nuclei (formerly ELA)

Other names

Revolutionary Cells

Description

Revolutionary Nuclei (RN) emerged from a broad range of antiestablishment and anti-U.S./NATO/EU leftist groups active in Greece between 1995 and 1998. The group is believed to be the successor to or offshoot of Greece's most prolific terrorist group, Revolutionary People's Struggle (ELA), which has not claimed an attack since January 1995. Indeed, RN appeared to fill the void left by ELA, particularly as lesser groups faded from the scene. RN's few communiqués show strong similarities in rhetoric, tone, and theme to ELA proclamations. RN has not claimed an attack since November, 2000.

Activities

Beginning operations in January 1995, the group claimed responsibility for some two dozen arson attacks and explosive low-level bombings targeting a range of U.S., Greek, and other European targets in Greece. In its most infamous and lethal attack to date, the group claimed responsibility for a bomb it detonated at the Intercontinental Hotel in April 1999 that resulted in killing a Greek woman and injuring a Greek man. Its modus operandi includes warning calls of impending attacks, use of rudimentary timing devices; and strikes during the late evening–early morning hours. RN last attacked U.S. interests in Greece in November 2000 with two separate bombings against the Athens offices of Citigroup and the studio of a Greek-American sculptor. The group also detonated an explosive device outside the Athens offices of Texaco in December 1999. Greek targets included court and other government office buildings, private vehicles, and the offices of Greek firms involved in NATO-related defense contracts in Greece. Similarly, the group attacked European interests in Athens, including Barclays Bank in December, 1998 and November, 2000.

Strength

Group membership is believed to be small, probably drawing from the Greek militant leftist or anarchist milieu.

Location/area of operation

The primary area of operation is in the Athens metropolitan area.

External aid

Unknown, but believed to be self-sustaining.

Revolutionary Organization 17 November (17 November)

Description

This is a radical leftist group established in 1975 and named for the student uprising in Greece in November, 1973 that protested the military regime. It is anti-Greek, anti-U.S., anti-Turkey, anti-NATO, and is committed to the ousting of U.S. bases, removal of Turkish military presence from Cyprus, and severing of Greece's ties to NATO and the European Union (EU).

Activities

Initial attacks were assassinations of senior U.S. officials and Greek public figures. The group added bombings in 1980s. Since 1990, the group expanded targets to include EU facilities and foreign firms investing in Greece and added improvised rocket attacks to its methods. The most recent attack claimed was the murder in June 2000 of British Defense Attache Stephen Saunders.

Strength

Unknown, but presumed to be small.

Location/area of operation

Athens, Greece.

External aid

Unknown.

Revolutionary Peoples' Liberation Party/Front (DHKP/C)

Other Names

> Devrimci Sol (Revolutionary Left)
> Dev Sol

Description

The group was originally formed in 1978 as Devrimci Sol, or Dev Sol, a splinter faction of the Turkish People's Liberation Party/Front. Renamed in 1994 after factional infighting, it espouses a Marxist ideology and is virulently anti-U.S. and anti-NATO. The group finances its activities chiefly through armed robberies and extortion.

Activities

Since the late 1980s the group has concentrated attacks against current and retired Turkish security and military officials. The group began a new campaign against foreign interests in 1990. Members assassinated two U.S. military contractors and wounded a U.S. Air Force officer to protest the Gulf War. It launched rockets at the U.S. Consulate in Istanbul in 1992. It assassinated a prominent Turkish businessman and two others in early 1996, its first significant terrorist act as DHKP/C. Turkish authorities thwarted a DHKP/C attempt in June 1999 to fire-light an antitank weapon at the U.S. Consulate in Istanbul. The DHKP/C conducted its first suicide bombings, targeting Turkish police, in January and September 2001. A series of safe-house raids and arrests by Turkish police since 2000 has weakened the group significantly.

Strength

Unknown.

Location/area of operation

The DHKP/C conducts attacks in Turkey, primarily in Istanbul. It raises funds in Western Europe.

External aid

Unknown.

Salafist Group for Call and Combat (GSPC)

Description

The Salafist Group for Call and Combat (GSPC) splinter faction that began in 1996 eclipsed the GIA since approximately 1998, and currently is assessed to be the most effective remaining armed group inside Algeria. In contrast to the GIA, the GSPC gained popular support through its pledge to avoid civilian attacks inside Algeria (although, in fact, civilians have been attacked). Its adherents abroad appear to have largely co-opted the external networks of the GIA, active particularly throughout Europe, Africa, and the Middle East.

Activities

The GSPC continues to conduct operations aimed at government and military targets, primarily in rural areas. Such operations include false roadblocks and attacks against convoys transporting military, police, or other government personnel. According to press reporting, some GSPC members in Europe maintain contacts with other North African extremists sympathetic to al-Qaeda, a number of whom were implicated in terrorist plots during 2001.

Strength

Strength is generally unknown; there are probably several hundred to several thousand inside Algeria.

Location/area of operation

Algeria.

External Aid

Algerian expatriates and GSPC members abroad, many residing in Western Europe, provide financial and logistics support. In addition, the Algerian government accused Iran and Sudan of supporting Algerian extremists in previous years.

Sendero Luminoso (SL)

Other names

Shining Path

Description

Former university professor Abimael Guzman formed Sendero Luminoso in the late 1960s, and his teachings created the foundation of SL's militant Maoist doctrine. In the 1980s SL became one of the most ruthless terrorist groups in the western hemisphere — approximately 30,000 persons have died since Shining Path took up arms in 1980. Its stated goal is to destroy existing Peruvian institutions and replace them with a communist peasant revolutionary regime. It also opposes any influence by foreign governments as well as by other Latin American guerrilla groups, especially the Tupac Amaru Revolutionary Movement (MRTA).

In 2001, the Peruvian National Police thwarted an SL attack against "an American objective," possibly the U.S. Embassy, when they arrested two Lima SL cell members. Additionally, government authorities continued to arrest and prosecute active SL members, including Ruller Mazombite, aka "Camarada Cayo," chief of the protection team of SL leader Macario Ala, aka "Artemio," and Evorcio Ascencios, aka "Camarada Canale," logistics chief of the Huallaga Regional Committee. Counterterrorist operations targeted pockets of terrorist activity in the Upper Huallaga River Valley and the Apurimac/Ene River Valley, where SL columns continued to conduct periodic attacks.

Activities

The SL has conducted indiscriminate bombing campaigns and selective assassinations. The group detonated explosives at diplomatic missions of several countries in Peru in 1990 and included an attempt to car bomb the U.S. Embassy in December. Peruvian authorities continued operations against the SL in 2001 in the countryside, where the SL conducted periodic raids on villages.

Strength

Membership is unknown but estimated to be 100 to 200 armed militants. SL's strength was vastly diminished by arrests and desertions.

Location/area of operation

Peru, with most activity in rural areas.

External aid

None.

United Self-Defense Forces of Colombia (AUC)

Description

The AUC — commonly referred to as the paramilitaries — is an umbrella organization formed in April, 1997 to consolidate most local and regional paramilitary groups, each with the mission to protect economic interests and combat insurgents locally. The AUC — supported by economic elites, drug traffickers, and local communities lacking effective government security — claims its primary objective is to protect its sponsors from insurgents. The AUC now asserts itself as a regional and national counterinsurgent force. It is adequately equipped and armed and reportedly pays its members a monthly salary. AUC political leader Carlos Castaño claimed that 70% of the AUC's operational costs are financed with drug-related earnings, the rest from "donations" from its sponsors.

Activities

AUC operations vary from assassinating suspected insurgent supporters to engaging guerrilla combat units. Colombian National Combat operations generally consist of raids and ambushes directed against suspected insurgents. The AUC generally avoids engagements with government security forces and actions against U.S. personnel or interests.

Strength

Strength of the AUC is estimated to be 6000 to 8150, including former military and insurgent personnel.

Location/area of operation

AUC forces are strongest in the northwest in Antioquia, Córdoba, Sucre, and Bolívar departments. Since 1999, the group demonstrated a growing presence in other northern and southwestern departments. Clashes between the AUC and the FARC insurgents in Putumayo in 2000 demonstrated the range of the AUC to contest insurgents throughout Colombia.

External aid

None.

Communist Party of the Philippines (CPP)
New Peoples' Army (NPA)

Description

The military wing of the Communist Party of the Philippines (CPP), the NPA is a Maoist group formed in March, 1969 with the aim of overthrowing the government through protracted guerrilla warfare. The chairman of the CPP's Central Committee and the NPA's founder, Jose Maria Sison, directs all CPP and NPA activity from the Netherlands, where he lives in self-imposed exile. Fellow Central Committee member and director of the CPP's National Democratic Front (NDF) Luis Jalandoni also lives in the Netherlands and has become a Dutch citizen. Although primarily a rural-based guerrilla group, the NPA has an active urban infrastructure to conduct terrorism and uses city-based assassination squads. The NPA derives most of its funding from contributions of supporters in the Philippines, Europe, and elsewhere, and from so-called "revolutionary taxes" extorted from local businesses.

Activities

The NPA primarily targets Philippine security forces, politicians, judges, government informers, former rebels who wish to leave the NPA, and alleged criminals. The group opposes any U.S. military presence in the Philippines and attacked U.S. military interests before the U.S. base closures in 1992. Press reports in 1999 and in late 2001 indicated that the NPA is again targeting U.S. troops participating in joint military exercises as well as U.S. Embassy personnel. The NPA claimed responsibility for the assassination of congressmen from Quezon (in May, 2001) and Cagayan (in June, 2001) and many other killings.

Strength

The strength of the NPA is slowly growing and is now estimated at over 10,000.

Location/area of operations

The NPA operates in rural Luzon, Visayas, and parts of Mindanao. It has cells in Manila and other metropolitan centers.

External aid

Unknown.

appendix e

Explosive materials

Department of the Treasury, Bureau of Alcohol, Tobacco and Firearms

COMMERCE IN EXPLOSIVES: List of Explosive Materials

The information listed in this appendix was updated on April 26, 2002, and comes from the ATF Web site at http://www.atf.treas.gov/pub/fire-explo_pub/listofexp.htm.

Pursuant to the provisions of section 841(d) of title 18, United States Code (U.S.C.), and 27 CFR 55.23, the Director, Bureau of Alcohol, Tobacco and Firearms, must publish and revise at least annually in the *Federal Register* a list of explosives determined to be within the coverage of 18 U.S.C. chapter 40, Importation, Manufacture, Distribution, and Storage of Explosive Materials. This chapter covers not only explosives, but also blasting agents and detonators, all of which are defined as explosive materials in section 841(C) of title 18, U.S.C. Accordingly; the following is the 2002 List of Explosive Materials subject to regulation under 18 U.S.C. Chapter 40. It includes both the list of explosives (including detonators) required to be published in the *Federal Register*, and blasting agents.

The list is intended to include any and all mixtures containing any of the materials on the list. Materials constituting blasting agents are marked by an asterisk. While the list is comprehensive, it is not all inclusive. The fact that an explosive material may not be on the list does not mean that it is not within the coverage of the law if it otherwise meets the statutory definitions in section 841 of title 18, U.S.C. Explosive materials are listed alphabetically by their common names followed, where applicable, by chemical names and synonyms in brackets.

In the 2002 List of Explosive Materials, ATF has added five terms to the list of explosives, has further defined two explosive materials, and has made amendments to two explosive materials to more accurately reference these materials.

The five additions to the list are as follows:

1. Azide explosives
2. HMTD [hexamethylenetriperoxidediamine]
3. Nitrate explosive mixtures
4. Picrate explosives
5. TATP [triacetonetriperoxide]

The ATF staff has added these explosive materials to the list because their primary or common purpose is to function by explosion. ATF has encountered the criminal use of some of these materials in improvised devices. "Nitrate explosive mixtures" is intended to be an all-encompassing term, including all forms of sodium, potassium, barium, calcium, and strontium nitrate explosive mixtures.

The two explosive materials that we have further defined by including their chemical names are listed as follows:

1. DIPAM [dipicramide; diaminohexanitrobiphenyl]
2. EDNA [ethylenedinitramine]

The two amendments to previously listed explosive materials are as follows:

1. "Nitrates of soda explosive mixtures" has been deleted and replaced with "Sodium nitrate explosive mixtures" to reflect current terminology.
2. PBX was previously defined as "RDX and plasticizer." We are changing the definition to reflect that PBX is an acronym for "plastic bonded explosive."

This revised list supersedes the List of Explosive Materials dated September 14, 1999 (Notice No. 880, 64 FR 49840; correction notice of September 28, 1999, 64 FR 52378) and became effective on April 26, 2002.

List of Explosive Materials

A

Acetylides of heavy metals
Aluminum containing polymeric propellant
Aluminum ophorite explosive
Amatex
Amatol
Ammonal
Ammonium nitrate explosive mixtures (cap sensitive)
*Ammonium nitrate explosive mixtures (non-cap sensitive)
Ammonium perchlorate composite propellant
Ammonium perchlorate explosive mixtures
Ammonium picrate [picrate of ammonia, Explosive D]
Ammonium salt lattice with isomorphously substituted inorganic
    salts
*ANFO [ammonium nitrate-fuel oil]
Aromatic nitro-compound explosive mixtures
Azide explosives

B

Baranol
Baratol
BEAF [1,2-*bis* (2,2-difluoro-2-nitroacetoxyethane)]
Black powder
Black powder based explosive mixtures
*Blasting agents, nitro-carbo-nitrates, including non-cap sensitive
    slurry and water gel explosives
Blasting caps
Blasting gelatin
Blasting powder
BTNEC [*bis* (trinitroethyl) carbonate]
BTNEN [*bis* (trinitroethyl) nitramine]
BTTN [1,2,4 butanetriol trinitrate]
Bulk salutes
Butyl tetryl

C

Calcium nitrate explosive mixture
Cellulose hexanitrate explosive mixture
Chlorate explosive mixtures
Composition A and variations
Composition B and variations
Composition C and variations
Copper acetylide

Cyanuric triazide
Cyclonite [RDX]
Cyclotetramethylenetetranitramine [HMX]
Cyclotol
    Cyclotrimethylenetrinitramine [RDX]

D

DATB [diaminotrinitrobenzene]
DDNP [diazodinitrophenol]
DEGDN [diethyleneglycol dinitrate]
Detonating cord
Detonators
Dimethylol dimethyl methane dinitrate composition
Dinitroethyleneurea
Dinitroglycerine [glycerol dinitrate]
Dinitrophenol
Dinitrophenolates
Dinitrophenyl hydrazine
Dinitroresorcinol
Dinitrotoluene-sodium nitrate explosive mixtures
DIPAM [dipicramide; diaminohexanitrobiphenyl]
Dipicryl sulfone
Dipicrylamine
Display fireworks
DNPA [2,2-dinitropropyl acrylate]
DNPD [dinitropentano nitrile]
Dynamite

E

EDDN [ethylene diamine dinitrate]
EDNA [ethylenedinitramine]
Ednatol
EDNP [ethyl 4,4-dinitropentanoate]
EGDN [ethylene glycol dinitrate]
Erythritol tetranitrate explosives
Esters of nitro-substituted alcohols
Ethyl-tetryl
Explosive conitrates
Explosive gelatins
Explosive liquids
Explosive mixtures containing oxygen-releasing inorganic salts and
    hydrocarbons
Explosive mixtures containing oxygen-releasing inorganic salts and
    nitro bodies
Explosive mixtures containing oxygen-releasing inorganic salts and
    water-insoluble fuels

Explosive mixtures containing oxygen-releasing inorganic salts and water-soluble fuels
Explosive mixtures containing sensitized nitromethane
Explosive mixtures containing tetranitromethane (nitroform)
Explosive nitro compounds of aromatic hydrocarbons
Explosive organic nitrate mixtures
Explosive powders

F

Flash powder
Fulminate of mercury
Fulminate of silver
Fulminating gold
Fulminating mercury
Fulminating platinum
Fulminating silver

G

Gelatinized nitrocellulose
Gem-dinitro aliphatic explosive mixtures
Guanyl nitrosamino guanyl tetrazene
Guanyl nitrosamino guanylidene hydrazine
Guncotton

H

Heavy metal azides
Hexanite
Hexanitrodiphenylamine
Hexanitrostilbene
Hexogen [RDX]
Hexogene or octogene and a nitrated N-methylaniline
Hexolites
HMTD [hexamethylenetriperoxidediamine]
HMX [cyclo-1,3,5,7-tetramethylene 2,4,6,8-tetranitramine; Octogen]
Hydrazinium nitrate/hydrazine/aluminum explosive system
Hydrazoic acid

I

Igniter cord
Igniters
Initiating tube systems

K

KDNBF [potassium dinitrobenzo-furoxane]

L

Lead azide
Lead mannite
Lead mononitroresorcinate
Lead picrate
Lead salts, explosive
Lead styphnate [styphnate of lead, lead trinitroresorcinate]
Liquid nitrated polyol and trimethylolethane
Liquid oxygen explosives

M

Magnesium ophorite explosives
Mannitol hexanitrate
MDNP [methyl 4,4-dinitropentanoate]
MEAN [monoethanolamine nitrate]
Mercuric fulminate
Mercury oxalate
Mercury tartrate
Metriol trinitrate
Minol-2 [40% TNT, 40% ammonium nitrate, 20% aluminum]
MMAN [monomethylamine nitrate]; methylamine nitrate
Mononitrotoluene-nitroglycerin mixture
Monopropellants

N

NIBTN [nitroisobutametriol trinitrate]
Nitrate explosive mixtures
Nitrate sensitized with gelled nitroparaffin
Nitrated carbohydrate explosive
Nitrated glucoside explosive
Nitrated polyhydric alcohol explosives
Nitric acid and a nitro aromatic compound explosive
Nitric acid and carboxylic fuel explosive
Nitric acid explosive mixtures
Nitro aromatic explosive mixtures
Nitro compounds of furane explosive mixtures
Nitrocellulose explosive
Nitroderivative of urea explosive mixture
Nitrogelatin explosive
Nitrogen trichloride
Nitrogen tri-iodide
Nitroglycerine [NG, RNG, nitro, glyceryl trinitrate, trinitroglycerine]
Nitroglycide
Nitroglycol [ethylene glycol dinitrate, EGDN]
Nitroguanidine explosives

Nitronium perchlorate propellant mixtures
Nitroparaffins Explosive Grade and ammonium nitrate mixtures
Nitrostarch
Nitro-substituted carboxylic acids
Nitrourea

O

Octogen [HMX]
Octol [75% HMX, 25% TNT]
Organic amine nitrates
Organic nitramines

P

PBX [plastic bonded explosives]
Pellet powder
Penthrinite composition
Pentolite
Perchlorate explosive mixtures
Peroxide based explosive mixtures
PETN [nitropentaerythrite, pentaerythrite tetranitrate, pentaerythri-
    tol tetranitrate]
Picramic acid and its salts
Picramide
Picrate explosives
Picrate of potassium explosive mixtures
Picratol
Picric acid (manufactured as an explosive)
Picryl chloride
Picryl fluoride
PLX [95% nitromethane, 5% ethylenediamine]
Polynitro aliphatic compounds
Polyolpolynitrate-nitrocellulose explosive gels
Potassium chlorate and lead sulfocyanate explosive
Potassium nitrate explosive mixtures
Potassium nitroaminotetrazole
Pyrotechnic compositions
PYX [2,6-*bis*(picrylamino)]-3,5-dinitropyridine

R

RDX [cyclonite, hexogen, T4, cyclo-1,3,5,-trimethylene-2,4,6,-trinitra-
    mine; hexahydro-1,3,5-trinitro-S-triazine]

S

Safety fuse
Salts of organic amino sulfonic acid explosive mixture
Salutes (bulk)

Silver acetylide
Silver azide
Silver fulminate
Silver oxalate explosive mixtures
Silver styphnate
Silver tartrate explosive mixtures
Silver tetrazene
Slurried explosive mixtures of water, inorganic oxidizing salt, gelling
    agent, fuel, and sensitizer (cap sensitive)
Smokeless powder
Sodatol
Sodium amatol
Sodium azide explosive mixture
Sodium dinitro-ortho-cresolate
Sodium nitrate explosive mixtures
Sodium nitrate-potassium nitrate explosive mixture
Sodium picramate
Special fireworks
Squibs
Styphnic acid explosives

T

Tacot [tetranitro-2,3,5,6-dibenzo- 1,3a,4,6a tetrazapentalene]
TATB [triaminotrinitrobenzene]
TATP [triacetonetriperoxide]
TEGDN [triethylene glycol dinitrate]
Tetranitrocarbazole
Tetrazene [tetracene, tetrazine, 1(5-tetrazolyl)-4-guanyl tetrazene hy-
    drate]
Tetryl [2,4,6 tetranitro-*N*-methylaniline]
Tetrytol
Thickened inorganic oxidizer salt slurried explosive mixture
TMETN [trimethylolethane trinitrate]
TNEF [trinitroethyl formal]
TNEOC [trinitroethylorthocarbonate]
TNEOF [trinitroethylorthoformate]
TNT [trinitrotoluene, trotyl, trilite, triton]
Torpex
Tridite
Trimethylol ethyl methane trinitrate composition
Trimethylolthane trinitrate-nitrocellulose
Trimonite
Trinitroanisole
Trinitrobenzene
Trinitrobenzoic acid
Trinitrocresol

Trinitro-meta-cresol
Trinitronaphthalene
Trinitrophenetol
Trinitrophloroglucinol
Trinitroresorcinol
Tritonal

U

Urea nitrate

W

Water-bearing explosives having salts of oxidizing acids and nitrogen
bases, sulfates, or sulfamates (cap sensitive)
Water-in-oil emulsion explosive compositions

X

Xanthamonas hydrophilic colloid explosive mixture

FOR FURTHER INFORMATION CONTACT: Arson and Explosives Programs Division, Bureau of Alcohol, Tobacco and Firearms, 650 Massachusetts
Avenue, NW, Washington, D.C. 20226 (Phone: 202-927-7930).

appendix f

Homeland security state contact list

Contact information telephone numbers and Web site details are from the official White House Web site.

Alabama

  800-361-4454
  http://www.homelandsecurity.alabama.gov

Alaska

  907-428-6003
  http://www.gov.state.ak.us/omb/Homeland1.pdf

Arizona

  602-542-1302

Arkansas

  501-730-9750
  http://www.adem.state.ar.us

California

  916-324-8908

Colorado

  303-273-1680
  http://www.ops.state.co.us

Connecticut

  203-805-6600

Delaware

    302-744-4101

District of Columbia

    202-727-1000
    http://dc.gov

Florida

    850-410-7233
    http://www.fdle.state.fl.us

Georgia

    404-824-7030
    http://www.gahomelandsecurity.com/

Hawaii

    808-733-4301 ext. 452
    http://www.scd.state.hi.us

Idaho

    208-422-5242
    http://www.state.id.us/government/executive.htm

Illinois

    312-814-2166

Indiana

    317-232-8303
    http://www.in.gov/c-tasc

Iowa

    515-281-3231
    http://www.iowahomelandsecurity.org

Kansas

    785-274-1121/1109

Kentucky

    502-607-1257
    http://homeland.state.ky.us

Louisiana

>225-925-7501
>http://www.loep.state.la.us/homeland

Maine

>207-626-4440

Maryland

>410-974-5024
>http://www.mema.state.md.us

Massachusetts

>617-727-3600 ext. 556

Michigan

>517-336-6198
>http://www.msp.state.mi.us

Minnesota

>651-296-6642
>http://www.dps.state.mn.us/homsec/mohshome.asp

Mississippi

>601-960-9999

Missouri

>573-522-3007
>http://www.homelandsecurity.state.mo.us

Montana

>406-841-3911
>http://www.discoveringmontana.com/css/default.asp

Nebraska

>402-471-2256

Nevada

>775-687-4240
>http://dem.state.nv.us/

New Hampshire

603-271-3294

New Jersey

609-341-3434

New Mexico

505-827-3370

New York

212-867-7060

North Carolina

919-733-2126
http://www.ncgov.com/asp/subpages/safety_security.asp

North Dakota

701-328-8100
http://www.nd.us/dem/homesec.html

Ohio

614-466-4344
http://www.state.oh.us/odps/sos/ohshome.htm

Oklahoma

405-425-2324

Oregon

503-378-3725

Pennsylvania

717-651-2715
http://www.homelandsecurity.state.pa.us

Puerto Rico

787-723-7924

Rhode Island

401-275-4102

South Carolina

803-737-3886

South Dakota

1-866-homland

Tennessee

615-532-7825
http://www.state.tn.us/homelandsecurity

Texas

512-936-1882

Utah

801-538-3400
http://www.cem.utah.gov

Vermont

802-828-3333

Virginia

804-225-3826
http://www.commonwealthpreparedness.state.va.us

Washington

Joe.Huden@MIL.wa.gov

West Virginia

No information available

Wisconsin

608-242-3210
http://www.wisconsin.gov/state

Wyoming

307-772-5234

Guam

671-475-0802

Northern Mariana Islands

    670-664-2280

Virgin Islands

    340-712-7711

American Samoa

    011-684-633-4116

appendix g

Publication references

107th Congress, HR 3162:
Uniting and Strengthening America by Providing Appropriate Tools Required to Intercept and Obstruct Terrorism Act of 2001 (also known as The PATRIOT ACT of 2001)

Presidential Decision Directive-39
Provides an unclassified synopsis of the U.S. national policy on terrorism and counterterrorism as laid out in Presidential Decision Directive-39 (PDD-39)

Presidential Decision Directive-62
"Protection Against Unconventional Threats to the Homeland and Americans Overseas," dated May 22, 1998

The National Strategy for Homeland Security: Office of Homeland Security (PDF)
Office of Homeland Security, July 2002
This document is the first national strategy for addressing homeland security issues in the United States. Topical material includes threat and vulnerability, organizing for a secure homeland, critical mission areas such as intelligence and warning, border and transportation security, domestic counterterrorism, protecting critical infrastructures and key assets, defending against catastrophic threats, and emergency preparedness and response.

Patterns of Global Terrorism
United States Department of State, published each year since 1993
This provides a chronological breakdown and dates of significant terrorist incidents as well as provides excerpts of the terrorist activity that took place and the locations.

*The National Strategy for the Physical Protection of Critical Infrastructures
and Key Assets* (PDF)
White House, published February 2003
This identifies the road ahead for a core mission area identified in
the President's National Strategy for Homeland Security. It covers
cross-sector priorities, securing critical infrastructures, and protecting key assets.

National Strategy for Combating Terrorism (PDF)
White House, published February 2003
This publication looks at the nature of the terrorist threat today and
the availability of weapons of mass destruction. Reviewed are the
goals and objectives of defeating, denying, and diminishing terrorist activities.

Project Megiddo — FBI
"Project Megiddo" is the culmination of an FBI research initiative
that analyzed the potential for extremist criminal activity in the
U.S. by individuals or domestic groups who attach special significance to the year 2000.

The Directory of Homeland Security
Provided is contact information for over 500 state and federal agencies. The following is provided: over 150 pages of contacts; key
local and federal personnel for each office; information on national organizations working on homeland security; agency-specific
procurement information and contacts; helpful resources on sell-
ing products to the federal government; and a listing of select
companies, including names of homeland security directors,
number of employees, homeland security products/services, and
key personnel.

The documents listed below are readily available on various Web sites, but
the majority can be found on the government's counterterrorism training
Web site www.counterterrorismtraining.gov, which was based on a work-
group convened by the Department of Justice's Bureau of Justice
Assistance.

Assessing the Threats (PDF)
Center for Defense Information, 2002
Examined in this book are threats to security and stability as perceived from four perspectives: American, West European, Russian, and Northeast Asian. Chapters include information focusing
on current security problems, weapons of mass destruction, and
various terrorist activities.

Assessing Threats of Targeted Group Violence: Contributions from Social Psychology (PDF)
National Threat Assessment Center, 1999
Recent increases in domestic and international acts of extremist violence perpetrated against American citizens prompted an increased need for information. To help understand and evaluate the threat posed to U.S. targets by extremist groups and their individual members, this article summarizes research on group behavior and the effects of group membership on individual behavior, proposes specific questions to consider in evaluating the risk for violence by groups and by individuals influenced by groups, and suggests further research needs.

Bioterrorism in the United States: Threat, Preparedness, and Response (PDF)
Chemical and Biological Arms Control Institute, 2000
Reviewed in this report are current programs that address the health and medical dimensions of national response to bioterrorism in the United States.

Combating Terrorism: Assessing the Threat of Biological Terrorism (PDF)
RAND, October 2001
Presented in this report is testimony before the House Subcommittee on National Security, Veterans Affairs, and International Relations on biological terrorism, the feasibility and likelihood of terrorist groups using biological or chemical weapons, and what the government can and should do to deal with biological or chemical threats.

Combating Terrorism: Assessing Threats, Risk Management, and Establishing Priorities
Center for Nonproliferation Studies, July 2000
Presented in this report is testimony before the House Subcommittee on National Security, Veterans Affairs, and International Relations on terrorism threat assessments and risk management strategies.

Cyber Protests: The Threat to the U.S. Information Infrastructure (PDF)
National Infrastructure Protection Center, 2001
Discussed in this report is the growing threat of cyber protests. Examples of recent events are provided.

Defending America: Asymmetric and Terrorist Attacks with Biological Weapons (PDF)
Center for Strategic and International Studies, February 2001
Explored in this report are various aspects of bioterrorism, including possible avenues of attack, potential threats, and possible solutions and preventative measures.

Defending America: Redefining the Conceptual Borders of Homeland Defense: The Risks and Effects of Indirect, Covert, Terrorist, and Extremist Attacks with Weapons of Mass Destruction (Final Draft) (PDF)
Center for Strategic and International Studies, February 2001
Examined in this report is the threat of terrorist attacks as well as more conventional means of attack (including how the two might overlap), the impact of technological change on homeland defense, and challenges for response planning.

Domestic Terrorism: Resources for Local Governments (PDF)
National League of Cities, 2000
This guidebook helps local decision makers develop and implement domestic terrorism preparedness plans. It surveys national strategy and describes the resources available to state and local governments for planning, training and exercises, equipment, intelligence, and medical services.

Homeland Security: Key Elements of a Risk Management Approach (PDF)
U.S. General Accounting Office, October 2001
Described in this report are key elements of a good risk management approach, including assessment of threat, vulnerability, and criticality.

International Crime Threat Assessment
President's International Crime Control Strategy, 1998
This global assessment examines the threat posed by international crime to Americans and their communities, U.S. business and financial institutions, and global security and stability. It was prepared by a U.S. federal interagency working group in support of the President's International Crime Control Strategy.

Protective Intelligence and Threat Assessment Investigations: A Guide for State and Local Law Enforcement Officials (ASCII or PDF)
National Institute of Justice, January 2000
Described in this report are protective intelligence and threat assessment investigations, focusing on protocols and procedures for law enforcement and security agencies responsible for protecting public persons and others who are vulnerable to targeted violence.

The Sociology and Psychology of Terrorism: Who Becomes a Terrorist and Why?
Federal Research Division, Library of Congress, September 1999
Examined in this study are the types of individuals and groups that are prone to terrorism in an effort to help improve U.S. counterterrorism methods and policies. The relevant literature with which to assess the current knowledge of the subject is examined, and psychological and sociological profiles of foreign terrorist

individuals and selected groups are developed to use as case studies in assessing trends, motivations, and likely behavior, as well as in revealing vulnerabilities that would aid in combating terrorist groups and individuals.

The World Factbook 2002
Central Intelligence Agency, 2002
The first classified *Factbook* was published in August 1962, and the first unclassified version was published in June 1971. The 1975 *Fact book* was the first to be made available to the public with sales through the U.S. Government Printing Office (GPO). This publication provides statistical information on all the countries in the world, including data on populations, militaries, geography, governments, and transnational issues.

Patterns of Global Terrorism, 2001
U.S. Department of State, May 2002
Examined in this report is the danger that terrorism poses to the world and efforts of the United States and international partners to defeat it. Aspects of the war on terrorism include diplomatic actions to form a global coalition against terror, cooperation among intelligence agencies, enhanced and cooperative law enforcement efforts, economic actions to deny financial support to terrorism, and military operations and assistance. The report is issued annually per congressional mandate. See the archive for reports from 1995 through 1999.

Political Violence Against Americans, 1998 (PDF)
U.S. Department of State, 1998
An overview of the political violence that American citizens and interests encountered abroad in 1998 is provided in this report. Incidents included were selected based on their seriousness, the use of unusual tactics or weapons, or the specific targeting of representatives of the United States.

Significant Incidents of Political Violence against Americans, 1997 (PDF)
U.S. Department of State, 1997
Provided in this report is an overview of the political violence that American citizens and interests encountered abroad in 1997.

The Sociology and Psychology of Terrorism: Who Becomes a Terrorist and Why?
Library of Congress, Federal Research Division, 1999
This report was prepared under an Interagency Agreement, and it provides approaches to terrorism analysis, general hypotheses of terrorism, psychology of the terrorist, and terrorist profiling, based on research.

Terrorism in the United States, 1999 (PDF)
> Federal Bureau of Investigation, 1999
>> This annual publication reviews the current year's terrorist incidents, suspected terrorist incidents, arrests that prevented terrorist attacks, and other significant events. The report also describes 30-year feuds in domestic and international terrorism and the FBI's response.

1997 Bombing Incidents (PDF)
> Federal Bureau of Investigation (FBI) Bomb Data Center
>> This bulletin provides statistics on criminal bombing incidents that occurred in the United States in 1997. Bombing data are presented by state, region, target, time of occurrence, and time of year.

Office for Domestic Preparedness (ODP) Information Clearinghouse
> The ODP Information Clearinghouse is a searchable virtual library of publications and other resources on domestic preparedness, counterterrorism, and weapons of mass destruction. The clearinghouse also offers an electronic newsletter that provides e-updates on domestic preparedness news, such as conference or training events, new ODP programs, and new publications.

Homeland Security Act of 2002 (H.R. 5005)
> Signed into law on November 25, 2002, this act restructures and strengthens the executive branch of the Federal Government to better meet the threat posed by terrorism. In establishing a new Department of Homeland Security, the act, for the first time, creates a federal department with a primary mission that will be to help prevent, protect against, and respond to acts of terrorism.

Protecting Democracy: States Respond to Terrorism
> The National Conference of State Legislatures created Web pages for counterterrorism legal issues of interest on the state level. Its state legislation database is updated monthly and is searchable by state, category, date/range, status, bill number/type, and keyword.

appendix h

Government legislative references

The origins of the listed documents are from the http://www.counterterror-ismtraining.gov Web site (unless otherwise noted). The counterterrorism training Web site documents are based on recommendations made by the Counter-Terrorism Training Coordination Working Group convened by the U.S. Department of Justice's (DOJ's) Office of Justice Programs to examine the counterterrorism tools available to law enforcement and first responder communities.

Working group participants included the Bureau of Justice Assistance, the Executive Office for U.S. Attorneys, the Federal Bureau of Investigation, the Federal Emergency Management Agency, the Federal Law Enforcement Training Center, the National Institute of Justice, the Office for Domestic Preparedness, the Office of Community Oriented Policing Services, the Office of Homeland Security, the Office of Justice Programs, the Office of the Police Corps and Law Enforcement Education, the U.S. Customs Service, and the U.S. Department of Labor. Working group membership will expand to include other federal agencies as well as nongovernmental organizations that represent affected constituencies.

National Security Institute: Counter-Terrorism Legislation
   http://nsi.org/terrorism.html
   This is a one-stop shop for links to counterterrorism legislation, executive orders, terrorism facts, terrorism precautions, and related sites.

Code of Federal Regulation-28 CFR Part 23
   http://www.iir.com/28cfr/guideline.htm and www.iir.com/28cfr
   This provides complete text and guidelines from the Institute for Intergovernmental Research.

United States Code Title 18 — Crimes and Criminal Procedure
   http://www.access.gpo.gov/uscode/title18/title18.html and http:/
   /uscode.house.gov/usc.htm
   Provided is a complete detailed listing of guidelines and procedures
   for a wide array of crimes in five parts, covering crimes, criminal
   procedures, prisons and prisoners, correction of youthful offenders, and immunity of witness. Chapters cover a wide range of
   material, including biological and chemical weapons, terrorism,
   and sabotage.

*Cyber Security Research and Development Act (H.R. 3394, Public Law
   107–305)*
   Signed into law on November 27, 2002, this legislation will establish
   computer security research centers and fellowship programs
   through the National Science Foundation and the National Institute of Standards and Technology.

Effective Counterterrorism Act of 1996 (H.R. 3071)
   Signed into law on April 24, 1996 (as S.735, Public Law No. 104–132),
   this bill sets penalties for providing terrorist organizations with
   material support, expands federal jurisdiction over bomb threats,
   adds terrorism offenses to the money laundering statute, and
   establishes or increases other penalties related to acts of terrorism.
   It also authorizes funding for specialized training or equipment
   to enhance the capability of metropolitan fire and emergency
   service departments to respond to terrorist attacks.

*Foreign Intelligence Surveillance Act of 1978 (FISA) (U.S. Code Title 50,
   Chapter 36)*
   Under a November 18, 2002, FISA ruling by an appeals panel of the
   U.S. Foreign Intelligence Surveillance Court of Review, police
   were given broader power in the use of surveillance against terror
   and espionage suspects. This action affirms the implementation
   of new U.S. Department of Justice procedures that allow easier
   information access between federal domestic police agencies and
   intelligence agencies.

Homeland Security Act of 2002 (H.R. 5005)
   Signed into law on November 25, 2002, this act restructures and
   strengthens the executive branch of the Federal Government to
   better meet the threat posed by terrorism. In establishing a new
   Department of Homeland Security, the act, for the first time, creates a federal department with a primary mission that will be to
   help prevent, protect against, and respond to acts of terrorism.

Illegal Immigration Reform and Immigrant Responsibility Act of 1996, Program to Collect Information Relating to Nonimmigrant Foreign Students and other Exchange Program Participants (Public Law No. 104–208, Section 641)

A final rule promulgated under this law established the Student and Exchange Visitor Information System (SEVIS), an Internet reporting and tracking system that will track "F," "M," and "J" visa participants from the time they receive their documentation until they graduate/leave school or conclude/leave their programs. Schools have until January 30, 2003, to enter data on new, nonimmigrant students and until August 1, 2003, to complete entries on current students. This information will be available to law enforcement, school officials, and certain U.S. State Department and Immigration and Naturalization Service personnel.

Immigration and Nationality Act of 1952 (U.S. Code Title 8)

The U.S. Immigration and Naturalization Service (INS) asked state and local police to voluntarily arrest aliens who violated criminal provisions of the U.S. Immigration and Nationality Act or civil provisions that render an alien deportable, and who are wanted as recorded by the National Crime Information Center. The National Security Entry–Exit Registration System Fact Sheet details the purpose and procedures called for by the INS National Security Entry–Exit Registration System. On December 6, 2002, the INS issued a statement emphasizing the registration requirements for visiting foreign nationals from the 18 countries affected. On December 18, 2002, the INS updated special registration requirements to include certain nonimmigrants from Pakistan and Saudi Arabia.

Maritime Transportation Security Act of 2002 (Public Law 107–295) (PDF)

Signed into law on November 25, 2002, this bill amends the Merchant Marine Act of 1936 to establish a program to ensure greater security for U.S. seaports. The act directs the Secretary of Transportation to assess port vulnerability and to prepare a National Maritime Transportation Antiterrorism Plan for deterring catastrophic emergencies.

Preparedness against Terrorism Act of 2000 (H.R. 4210)

Referred to the Senate committee on July 26, 2000, this bill requires the President to ensure that federal emergency preparedness plans and programs are adequate and carried out in the event of an act of terrorism or other catastrophic event.

Safe Explosives Act (Homeland Security Act of 2002, Public Law No. 107–296, Section 1121)

Included as part of the Homeland Security Act of 2002 and signed by President George W. Bush on November 25, 2002, the Safe Explosives Act empowers the Bureau of Alcohol, Tobacco and Firearms (ATF) to apply stricter controls on the purchase of explosives. Effective May 24, 2002, any person who wants to transport, ship, cause to be transported, or receive explosive materials must first obtain a federal permit. ATF prepared a special online reference page to keep the public informed of resulting regulations.

Terrorist Bombings Convention Implementation Act of 2002 (Title I) and Suppression of the Financing of Terrorism Convention Implementation Act of 2002 (Title II) (H.R. 3275, Public Law No. 107–197)

This bill was enacted as Public Law Number 107–197 on June 25, 2002. Title I implements the International Convention for the Suppression of Terrorist Bombings, which was signed by the United States on January 12, 1998. This convention imposes legal obligations on state parties to submit for prosecution or to extradite any person within their jurisdiction who unlawfully and intentionally delivers, places, discharges, or detonates an explosive or other lethal device in, into, or against a place of public use, a state or government facility, a public transportation system, or an infrastructure facility. Title II implements the International Convention for the Suppression of the Financing of Terrorism, which was signed by the United States on January 10, 2000. This convention imposes legal obligations on state parties to submit for prosecution or to extradite any person within their jurisdiction who unlawfully and willfully provides or collects funds with the intention that they should be used to carry out various terrorist activities. State parties are subject to the obligations of these conventions without regard to the place where the alleged acts included in these conventions take place.

The below-listed legislative hate crime references can be located on the Department of Justice's National Criminal Justice Reference Service Web site at http://www.ncjrs.org/hate_crimes/legislation.html.

Hate Crimes Prevention Act of 1999 Bill (H.R. 1082)

This act amends 18 U.S.C. 245 that prohibits persons from interfering with an individual's federal rights (e.g., voting or employment) by violence or threat of violence due to his or her race, color, religion, or national origin. This act allows for more authority for the federal government to investigate and prosecute hate crime offenders who committed their crime because of perceived sexual orientation, gender, or disability of the victim. It also permits the federal government to prosecute without having to prove that the victim was attacked because he or she was performing a federally protected activity.

Church Arson Prevention Act of 1996 (18 U.S.C. 247)

This act created the National Church Arson Task Force (NCATF) in June 1996 to oversee the investigation and prosecution of arson at houses of worship around the country. The NCATF brought together the FBI, the ATF, and Department of Justice prosecutors in partnership with state and local law enforcement officers and prosecutors. In addition to the NCATF's creation, the law allowed for a broader federal criminal jurisdiction to aid criminal prosecutions, and established a loan guarantee recovery fund for rebuilding.

Hate Crimes Sentencing Enhancement Act (Section 280003 of the Violent Crime Control and Law Enforcement Act of 1994)

As a part of the 1994 Crime Act, the Hate Crimes Sentencing Enhancement Act provides for longer sentences when the offense is determined to be a hate crime. A longer sentence may be imposed if it is proven that a crime against person or property was motivated by "race, color, religion, national origin, ethnicity, gender, disability, or sexual orientation."

Hate Crime Statistics Act of 1990 (28 U.S.C. 534)

This act requires the Department of Justice to collect data on hate crimes. Hate crimes are defined as "manifest prejudice based on race, religion, sexual orientation, or ethnicity." The FBI, using the Uniform Crime Reporting system, compiles these statistics. The Crime Act of 1994 also required the FBI to collect data on hate crimes involving disability.

appendix i

Glossary of terminology

Back door A hole in the security of a computer system deliberately left in place by designers or programmers or established maliciously by manipulating a computer system.

Berserker Term considered and posed by Jonathan White in 2000 to better explain actions of a single-event terrorist. These individuals are crazed true believers who went too far and possibly crazy for their cause.

Code master An individual who epitomizes the art of computer usage, programming, and in the case of cyber terror, malicious activity.

Denial of service (DOS) A malicious activity that renders a server, or a service, useless. This is often done through transmission of a virus or a repetitive electronic attack.

Hacker An individual who gains unauthorized access to a computer system.

Hard target A well-fortified and secure location that is extremely difficult to penetrate, e.g., military installation, government facility, and nuclear site.

Lone wolf Considered a one-hit wonder and an extremist. This type of terrorist is often leaderless, acts on his own, and once he commits the violent act, will vanish.

Militia Any number of American paramilitary right-wing groups that focus their beliefs and issues on taxes, white supremacy, gun control, abortion, and antigovernment.

Phreak A technologically savvy individual who understands the inner workings of communication and phone systems and uses that knowledge to exploit illicit cyber activity. (phreaking, *verb*)

Ping A networking computer program that verifies Internet protocol (IP).

Script kiddie Individuals who break security on computer systems without truly understanding the exploit they are using.

Soft target A less-fortified and often more attractive target for a terrorist due to its relative ease of accessibility, e.g., hotel, market, and arena.

Trojan horse A hidden script attached to a program that appears legitimate but contains code allowing unauthorized collection, exploitation, falsification, or destruction of data on a host computer.

Wolf packs American right-wing extremist term for small groups of activists operating below a militia.

Worm A type of virus that acts as an independent program that replicates itself from machine to machine across network connections in an effort to cause a denial of service.

The culture and make-up of many domestic groups has led to them developing their own terminology and lingo. In his book *Blood in the Face*, James Ridgeway provides an example of what is referred to as "Klanspeak."* The following terms and definitions are shown as represented in his work and are provided as an example of just one group's use of distinct terms.

Klanspeak

Empire The national Ku Klux Klan organization

Realm The Klan in a particular state

Dominion Five or more counties of a Realm

Klanton or Den Local chapter

Klavern Local meeting place

Imperial Wizard Head of National Ku Klux Klan

Grand Dragon Head of a Realm

Great Titan Head of a Dominion

Giant Head of a Province

Exalted Cyclops Head of a Klanton

Klaliff Vice president to Exalted Cyclops

---

* Ridgeway, J., *Blood in the Face*, Thunder's Mouth Press, New York, 1990, p. 70.

Kladd Assistant to Exalted Cyclops

Kleagle An organizer

Kludd Chaplain

Klokard National lecturer

Index